The Regulators

D0769665

FOR DAVID

The Regulators

Anonymous Power Brokers in American Politics

Cindy Skrzycki

Illustrations by Keith Bendis

ROWMAN & LITTLEFIELD PUBLISHERS, INC.
Lanham • Boulder • New York • Oxford

ROWMAN & LITTLEFIELD PUBLISHERS, INC.

Published in the United States of America
by Rowman & Littlefield Publishers, Inc.
A Member of the Rowman & Littlefield Publishing Group
4501 Forbes Boulevard, Suite 200, Lanham, Maryland 20706
www.rowmanlittlefield.com

P.O. Box 317, Oxford OX2 9RU, United Kingdom

Copyright © 2003 by Rowman & Littlefield Publishers, Inc.

All newspaper columns are © *The Washington Post*. Reprinted with permission.

All rights reserved. No part of this publication may be reproduced, stored in a retrieval system, or transmitted in any form or by any means, electronic, mechanical, photocopying, recording, or otherwise, without the prior permission of the publisher.

British Library Cataloguing in Publication Information Available

Library of Congress Cataloging-in-Publication Data

Skrzycki, Cindy, 1955–
    The regulators : anonymous power brokers in American politics / Cindy Skrzycki ; illustrations by Keith Bendis.
        p.   cm.
Includes bibliographical references and index.
    ISBN 0-7425-1907-4 (cloth : alk. paper) — (ISBN 0-7425-1908-2 (pbk. : alk. paper)
    1. Administrative procedure—United States. 2. Administrative agencies—United States. 3. Industrial laws and legislation—United States. 4. Social legislation—United States. I. Title.
    KF5407.S59 2003
    342.73'066—dc21   2002151022

Printed in the United States of America

♾™ The paper used in this publication meets the minimum requirements of American National Standard for Information Sciences—Permanence of Paper for Printed Library Materials, ANSI / NISO Z39.48-1992.

Contents

Figures and Tables

Figures

Tables

Columns from *The Washington Post*

Introduction

Chapter 1

Chapter 2

Chapter 3

Chapter 4

Chapter 5

Chapter 6

Acronyms

U.S. Government Acronyms

ATF   Bureau of Alcohol, Tobacco and Firearms
CBO   Congressional Budget Office
CPSC   Consumer Product Safety Commission
DOE   Department of Energy
DOT   Department of Transportation
EPA   Environmental Protection Agency
FAA   Federal Aviation Administration
FCC   Federal Communications Commission
FDA   Food and Drug Administration
FTC   Federal Trade Commission
GAO   General Accounting Office
HHS   Department of Health and Human Services
HUD   Department of Housing and Urban Development
NASA   National Aeronautics and Space Administration
NHTSA   National Highway Traffic Safety Administration
OFCCP   Office of Federal Contract Compliance Programs
OIRA   Office of Information and Regulatory Affairs
OMB   Office of Management and Budget
OSHA   Occupational Safety and Health Administration
SEC   Securities and Exchange Commission
USDA   Department of Agriculture

Other

APA   Administrative Procedure Act
ATA   American Trucking Associations
CRA   Congressional Review Act
GSA   General Services Administration
NAFTA   North American Free Trade Agreement
NAM   National Association of Manufacturers
NFIB   National Federation of Independent Business
NRDC   Natural Resources Defense Council
WTO   World Trade Organization

Preface

The idea for this book grew out of speeches that I have given over the years to students at liberal arts colleges around the country. Every time I left Washington and my job as a reporter for *The Washington Post* to speak to classes studying political science, economics, government, and administrative law, the students were astonished at the magnitude of federal regulation and the role that it plays in our lives. They got excited about the topic when they realized that federal regulation is where some of the best lessons in government are taught and learned.

For more than a decade at *The Washington Post,* I have written about almost every federal agency and the rules they have issued in a column aptly named "The Regulators." I tried to give readers insight into how the regulatory machinery of the federal government grinds along and why the people who hold regulatory posts in the federal government have so much power. Many of my readers are the regulators themselves.

Over the years, I have written about government initiatives that have caused great controversy throughout the country and some that were completely overlooked. Questions about how we should regulate clean air and clean water, how much arsenic should be in our water, what safety rules should apply to Mexican trucks crossing the border, how air bags should be tested for safety, and what standards there should be for the marketing of bear repellent were answered, ultimately, by regulations. I also have written extensively about the relationship among federal regulators, the business community, and consumers. These often are long-term relationships that are built around issues that are very specific to a single industry. Vintners have an intense interest in how the federal government mandates labeling of alcohol and health claims that can be made about alcohol consumption. Candy makers fight over the size of breath mints, which are governed by the Food and Drug Administration. Advocates for saving water square off against the plumbing industry in the battle over how much water should be allowed for the clean flush of a toilet.

I hope to do in this book what I have been doing for readers of "The Regulators": take a complicated and sometimes inscrutable topic and make it a comprehensible, important lesson in government. For this book, I have selected cases of regulatory authority—or campaigns against that authority—to make various points about the history of regulation, the influence of special interests, and the role of Congress in rulemaking, to name a few. I include the practical side of regulation as well as the seemingly frivolous side. Some of these issues go back several years, but they illustrate or prove pertinent, enduring points about regulation and how it works regardless of the dates on the columns. Yesterday's fight over arsenic in the nation's drinking water is not unlike current regulatory strife over letting Mexican trucks roll over the border.

I chose cases that illustrate how economic considerations shape rules or how businesses respond to rules. I have tried to highlight the interplay between regulators and the people and businesses they regulate, as well as the intense political atmosphere that envelops any major regulatory initiative. My columns form the organizational spine of this book, but I also chose a few articles that were collaborations with *Washington Post* colleagues Helen Dewar, Carrie Johnson, and Eric Pianin; those were instances when an event called for a news story rather than a column. The headlines on the columns, in some cases, have been edited lightly for use in the book.

Not only are these good stories for a newspaper that covers Washington carefully, but they are case studies for students of government, economics, law, and public affairs about how government applies to real life. The rule-makings that grow out of these issues are laboratories for examining the nitty-gritty of regulation, a governmental function that has been around in one form or another since the beginnings of the republic—though the founders never envisioned anything like the regulatory state we live in now.

Regulation is important to examine up close for another reason: It involves all the political machinery of Washington—the White House, Congress, lobbyists, the judiciary, and the widest possible range of public interest and business groups. In many ways, the debate over a rulemaking and the resolution of that debate constitute the real policy work of Washington; it is unlike anything that the congressional or judicial branches of government do because of the unusual delegation of power from Congress to unelected bureaucrats. They often determine how federal laws are carried out and shape new regulatory initiatives. They are responsible for thousands of rules that are issued every year influencing the safety of a product, the economic viability of a company, the marketing of a drug, the competitive advantage of an industry, and even how the government responds to terrorism. What they decide matters in your life or will come to matter as the years go by.

In his influential book, *Rulemaking: How Government Agencies Write Law and Make Policy,* Cornelius M. Kerwin argues that "rulemaking affects every institution and process of government, every participant in policy deliberations, and every person affected by rules."[1] Indeed, rulemaking is an agency's single most important function. It gives it power, purpose, and a loud voice in important public policy issues. It is a way to respond to social and economic problems and to make domestic policy. A decision not to regulate can be equally as powerful a statement.

My coverage of this sometimes invisible subsidiary of the executive branch has led me to believe that we are now as much a nation of rules as we are one of laws. The regulators, among them career civil servants and political appointees, are a power center in Washington and a fundamental part of the political system. Many of them are like the Wizard of Oz, pushing and pulling the levers of power behind the curtain. They have great influence and, in many cases, anonymity—a combination that makes their role in setting public policy so hard to grasp and sometimes so hard to oversee.

Many commentators and political scientists believe that the study of regulation often isn't as exciting as the horserace of a national election, the making of foreign policy, or the examination of the inner workings of the Supreme Court. I disagree. Any student of government would have an incomplete education without an understanding of the day-to-day work of the regulators, who are some of the most interesting bureaucrats in Washington—and sometimes the most dedicated to their cause. In many respects, this is where the real work of government is done or avoided, where the intent of Congress is carried out or stymied, and where presidents leave their stamp on important health, safety, environmental, and financial issues through the people they appoint to important regulatory posts and their executive fiats.

Many people encouraged me to write this book and offered me help to get it done. First and foremost, *The Washington Post,* the hometown newspaper of "The Regulators," allowed me to step back from daily and weekly coverage of the regulatory world to write a book to explain why this is all worth understanding. I thank the highly skilled research professionals at *The Washington Post* for their excellent work, which is always delivered with speed and accuracy, especially Richard Drezen and Robert Lyford. Also, I am grateful to Jill Dutt, assistant managing editor of the *Post* business section and a longtime supporter of the column; David Ignatius, who conceived the column; and Len Downie, Tom Wilkinson, and Sandra Lee for making my leave possible and supporting the book. Fred Barbash, a former *Post* colleague, insisted long ago that these columns added up to a book. I also thank L. Sandy Maisel, a political science professor at Colby College, for imagining this book in the first place and for his prodding, help along the way, and sharing of contacts in the publishing world.

I am grateful to American University for giving me a home while I wrote this book, allowing me access to the library, a quiet space, and staff who were generous with their time. I give special thanks to Kay Mussell, dean of the College of Arts and Sciences, who welcomed me on campus and took care of every need. Special thanks go to the American University Economics Department: Larry Sawers, chairman of the department, who allowed me to use precious office space, and the administrative staff of the Economics Department, especially Sharon Childs-Patrick and Glen Arnold, who helped me out of many jams. Also, my gratitude goes to James McCabe, manager of computer training and documentation at American, who fixed computer problems and made house calls. Thanks also go to Karen Froslid-Jones, who was an all-around fixer for me while at American University, and American University Washington College of Law and Government Fellow Jeffrey S. Lubbers, who shared his insights on the book.

Others who contributed time and research along the way are Curtis Copeland, Paul Noe, Melinda Warren, Gary Bass, and Madeline Nelson. Each is an expert in the field of federal regulation, and all were generous with their time and patient in answering my questions.

The project never would have been started or finished without the professional support of my editor at Rowman and Littlefield Publishers, Jennifer Knerr, who took a chance on a different kind of book and encouraged me as I wrote it. She is a patient, kind, and wise editor. Also, thanks go to Renee Legatt, Knerr's assistant, who was capable of cheerfully answering any question, any time.

Finally, thank you to my daughters—Elizabeth and Natalie—for understanding how important this is to me and allowing me to get home late more times than I would like to remember. And, finally, I thank my husband, David Shribman, a born editor, writer, manager, and patient soul who did double duty on the home and work front so that this could be completed in a timely way.

Note

1. Cornelius M. Kerwin, *Rulemaking: How Government Agencies Write Law and Make Policy* (Washington, D.C.: CQ Press, 1994), 292.

Introduction

Parting Policy: "Midnight Regulations" Swell *Register*

The Washington Post, January 23, 2001—Former president Bill Clinton may be eating egg salad from a deli in Chappaqua, but his influence is still being felt in official Washington: Yesterday's *Federal Register,* a whopping 944 pages in two volumes, is the Clinton administration's last regulatory hurrah.

Technically, President Bush is in charge now. But because of the production and printing schedule of the *Federal Register,* Clinton and his appointees were able last Friday to rush through scores of new rules and proposals that didn't see the light of day until Monday.

The *Federal Register,* read closely by lobbyists, businesses and other groups subject to regulation, is the government's daily compendium of proposed and final rules, special regulatory notices, and executive orders. Once a final rule is printed, it has the force of law.

The material sent over by Clinton appointees Friday took three nights to print and bind, said Andy Sherman, spokesman for the Government Printing Office.

The printing crew was put on overtime to finish it and produce about 15,000 copies.

Those rules were preceded by three other double-volume editions of the *Register* last Wednesday, Thursday and Friday that added up to 2,568 pages.

Many of the regulations published yesterday are still in the proposal stage, so they will be subject to the 60-day delay the new Bush administration imposed Saturday.

But some are final rules that will be difficult to undo. Among them: standards for the use of bodily restraint and seclusion at residential psychiatric treatment facilities for those under 21 years of age; eight new national monuments that prohibit development on various pieces of land; and how the National Park Service will interpret snowmobile limitations in certain parks.

Other Clinton administration rules arrived Friday and were scheduled for publication later this week. But the Bush administration moved quickly yesterday, instructing agencies to write to the *Federal Register* to stop publication.

Frances McDonald, managing editor of the regulatory publication, said five agencies sent notices to stop various proposals from appearing in print. Anyone who wanted to view those rules would have had to do so in person yesterday at the *Register*'s office, where they were open for public inspection.

The Federal Aviation Administration asked that a proposed rule governing the flights of air-tour operators over smaller national parks be withdrawn from publication tomorrow. That proposal was filed by the Clinton administration Friday at 10:33 a.m.

The Environmental Protection Agency asked that a broad proposal to regulate pesticides created through plant bioengineering be withheld from publication. The Department of Housing and Urban Development, the Forest Service and the Office of the U.S. Trade Representative also asked that a variety of proposals be withheld and the documents sent back to the agencies.

It wasn't clear who was coordinating the effort. A call to the Office of Management and Budget press office resulted in this reply from a person who would not give his name: "We don't have a communications person yet. Let's just leave it at that. I have a million things I have to do. Bye." Click.

It wasn't easy to get answers at the agencies, either.

Some agencies don't have anyone in the administrator's corner office yet. For example at EPA, Michael McCabe, a Clinton political appointee is acting administrator for a few days. At the National Highway Traffic Safety Administration, Executive Director L. Robert Shelton is running the show. He is a career civil servant.

Though not printed in the *Federal Register*, the Clinton administration took other last-minute actions. Justice Department lawyers filed papers at the Supreme Court on a red wolves endangered species case for the Interior Department—ahead of this Friday's filing deadline.

At the Department of Transportation, then-Secretary Rodney E. Slater gave away millions in grant money late last week. Last Thursday, he awarded $61.6 million in discretionary funds for 15 bridge projects in 14 states. The Chicago Transit Authority got $320 million on Friday. Another $7.5 million was handed out to states for child-passenger safety education.

He also made a final decision adding Continental Airlines and Delta Air Lines to the carriers serving Argentina from the United States.

Not to be outdone, the Agriculture Department spread around some government largess of its own. It awarded $48 million, including an $18 million grant to help the state of California pay farmers to retire 12,000 acres of environmentally sensitive cropland.

I start with this column to give you an idea of what is to come and to show you how outgoing administrations scramble to get some of the most important work of the federal government done before the lights go out. They regulate, issuing a special brand of rules called "midnight regulations." These often are some of the most important and controversial rules that an administration worked on during its tenure in Washington.

One of the first things the new administration of George W. Bush did on January 20, 2001, was to undo everything the Clinton administration did at the proverbial stroke of midnight on the regulatory front. It issued what came to be known as the "Card Memo," freezing hundreds of rules for at least two months so they could be reviewed. Eventually many of them were delayed, changed, or stopped altogether. Some Clinton-era rules did go forward.

The move by the new administration is indicative of how important the management of regulation is to the country. Even before the Bush White House had nominated candidates to head the agencies and departments, it was regulating. Prior administrations had taken similar steps to quickly align regulatory policy with political objectives.

With the midnight regulations episode as a starting point, this book draws on a collection of important, real-life regulatory experiences that offer insight into how this part of the federal government really works. What follows is an attempt to cover what I consider to be the essentials of understanding federal regulation and the role it plays in business and everyday life.

Though you may not give it much thought, federal regulators—unelected bureaucrats who often stay in Washington for life or reside there briefly as political appointees—shape decisions that influence the quality of air you breathe, how safe your car is, which immigrants will enter and stay in this country, how airports will be protected from terrorism, what you can expect from your employer in terms of working conditions and pensions, and how safe that hamburger is that you just put in your mouth. Regulation is everywhere partly because Americans have come to look to their government to set rules, especially at times of crisis. In the aftermath of the accounting and corporate scandals of 2002, the response was to regulate so that Americans would have some assurance that the unsavory financial machinations at companies like the Houston-based Enron Corporation would not happen again.

Broadly, I will address these issues in several contexts: the scope of federal regulation and its influence, historical perspective on how the regulatory state was created and the roles that people play within it, an examination of efforts to change the system, and the challenges of regulating in the future. These are the broad confines within which individual regulatory decisions are made.

The structure of this book is such that it will enhance the body of serious work that already exists in this area and is taught across several disciplines. It is intended to be a stand-alone introduction to regulation or a stepping-off point for broader commentary on the politics of regulation. It also could be assigned as a supplement to numerous excellent graduate texts that examine how the administrative process works, the case law that has been created in the regulatory field, and the economic and political considerations of regulation.

The first chapter looks broadly at the reach of regulation in practice and application; it examines the many ways of trying to estimate the extent of regulation. It discusses why regulation has become a fact of everyday life. It makes no judgments about whether this is a good or a bad thing but, rather, provides examples for the reader to make up his or her own mind.

Chapter 2 focuses on the history of the regulatory state. It looks at the creation and work of various federal agencies and the role they play in setting important national policies. It examines who the rulemakers are, how much power they have, and how they make rules. It discusses the challenges that regulators face in getting and keeping their jobs.

Chapter 3 discusses what role special interests—some of them extraordinarily esoteric—play in shaping regulation and why they can be one of the most influential factors in the outcome of a rule. Similarly, Congress, and its political makeup, wields significant influence in the regulatory process and helps shape regulatory policy through funding, oversight, and legislation.

Chapter 4 centers on attempts to change or "reform" the regulatory process. It looks at the efforts of Congress, business lobbyists, scientists, and economists to change the process of making rules, as well as the threshold for proposing a rule in the first place. It examines the procedures that exist for eliminating rules, especially the Congressional Review Act. And it discusses at length the legislative forays in the 1990s to effect change on the structure and application of regulations.

Regulation costs money. Chapter 5 discusses contemporary attempts to put a price tag on regulation and why it is difficult to assess the cost, not to mention the benefit, of federal regulation. Estimates often vary wildly between the regulators and the regulated. Science and economics, increasingly, are the yardsticks used to weigh the necessity of a rulemaking.

The final chapter considers how the George W. Bush administration has faced regulatory challenges, before and after the events of September 11, 2001. It explores the economic and regulatory aftermath of the collapse of the Enron Corp., the bankruptcy of WorldCom Inc., and accounting irregularities in the corporate world—some of them deemed to be criminal behavior. These events had a major impact on the future direction of regulatory policy, especially as financial regulation and the creation of an entire new bureaucracy created to fight terrorism moved to center stage. Finally, the book looks forward to the ultimate future challenge to regulation: globalization of the world economy, "harmonization" of standards, and the effect those movements have on domestic regulatory policy.

The Long Arm of the Regulators: The Ubiquitous Regulatory State

---

The Hole Truth: With Swiss Cheese, It's All in the Eyes

The Washington Post, August 1, 2000—"I'll have a ham and cheese on rye with three-eighths-of-an-inch eyes, please. Easy on the mustard."

The next time you order the old standby, you might take a look at the holes in the cheese. The Department of Agriculture has proposed allowing producers to make smaller holes—or, as the regulators call them, eyes—in Swiss cheese.

The idea is to stop gumming up slicers and get a neater piece of cheese that isn't all tattered at the edges. "According to the cheese industry, the whole trend in American Swiss cheese is to the smaller eye," said Kathleen Merrigan, administrator of the Agricultural Marketing Service. "Europeans like bigger holes. But it's used for sandwiches here, and if you have really big holes there is a lot of trim and waste in the product."

The real issue, of course, is money. Sales of Swiss have been declining in recent years, and American makers want a bigger slice of the cheese market. (Americans eat about 30 pounds of cheese a year, including about 10 pounds of Cheddar but only 1 pound of Swiss.)

The price Swiss makers are able to get for their Swiss depends, in part, on the grade that Agriculture Department inspectors give it. And, for now at least, Grade A Swiss does not allow the smaller holes that large buyers crave.

As huge buyers such as Kraft Foods started asking for smaller holes, producers found themselves selling a lower grade of cheese with smaller holes. But because of the lower grade, they didn't get paid as much for it. They then found that wholesalers were selling the small-eyed Swiss at Grade A prices—a difference that can be about 10 cents a pound, said John Umhoefer, executive director of the 130-member Wisconsin Cheese Makers Association.

The cheesemakers responded by pushing for smaller holes in their product last year. They asked the Agriculture Department, which sets the standards for grades, for more freedom on eye size. "Swiss is the only major U.S. cheese variety in decline," said a letter from the Wisconsin Cheese Makers. " . . . Eye size requirements for Swiss cheese are out of step with the demands of the consumer and the marketer/processor."

The regulators heard. The fifteen-page proposal issued July 20 calls for allowing the majority of the holes in Swiss to be in the range of 3/8 to 13/16 of an inch in diameter. The current standard for Grade A Swiss calls for a narrower range that produces a bigger hole: 11/16 to 13/16 of an inch, or about the size of a nickel.

"The cheese shall be properly set and shall possess well-developed round or slightly oval-shaped eyes which are uniformly distributed," the current Grade A standard reads. Federal inspectors use the standard in rating Swiss to determine flavor, body, finish, appearance and color.

The new proposal states: "The Department feels that uniformity of eye size is a measure of quality in Swiss cheese and therefore proposes to recognize the significance of uniformity of eye sizes within this larger range for Grade A Swiss."

That means every eye has to be about the same size. As for Grade B Swiss, there's room for more flexibility. The eyes could be any size within that range. (The proposed changes also specify that the color of Swiss should be white to light yellow.)

And advances in science are helping cheesemakers deal with their eye problem.

The holes in Swiss cheese are caused by carbon dioxide expanding within the cheese curd during a ripening period in a warm room. "We have perfected the culturing so the eyes are more uniformly distributed and you can somewhat change the size of the eyes. You find cultures that do the things you want them to do," said Allen Sayler of the International Dairy Foods Association.

Brewster Dairy Inc., the largest domestic maker of Swiss cheese, said the holes can be made smaller by removing the cheese from the gas-making process earlier and refrigerating it. "You really have to know what you're doing," said Gene Hong, research and quality assurance director for the Ohio company.

Though the "eye" standards do not have any food-safety implications, they do provide common terminology for buyers and sellers. The first official standard for Swiss was set in 1953, and the standard was last revised in 1987. The government also sets standards for American, Cheddar, Colby and Monterey Jack cheese. Though the standards are voluntary, many cheese plants ask for the USDA imprimatur on their product.

The graders who taste and spit out the cheese have a checklist of 22 "classifications" that determine the quality of a Swiss cheese eye. They dis the Swiss with eyes they describe as cabbage, collapsed, dull, dead, frog mouth, gassy, nesty, one-sided, underset or uneven. Instead of an A, such cheese would receive a B or a C.

The lingo, developed by graders who are the equivalent of experienced wine stewards, has been used for decades by state and federal officials to classify Swiss in a uniform and consistent way.

Industry experts said the change will not affect prices, or taste, at the deli counter, especially if store buyers stick to Swiss with bigger holes.

"People want a piece of Swiss cheese that holds together," said Joseph Zuercher, a Chicago-based importer and wholesaler of cheese. He said Swiss made in Switzerland can have holes as big as quarters and half-dollars. But that cheese is often eaten in chunks or melted, he said.

Ham and cheese lovers may not be as picky about the holes in their Swiss, or care if it's gassy. But buyers of big blocks of Emmentaler, as it's also called, do pay close attention. That's because cheese whose holes are too big creates waste when sliced, and waste means lost profit.

"Retail wants big, and some buyers want small because it's less likely to crumble and fall apart," said the Wisconsin cheesemakers' Umhoefer. "Some are even demanding a certain eye size."

Producers hope the proposed changes will address the needs of buyers who use high-tech slicers that can spit out up to 1,000 slices a minute. Smaller holes work better in these slicers with much of the cheese bound for high-volume food service operations.

"You can't be strangled by these outmoded regulations," said Brad Legreid, executive director of the Wisconsin Dairy Products Association.

There are many areas of life, Swiss cheese among them, that federal regulation touches. The role of federal regulators in deciding the size of the holes in Swiss cheese is a vivid example of the pervasiveness of federal regulation, its effect on the smallest details of common, everyday things, its implications for business, and its reach all the way to hungry consumers ordering at the deli counter.

I devoted an entire edition of my *Washington Post* weekly column, "The Regulators," to writing about the change in the size of holes in Swiss cheese to offer an intimate, inside look at the breath of the regulatory establishment, its incredible specialization, and its sometimes impractical application. Not to mention cost. The expansion of the regulatory state that has been going on since the New Deal has engendered impassioned debate over who should control federal agencies and to what extent their authority should reach. In a report for the Senate Committee on Governmental Affairs in 1986, Morton Rosenberg, a specialist in American public law at the Congressional Research Service, writes,

> The signal American socio-political development of the last half century has been the rejection of passive, minimalist governance and the

acceptance of, and ever increasing demand for, the exertion of governmental efforts to ameliorate perceived social, economic and political wrongs. One of the most prominent characteristics of this active political philosophy has been the emergence of a pattern of pervasive governmental economic and social regulation. In short, we are in the era of the administrative state.[1]

Hence, even regulatory decisions as small as the adjustment of the diameter of holes in Swiss cheese are not too insignificant to be addressed by federal regulators. But some of the biggest events in our lives have also come to be controlled or influenced by federal regulation. Decisions affecting auto and air safety, privacy in the age of the Internet, attempts to ban tobacco, homeland security, and how to rein in corporate wrongdoers in the age of Enron Corp. and its spectacular accounting hijinks have come to dominate the new century. In fact, the largest expansion of the federal government and the regulatory state occurred after September 11, 2001, with the idea of creating the Homeland Security Department and the merging of thousands of federal employees and their regulatory responsibilities.

Historically, regulating—the purview of bureaucrats—has been regarded as not very meaningful work. But most regulatory determinations, whatever their size, are very important to the parties affected, and that includes private citizens as well as business. This is why this little-appreciated area of American politics often provides the rawest look at the collision among government, business, and consumers. The regulators, and the decisions they make, have been a growing influence over the last half century, affecting the direction of social and economic policy to an extent the Founding Fathers never accounted for or imagined. And, unlike the legislative process, which involves electing officials who can be held accountable, and legislation, which is largely created in public view, the regulatory process is largely an anonymous one with a high level of unaccountability attached to it—despite congressional oversight and executive and judicial review of rules.

The origins of federal departments, agencies, and commissions are diverse, but there is commonality among them. Though they are creatures of Congress and are supervised by the judiciary and executive branches both directly and indirectly, some agencies do have what James Q. Wilson calls in his book *The Politics of Regulation* a "substantial autonomy, at least with respect to congressional or executive direction." He attributes this to the "largely unsupervised nature of most regulatory activity."[2] Recent academic literature is replete with analyses of how the bureaucracy works, what influences it, and whether it is responsive to public demand. In his book, *Regulatory Politics in Transition,* Marc Allen Eisner does a historical survey of regulatory regimes dating to 1880. His conclusion is that, over time, agency autonomy has been enhanced by the hiring of highly specialized economists and researchers in place of policy generalists, who usually were lawyers. His point is that this specialization—which he calls "agency professionalism"—has given agencies increasing independence from congressional oversight and public and private influence. Interestingly, the work done by B. Dan Wood and Richard W. Waterman in *Bureaucratic Dynamics: The Role of Bureaucracy in a Democracy,* which involves using empirical research methods to examine eight agencies, shows that the bureaucracy does adapt and respond to hierarchical control—especially shared control from the Congress and the president.

The Effect on Business

We like to think that consumers drive demand in free markets and that free markets foster the best models of competition among companies. Those theories may have relevance, but they have not mitigated the countless behind-the-scenes regulatory decisions that can have a major impact on both consumers and the markets, influencing what businesses produce, how much products cost, and what is available to consumers. For many businesses and special interest groups that represent other parts of American society, the promulgation and implementation of a regulation may be more important than passage of the law that created the idea for the rule. Again, the autonomy of regulators and the power vested in them often result in policies that are a departure from what the principals ever expected.

For that reason, many businesses have organized important functions such as human resources and environmental strategies around the work of regulators. They know that compliance—or noncompliance—with the rules can cost time and money. Regulatory issues, and their growing reach, often determine whether companies or special interests have a large lobbying presence in Washington or a small one. They determine, too, how much they spend on monitoring federal regulation, which can be a full-time job. Many companies have large full-time staffs, or consultants, in Washington who do a highly specialized kind of jousting with federal regulators. General Electric Co., for example, spent years lobbying against clean-up costs for the Hudson River, where its plants are located. The company spent millions of dollars trying to convince federal regulators not to disturb the river, but it lost its case when the Environmental Protection Agency decided in summer 2001 that the company would have to clean up years of toxic PCB discharges into the river. Everyone from salt producers to cement makers has a presence in Washington keeping a watchful eye on the regulators.

For many companies, the monitoring of federal regulation and lobbying of regulators constitute one of their most critical tasks—more important, in some cases, than advertising, marketing, or public relations. For the airline industry, after the terrorist attacks of September 11, 2001, the lobbying prowess of dozens of seasoned professionals, including the chief executive officers of some of the airlines, resulted in a $15 billion relief package to keep airline companies afloat. Enron Corp., before its fall, benefited from the courting it did of federal regulators and members of Congress, allowing it to be absolved from complying with some of the same financial rules that may have kept it from collapse. Because of the lobbying the company did on a complicated financial issue, it was not subject to any regulation or oversight by the Commodity Futures Trading Commission in energy-related derivatives. In the end, this is an exemption that may have led to Enron's downfall when it filed for bankruptcy and spawned widespread congressional investigation: "In late 2000, Congress exempted from nearly all regulation these over-the-counter derivatives, which are contracts whose value is derived from the underlying assets such as commodities or currencies. Enron led the massive lobbying effort on Capitol Hill and, with the exemption, escaped federal oversight of its trading activities."[3] At the Department of Labor, Enron asked for a key change in its pension plan to reduce its costs while it reduced the value of the pensions that were earned by employees.

The company and its chief executive officer, Kenneth Lay, also had access to high-level officials in the Bush administration and offered advice on how the Bush administration should shape a national energy policy. The company was also influential in picking the top regulator at the Federal Energy Regulatory Commission. In short, Enron is a classic case of mastering the inner workings of the regulatory system in Washington and directing campaign contributions to important policy makers. Its savvy in understanding the regulatory system led to its ascendancy—and its demise—when Congress and regulators reacted by calling for more financial, accounting, and pension regulation.

From Microsoft Corp. to toilet makers, businesses have come to learn that it is as important to know their regulators as it is to be on a first-name basis with their representatives in Congress. The Wisconsin cheese makers, for example, knew where to turn and how the system worked when they needed a price adjustment for their product. They mounted an offensive, followed established rules of bureaucratic conduct, and won the change they sought. Microsoft, like many companies in the high-technology sector, wanted nothing more than to refrain from becoming involved in regulatory politics. But Microsoft and companies like it found that keeping their distance from Washington was unwise and, ultimately, impossible. Questions about electronic privacy, competition, taxes on Internet commerce, and telecommunications policy—all of them became part of the Washington policy and regulatory agenda and dominant factors in the growth and future of the New Age Economy. And all of this is quite apart from the huge antitrust action the government took against Microsoft.

Bridgestone/Firestone: A Case Study

The Bridgestone/Firestone Corp. found out the hard way about the reach of federal regulators, particularly when Congress supports more regulation. In summer 2000, when one of the biggest safety and regulatory crises of the last half century hit the Japanese tire company (which has its American headquarters in Nashville, Tennessee), it found itself flat-footed. The trouble began when federal regulators at the National Highway Traffic Safety Administration began investigating the company after a mounting number of deaths were linked to tread separations in the tires. With no official representation in Washington, Bridgestone/Firestone was at a disadvantage in the biggest challenge of its corporate life, trying to convince Congress, regulators, and the public that its tires were safe. The company's position as an outsider in Washington made it even harder for the company to persuade regulators to broaden their investigation to include the Ford Motor Co. and its best-selling sports utility vehicle, the Explorer. Firestone insisted that the problem was not with its tires but, rather, with the instability of the Explorer, on which millions of Firestone tires were mounted.

But Bridgestone/Firestone lacked the two most important weapons a company in a regulatory crisis requires in Washington—access and credibility. Until the year 2000, the company had depended on the Rubber Manufacturers Association, a Washington-based group to which most of the tire manufacturers belonged, to keep an eye on NHTSA and represent its interests, which, in ordinary times, were minimal.

Ford, on the other hand, has had a powerful presence in Washington for decades. Its representatives, many of them seasoned lobbyists, were on a first-name basis with key decision makers at the agency. It worked on countless safety rulemakings with regulators at NHTSA and was the subject of safety recalls overseen by the agency, just as many of its competitors in the auto business have been. It understood through years of experience—dating to the inception of the agency in 1966—that NHTSA is responsible for developing safety standards, identifying defects in vehicles (and tires), and researching everything from distracted drivers to how long it takes brakes to stop a vehicle. The company had a firm grasp of the regulatory process, the extent to which it could be regulated, and the extent to which it could avoid regulation.

To give it even more heft in Washington, Ford also had long-standing relationships with influential members of Congress, such as Democratic Congressman John Dingell, who lives not far from Ford headquarters in Detroit. Members of Congress overseeing agencies like NHTSA can play important roles in representing the interests of their constituents—the auto companies.

Firestone Gets in Gear on Lobbying

The Washington Post, June 19, 2001—Few companies are better than Ford Motor Co. at Washington politics. Bridgestone/Firestone Corp. learned that the hard way. Now the tiremaker is scrambling to catch up.

As it prepared for today's hearing into the deaths linked to Firestone tire failures on Ford Explorers, Firestone's new Washington representative arranged for the hand-delivery of the ultra-popular Precept MC Lady golf balls to several members of Congress. The golf balls, which are made by Bridgestone Sports USA in Atlanta, are virtually impossible to get in pro shops or elsewhere because they are in such demand by mostly male golfers who want to add distance to their shots. This is one product that Bridgestone can't make enough of.

"We've got balls," said Steven Akey, a former Department of Transportation official who opened Firestone's first Washington office on April 16. "It kind of symbolizes that we're being aggressive about this."

Firestone, on the other hand, had little to do with Washington until the first set of congressional investigations last fall on the deaths linked to Firestone tire failures on Ford Explorers.

"They had next to nothing in terms of relationships," said one of Firestone's new hires. "It wasn't on their radar. It wasn't a priority. It's like your roof. You take it for granted until something goes wrong and then you give it a lot of attention in a short period of time."

For example, Rep. Bart Gordon (D-Tenn.), who has a Firestone plant in his district, said he never heard from the tiremaker in the nine terms he has served in Congress—until Firestone chief executive John T. Lampe called last August after the initial recall of 6.5 million tires.

Before then, when it had business in Washington, Firestone relied mostly on the Rubber Manufacturers Association, a trade group of tire-makers. "Their profile, for the size of the company, was the lowest of our members," said Donald Shea, the group's president.

That's changing. Firestone now has nine lobbying and legal firms. It increased its lobbying expenditures to more than $1 million last year—still far behind Ford's reported spending of more than $8 million.

In preparation for the first congressional hearings on the recall last fall, Firestone brought on the law firm of King & Spalding. It hired Holland & Knight partner and former representative Gerry Sikorski (D-Minn.), who had 10 years of experience on Energy and Commerce's oversight and investigations subcommittee.

Firestone also added Public Strategies, an Austin-based public affairs firm that has in its ranks Jeff Eller, a former Clinton administration director of media affairs. He hired Akey and also Wallace Henderson, hunting buddy and former counsel to Rep. W. J. "Billy" Tauzin (R-La.), chairman of the committee.

Last October, Firestone continued its hiring spree by retaining Chesapeake Enterprises' Scott Reed, who was Sen. Robert J. Dole's presidential campaign manager. More firepower was added with Akin, Gump, Strauss, Hauer & Feld, whose ranks include former representative Bill Paxon (R-N.Y.) and Susan Lent, who served on the Bush–Cheney transition team. Akin Gump billed Firestone $500,000 last year.

Jack Rice, former National Highway Traffic Safety Administration chief counsel, who is now at Arent Fox Kintner Plotkin & Kahn, was tapped by Firestone to handle the agency. Ben Barnes, former lieutenant governor of Texas and a friend of Senate Majority Leader Thomas A. Daschle (D-S.D.), who now heads an Austin firm called Entrecorp, was hired as well.

The person who arranged the hand-delivery of the golf balls was Steven Akey, who was counselor to former Transportation Department Secretary Rodney E. Slater. Akey now directs and coordinates the company's lobbying effort, sharing an office with Public Strategies.

"Anything is an improvement over where they were," one lobbyist said of Firestone. "Unfortunately, for a lot of companies, they don't pay attention until the wolf is inside the door and it costs them."

This isn't to suggest that personal familiarity determines the outcome of an important regulatory decision or an investigation. But companies have a better chance of influencing the decision and being heard if they understand the broad scope and back doors of the regulatory landscape.

The NHTSA investigation was closed on October 4, 2001, with Bridgestone/Firestone agreeing to recall an additional 3.5 million tires at a cost of about $30 million. The original recall in August 2000 involved 6.5 million tires. The company, by this time, finally had gotten to know its regulators at NHTSA well: it took a half dozen meetings between July and October 2001, when the agreement was reached and the case was closed.

Firestone's refusal to recognize the extent and importance of federal regulation is an unusual but telling example of the power of the regulators as America's unelected arm of government. Not only did Firestone miscalculate the effect the recall would have on its own business, but it failed to understand how the tread separation problem would spark a spate of new tire and auto safety legislation.

The Firestone episode produced a firestorm, shining a light on the effectiveness—or ineffectiveness—of safety rules the government had put in place thirty years ago. Auto companies saw what was in store for them as a result of the Firestone problem and immediately began strategizing on how to limit the extent of new rules or at least contain ones that they considered problematic. One area of particular concern was the scope of a new rule to impose criminal penalties on company personnel who did not inform regulators of defects in their products, especially if they occurred overseas. The dispute was finally resolved in a way the auto companies could live with. For them, it was a regulatory fiat—but a manageable regulatory fiat.

High-Speed Legislation:
Auto-Safety Bill Reflects Industry's Interest

The Washington Post, October 24, 2001—In the end, it was as quick as running a red light: Auto-safety legislation sailed through the House and Senate earlier this month after a furious lobbying battle over how strong criminal penalties and safety-defect disclosure rules should be for the auto and tire industries.

It took just five weeks to get it all done—hold hearings, write reports, prepare legislation and pass a bill. The finished product, which imposes criminal penalties on auto and tire manufacturers, increases their reporting requirements to the National Highway Traffic Safety Administration, and gives the agency additional funding to do its job.

But along the way, its backers had to deal with the 16 lobbyists unleashed by the U.S. Chamber of Commerce to try to block or weaken the package, as well as the parade of victims of tire-related accidents that safety advocate Joan Claybrook brought to town to back the case for a stronger bill.

The legislation means new regulatory obligations for the tire and auto industries—a direct response to the August recall of 6.5 million Bridgestone/ Firestone Inc. tires and 119 accident deaths linked to them. But the bill also reflects the lobbying prowess of the automotive industry, the Chamber and other business groups that persevered until they got a bill they can live with. "Common sense prevailed," said R. Bruce Josten, the Chamber's executive vice president. "It was a solid victory."

Combining forces, the business interests pressed legislators to drop provisions they didn't like, add ones they preferred, and, in the end, persuade individual senators to "hold" or block passage of the entire Senate bill.

The idea was to bottle up Sen. John McCain's (R-Ariz.) bill, which had more onerous criminal penalties and broader disclosure requirements, and push a House bill, sponsored by Reps. Fred Upton (R-Mich.) and W. J. "Billy" Tauzin (R-La.), that business found more palatable.

Josten made no apologies for the strategy—or the result. The Chamber was fearful that the criminal provisions in the Senate bill would influence how other industries interact with regulators in designing and testing their products.

The Chamber also "fax and e-mail blasted around town to associations that shared the same interests," he said, and did "continuous lobbying across town with an awful lot of letter writing in between."

Between Sept. 20 and Oct. 5, the Chamber shot off five letters to the Senate and Rep. Thomas J. Bliley Jr. (R-Va.), chairman of the House Commerce Committee. Two of them warned that the Chamber would consider a vote for the Senate bill a "key vote" that would affect a senator's rating with the Chamber and the endorsement and political donations that go with it. The National Association of Manufacturers (NAM) sent a letter of its own, with much the same message.

Meanwhile, realizing that the auto industry wanted to keep a low profile in this fight, Josten fielded press calls.

Mike Stanton, lobbyist for the Alliance of Automobile Manufacturers, credited the Chamber with slowing down the Senate bill and shifting focus to "a more workable version in the House."

On the other side of the issue, public interest groups were working no less feverishly. Claybrook, a former NHTSA administrator who is president of Public Citizen, held numerous news conferences at major junctures in the legislative process. She flew in 25 victims and relatives involved in accidents with Ford Explorers and Firestone tires to talk to legislators.

"They made it clear the public was on the case, but the Chamber was intimately involved in all the strategy and they controlled the leadership," Claybrook said.

Public Citizen objects to limits the bill puts on public disclosure of information automakers have to file with NHTSA. And the group criticized the criminal-penalties provision. Though it increases fines to $15 million, they argue it would be tougher to prosecute misdeeds because it includes a provision that lets executives correct inadvertent misstatements about safety defects.

"We got as tough a bill as you could get out of this session in record time. You would think consumer advocates would be pretty happy, and some are," Tauzin said in an interview. He defended the criminal provisions in the House bill, saying they are stronger than the Senate's because they are "enforceable."

Tauzin spokesman Ken Johnson said the bill includes provisions that would have taken years to pass: NHTSA must rewrite its 30-year-old tire standard, mandate notice of foreign recalls, develop a dynamic test for rollover of vehicles and improve testing of child safety seats.

"Congress deserves a pat on the back, not a kick in the butt, for this," he said.

McCain isn't as happy. His frustration spilled over when he tried for the second time to have his bill passed—only to have it blocked by "holds," procedural maneuvers executed anonymously by his colleagues. Mark Buse, staff director for the Senate Commerce Committee, said the chamber and NAM were acting as "shills" for the auto industry.

Vowing to revisit the issue next year, McCain put forward the House bill. The Clinton administration also weighed in, supporting the Upton–Tauzin approach.

"I will tell you, in straight talk, what this is all about," McCain said on the Senate floor. "This is the trial lawyers against the automotive interests. Trial lawyers do not want it because . . . they want to be able to sue anybody for anything under any circumstances. And the automotive industry wants this thing killed, figuring the publicity around these accidents . . . will die out and they will be able to kill off the legislation next year."

Playing by the Rules

In his book *Private Power and American Democracy*, Grant McConnell develops the eye-opening argument that the companies that play interest group politics best actually are comfortable with their regulators and have learned how to manipulate them to a certain degree. "Hence," McConnell writes in his landmark 1966 work, "the railroad industry is largely content with regulation by the Interstate Commerce Commission, the securities trade is pleased to see extension of Securities and Exchange Commission policing, and the oil industry is happy to cooperate in the operation of the National Petroleum Council."[4]

Cornelius M. Kerwin, a professor of public policy and provost at American University, believes that there are special interest groups that accept and understand regulation; they realize it can have benefits. In his book, *Rulemaking: How Government Agencies Write Law and Make Policy*, Kerwin says:

> Interest groups are sufficiently sophisticated to understand the benefits and costs that may arise from rules. They have also developed the means for monitoring rulemaking processes and for communicating their views to the rulemakers. They prefer the relative calm and predictability of a process that operates according to fixed procedures, participation in which requires at least a modicum of technical expertise and a certain understanding of bureaucratic decisionmaking.[5]

In the case just mentioned, the auto companies and other business groups were savvy enough to contain what could have been—in their view—an even more onerous regulatory burden for them. The biggest companies, which have the resources to cope with it, are not entirely uncomfortable with the notion that regulation is pervasive because they feel they have some control over it. Small business has a different view and usually fights heavy doses of regulation head-on. The recognition that regulation is a fact of life pertains not only to old-line companies but also to newcomers that rapidly have grown into big corporate players. The biotechnology industry, organic food farmers, and online music providers have realized that what begins as policy debate in Washington often ends up as a sweeping regulatory program. Here are several examples: Deciding the formula for fuel efficiency can be an important factor in the future design of the automobile. Setting the threshold for an acceptable level of arsenic in drinking water is a public safety and economic issue for states, localities, and citizens. Declaring a plant or animal species endangered can affect the course of industrial and residential development if whole parcels of land are off-limits to new projects. The fledgling organic food industry now is regulated by the federal government.

Besides issuing prospective rules, agencies also regulate more informally. They inspect products, grant licenses, issue recalls, settle disputes, issue benefits, collect taxes, and offer guidance to companies and individuals on the implementation of their programs. All of these actions require informal decisions that can have widespread applicability. They are another way beyond formal rulemaking to extend the reach of regulators. Ernest Gellhorn and Ronald M. Levin, in their book *Administrative Law and Process in a Nutshell,* state that an agency that issues a press release or holds a news conference can have an effect that is "as potent as a formal rule or order."[6]

Getting Down to the Details

As regulation has become part of the fabric of government over the last century, the influence and reach of regulators have grown. There is great specialization among agencies and within them, leaving it up to companies and nonprofit groups that care about federal regulation to figure out where to apply pressure to lobby their causes. They have found that the time they spend on this task is often profitable because the issues tackled by regulatory experts within the agencies and departments of the federal government have become increasingly broad and deep.

At the Food and Drug Administration, for example, where there are hefty regulatory issues involving tobacco, food safety, and the approval of new drugs and medical devices, there also are regulatory experts who can address an issue as narrow as the labeling on breath mints or the tasting of tea samples to determine if imports comply with the guidelines set to determine if a tea is green, oolong, or pekoe. They have expertise in esoteric areas such as taste testing (they call it swish and spit) and the legal intricacies of labeling. This kind of expertise extends the reach of regulation to a level that is almost unimaginable to the average American who does not realize that what the label says on a product often is a years-long regulatory deliberation.

Sizing Up Breath Mints Leaves a Bad Taste in Some Mouths

The Washington Post, January 16, 1998—This is a story about bad breath, federal regulation and the six years it took to propose the appropriate serving size for small breath mints.

Back in 1991, the Food and Drug Administration, which implements the Nutrition Labeling and Education Act, needed to come up with a "reference amount" for hard candies and breath mints. A reference amount is a measurement that the agency uses to pinpoint how much of a food is consumed at a "single eating occasion." A company translates the amount into its serving size, which must be included on a product's nutrition label.

In this case, the FDA decided that 15 grams was the correct amount, which would equal a certain number of candies in each serving size, an amount the manufacturer would determine.

That was fine for peppermint drops or root beer barrels, but the full-size-breath-mint people—who don't consider themselves to be in the hard-candy camp—objected, pointing out that 15 grams equaled an entire package of full-size breath mints. Breath-mint fanatics may pop a whole roll, but most people ate one or two, mostly to banish bad breath, they told the FDA.

The FDA concurred and created a category for breath mints of two grams, which was about one full-size mint—for example, a Certs or a Breath Saver.

That satisfied many of the big-breath-mint makers, but the small-breath-mint people piped up: Two grams was still too big for their products. Ferrero USA Inc., maker of the tiny Tic Tac, said this equated to about five Tic Tacs.

Ferrero suggested that 0.5 grams or less was the correct reference amount for its product. That equated to one little mint.

The FDA said it couldn't decide until the company did a survey on consumption to support its petition for the change. Tic Tac did two surveys, which found that Tic Tac lovers used one mint and never got around to consuming five mints a day. Based on the surveys, Ferrero said users "place one breath mint in their mouth per freshening occasion."

Ferrero also hired I. Scott Bass, a lawyer at Sidley & Austin who is expert in FDA labeling issues. In 1994, Bass filed a petition for the company, saying that if the label requirement wasn't changed, it would damage the company's promotional campaign, which was built around one mint doing the job. With more than 235 million boxes of Tic Tacs sold annually in 1993, it didn't want to have to present labeling information using the five-mint serving size, especially when its bigger-mint brethren now were able to use one mint as their serving size.

Bass reminded the agency that Ferrero spent more than $130 million positioning Tic Tac as the one breath mint.

Other smaller mint makers also argued for a category change.

Frisk Refreshing Tablets complained that it would take 15 Frisks to meet the two-gram amount. Frisk said this would be misleading the consumer and the company feared "unlimited liability" if 15 were the serving size. It sent along some Frisk Peppermint and Eucalyptus tablets, weighing 0.13 grams, so the FDA could taste Frisk for itself.

But opposition to creating a 0.5-gram category surfaced faster than a bad case of morning breath.

Stuart M. Pape of Patton Boggs, a lawyer acting for an unnamed client that smelled a lot like a full-size-breath-mint company, said Ferrero was misusing the labeling laws by passing itself off as the 1.5-calorie breath mint.

Pape also trotted out the "waffle" argument. Waffles, he said, have been miniaturized. "Yet, appropriately, there is only one reference amount for waffles, 85 grams."

Kraft Foods chimed in on behalf of its product, Altoids, the "curiously strong peppermints." It worried that Altoids, a medium-size mint, would be stuck in the two-gram category, meaning the label would have to state three Altoids as a serving size while everyone else—producers of mints big and small—would be able to use one.

While popping samples of Tic Tacs and Frisks, agency staff got down to examining Ferrero's survey data.

The FDA was concerned that the analysis the company used was based on "the number of pieces put into the mouth at one time." The FDA wanted to focus on how many pieces were consumed in a single-eating occasion. That led to the jelly-bean analysis.

"A person may eat 10 jelly beans within a few minutes, but may only put one piece in his or her mouth at a time and finish each one before eating another. This situation would still represent 10 jelly beans eaten during a single eating occasion," the FDA theorized.

Thus, the FDA figured that people typically eat more small breath mints at a single eating occasion than if they were using a larger breath mint. The agency, quite logically it thought, concluded that Tic Tac consumption was closer to two mints than one. Yet five still seemed too many.

In the end, the agency decided not to create a 0.05-gram category for little mints. Instead it proposed changing the serving size to one unit—the same denomination it uses for ice cream cones, eggs and chewing gum. The serving size on the label would then also reflect the actual weight of one mint. In Tic Tac's case that probably would be 0.4 grams.

"It's very fair for consumers," Bass said. Ferrero, however, would also have liked the FDA to link the mint's "efficacy" with its small size.

But if consumers want to find the best bad-breath blaster, that's not possible from this label change. This is about serving sizes and nutrition, not "breath malodor elimination," as the FDA likes to call it.

"The consumer has to decide if the product works for them," said Ellen Anderson, the FDA's serving-size expert.

What Isn't Regulated?

At the end of the twentieth century and the beginning of the twenty-first, the regulatory establishment made major forays into controlling food safety, extending important environmental rules such as controlling ozone, setting standards for air bags in automobiles, creating a test to determine the likelihood of a rollover in a sport utility vehicle, establishing energy-efficiency levels for major appliances, and issuing the first-ever rule to limit ergonomic injuries in workplaces. It continues to deliberate how much sleep the nation's truck drivers need to do their jobs safely. It has decided the rules for how trucks coming from Mexico should be allowed to do business in this country under the terms of the North American Free Trade Agreement. Since September 11, 2001, the possibilities for federal regulators to address security and safety issues have grown exponentially to include issues such as whether pilots should carry guns in the cockpit. Scandals in the business world, such as the Enron affair, present challenges for agencies such as the Department of Labor, the Securities and Exchange Commission, and the Commodities Future Trading Commission that did not exist the previous year when the economy was booming and companies convinced regulatory overseers that they needed less oversight to continue thriving.

In the more routine world of regulation, prunes, soy milk, grits, unpasteurized juice, the water content in poultry, and eggs did not escape regulatory scrutiny. Nor did lead wicks in candles, the composition of crayons, imported cat and dog fur, pet ownership in public housing, tampon absorbency, the energy efficiency of air conditioners and hot water heaters, whether peanuts should be served on airplanes, and pollution control from weed whackers.

Besides its antitrust responsibilities, the Federal Trade Commission also is in charge of false claims in advertising and polices other areas of consumer concern, such as the funeral industry and how clothing manufacturers should label garments to help consumers care for them. Bank regulators are trying to manage the new frontier of electronic banking. The Federal Aviation Administration recently spoke of how "fractional aircraft" owners and managers should be regulated: these are investments akin to timeshares in business aircraft.

How Long Is the Reach?

The crudest way to track this annual blizzard of regulatory activity is to become a student of the *Federal Register,* which is now available online at www.access.gpo.gov/nara. For those who prefer paper, an annual subscription is $699, or $10 an issue. (Members of Congress get it free.) The National Archives and Records Administration publishes the *Register;* the U.S. Government Printing Office did the actual printing and binding of the 6,490 volumes that were in circulation in 2001.

The *Federal Register,* which is published Monday through Friday, is the federal government's legal accounting and public archive of regulatory proposals, final rules, meeting notices, paperwork collections, and executive orders from the president. The typical American might never have cause to browse the thin-paper pages of the volumes. But to those who have a stake or an interest in federal regulation, the *Federal Register* is closely watched to the point where interest groups check daily for rules that they expect to be published. They hover over their computers to get a first peek at the rule they are interested in seeing. Some special interests have staff who do nothing but look for the next rule.

On August 30, 2001, for example, no big regulatory initiatives were expected or announced, and yet there were 170 pages of proposed and final rules, along with other pronouncements. The Coast Guard announced a comprehensive review of boating safety regulations; the Consumer Product Safety Commission instructed the makers of a dermal patch that relieves pain about how it must be packaged to meet child-resistant packaging requirements; the Federal Reserve Board announced a discount rate change; the Fish and Wildlife Service proposed exemptions to its regulations protecting the Preble's Meadow Jumping Mouse, which is an endangered species; and the U.S. Patent and Trademark Office proposed a hearing to amend its rules to make mandatory the electronic filing of trademark documents. That is just an average day—and hardly the whole picture.

The *Federal Register*: The Book of Rules

The documentation of federal regulation began on March 14, 1936, for the same reason it exists now: Rapid-fire, presidents and bureaucrats make pronouncements and rules that take on the force of law. The federal government has been regulating since its inception, especially during wartime. There was little resolve to have any record of rulemakings until an episode occurred that illustrated how poorly the government cataloged and made available regulations. In July 1933, President Franklin D. Roosevelt began to issue a series of executive orders setting petroleum quota allowances. Panama Refining Company sued the government, saying that government inspectors exceeded the scope of the first order, which inadvertently was obliterated by a subsequent order.

Clearly, no one could keep track of what was going on. In 1934, the "Hot Oil Case" went to the Supreme Court, which chastised the Interior Department and the president for failing to give adequate notice of the orders. "When the oil company's attorney complained to the Court that the regulations in question could scarcely be found and that he had been forced to prepare his case using a tattered, unofficial copy of them, the Court ordered Justice Department attorneys to produce the original document. Despite an all-out search, the government was unable to locate the original," writes Michael White, director of the *Federal Register*'s legal and policy staff, in a 1996 article in the National Archives publication *The Record*.[7]

After that embarrassment, the Federal Register Act passed Congress quickly on July 26, 1935, and was signed by Roosevelt equally as fast. Since then, the *Federal Register* has grown fat. Regulatory devotees count not only substance but pages of the *Federal Register*. In 1936, the *Federal Register* was a manageable 2,620 pages, reflecting the work of far fewer federal agencies than exist today. By 1976, the page count increased to 50,505; in 2000, the tally was 74,258. It was the highest page count ever and reflected dozens of rules that the departing Clinton administration tried to get on the books before it left office—those "midnight regulations." In 2001, the page count receded to 69,591.

In 1976, the Office of the Federal Register began tracking the number of pages devoted to final rules, proposed rules, and notices. There was growth there, too: In 1976, there were 12,589 pages of final rules issued by the federal government. In 2001, the page number had almost doubled for final rules. Another way to look at it is that the Office of Management and Budget estimates that there are, roughly, four thousand five hundred regulatory actions taken by agencies every year.

There are those who religiously keep track of the size and growth of the *Register*s. It is a kind of sport as well as a road map of where the regulators are going. But many regulatory experts and practitioners in the field regard it as a misleading and imprecise measure of the extent and growth of federal regulation. Critics of regulation are fond of piling high stacks of *Federal Registers* on the floor of the House of Representatives or the Senate, or at a press conference, to prove their point that federal regulation has become expansive and overbearing. They complain, on behalf of their business constituencies, that regulation has become so complicated and prevalent that no small business person can comply with what is published within its covers; large corporations, on the other hand, have more of an advantage because they can hire entire staffs to catalog and interpret rules.

Conversely, supporters of regulation say that page count means nothing and is not representative of the quantity of rules actually being promulgated. Sally Katzen, former administrator of the Office of Management and Budget's Office of Information and Regulatory Affairs in the Clinton administration, made a point of stressing in an article in *The Washington Post* that "people not get hung up on the numbers of pages or the volume of regulations" in the *Federal Register* or the semiannual agenda of federal rules that outlines what regulatory actions agencies are contemplating.

Instead, high page counts may reflect the territory covered by just one rule: the ergonomics rule, for instance, took up 608 pages in the *Federal*

Register when it was published on October 9, 2001, though the substance of the rule was only eight pages long. The Clinton administration was quick to point out that most of the page tally was accounted for by supporting documents, such as the summary and explanation of the rule (161 pages), health effects (104 pages), and risk assessment (213 pages). The economic analysis used as the basis for the standard was 1,777 pages, but it was not published in the *Federal Register*. (Though the ergonomics rule had lots of verbiage, it was surpassed by the comments filed by the public in the federal government's antitrust case against Microsoft: a whopping 6,838 pages, filling twelve volumes.)

Another way to get a snapshot of regulatory activity is to look at the reports that the General Accounting Office compiles for every major rule—that is, one that has a $100 million impact on the economy annually. The GAO sends the reports to the committee in Congress that has jurisdiction over that area.

These brief reports provide accurate synopses of what each agency has issued, along with a calculation of the cost of the rule, its benefits, when it was proposed, and its relevance. For example, on September 11, 2001, the GAO sent to two congressional committees its report on a major rule issued by the Interior Department's Fish and Wildlife Service on early-season migratory bird hunting regulations for certain tribes on Indian reservations and ceded lands. The GAO reported that the rule would have an economic impact of more than $1.2 billion and that the agency followed all the correct procedural steps in issuing it.

The Growth of the Regulatory State

It is difficult to understand the scope of contemporary regulation without having some background on the metamorphosis of the regulatory state, which, the federal government itself now concedes, affects "virtually all individuals, businesses, State, local, and tribal governments, and other organizations in virtually every aspect of their lives or operations."[8] There are more than one hundred federal agencies with subagencies and departments under them, and they complete about four thousand five hundred new rules annually, according to the Office of Management and Budget.

The first "real" regulatory agency was the now-defunct Interstate Commerce Commission, an entity that was created in 1887 to curb abuse by the railroads in setting rates. The model of having a commission adjudicate decisions was duplicated in the Federal Trade Commission (1914) and other commissions like the Federal Power Commission (1920), a predecessor to today's federal Energy Regulatory Commission, and the Federal Radio Commission (1927), which became today's Federal Communications Commission. Supporters of the commission model of regulation viewed it as a scientifically capable body better suited to making technical decisions than the courts. They also thought it was the best way to combine the legislative, judicial, and executive forms of government into a single agency. Others believed that commissions would be professional and impervious to political influence. Some of this, but not all, would prove true.

The Federal Reserve Board (1913), the Tariff Commission (1916), the Commodities Exchange Commission (1922), and other financial regulators came into being before the idea of federal regulation really began to blossom in the 1930s. Before those earliest agencies were created, big federal departments like Labor (1913) and Commerce (1913) already were in place, outgrowths of President Theodore Roosevelt's Progressive attitude that professionals should head these departments.

The bureaucracy, as it is often disparagingly called today, is the creature of a new attitude Americans had about the role of government after the Great Depression and World War II. Americans looked to the federal government to solve what seemed like intractable economic problems. President Franklin Roosevelt's New Deal spawned regulatory bureaucracies such as the Securities and Exchange Commission, the National Labor Relations Board, and the Civil Aeronautics Authority (later renamed the Civil Aeronautics Board), a powerful agency that existed before the airlines were deregulated in 1978. The Federal Communications Commission and the Interstate Commerce Commission received from Congress expanded mandates to regulate. The Social Security Administration was created in 1933. The Food, Drug and Insecticide Administration was established in 1927 and was renamed the Food and Drug Administration in 1930.

Regulatory enthusiasts such as James Landis, a lawyer, regulator, and drafter of securities laws, encouraged the expansion of federal agencies as a fourth branch of government—the administrative branch, which would be staffed by experts and elites who would be intellectually equipped to handle the economic regulation of a rapidly expanding industrial economy. Landis staked his career on this notion and saw it firmly take hold during his time.

Starting in the 1950s, the regulatory state grew by leaps and bounds. President Lyndon Johnson's Great Society created government programs that found homes in the Departments of Health and Human Services (which earlier was the Department of Health and Education and Welfare, created in 1953), Housing and Urban Development (1965), and Transportation (1966). The consumer movement resulted in the National Credit Union Administration in 1970 and the Consumer Product Safety Commission in 1972. The Department of Transportation also was a response to the consumer movement and concerns voiced by activist Ralph Nader about the safety of automobiles. The Department of Energy was created in 1977 to gather under one roof many agencies and commissions that were addressing concerns about energy supplies and management. And the Environmental Protection Agency and the Occupational Safety and Health Administration were created in the 1970s to come up with answers to what we consider the modern-day problems of pollution and workplace hazards.

This new generation of federal agencies did not operate like the independent commissions created before them. Instead, Congress provided the instruction manual for how these agencies would operate by passing detailed statutes that often included deadlines for when rules had to be issued. A single administrator, rather than a clutch of commissioners, ran each new agency. All of these agencies are the foundation of the regulatory state that we have today. As the President's Committee on Administrative Management noted in 1937: "The rule-making power, like Topsy, just grew."[9]

The Expansion of the Agencies and Their Rules

The growth in rulemaking also is linked to the size of the federal regulatory bureaucracy, which now has fourteen cabinet-level departments and fifty-five independent agencies and commissions. A study by the Center for the Study of American Business at Washington University notes that staffing in regulatory agencies grew from 69,946 in fiscal year 1970 to an estimated 131,983 in 2000.

The number of agencies multiplies quickly when one opens the door to the parent department or agency. The Department of Health and Human Services has a sixty-eight-page listing in the *Federal Yellow Book*, a directory of federal agencies. Under the umbrella of HHS is the Administration on Aging, the Administration for Children and Families, the Centers for Disease Control and Prevention, the Food and Drug Administration, the Indian Health Service, the Centers for Medicare and Medicaid Services (formerly the Health Care Financing Administration), and the National Institutes of Health. Each in its own right is an imposing bureaucracy and a prolific regulator.

People think that the Treasury Department is consumed with economic policy and management. That is only partly true. Besides tax and economic policy, the Treasury is responsible for the Bureau of Alcohol, Tobacco and Firearms, which is a major tax collector, labeling regulator, and investigator (especially dealing with illegal use of firearms and explosives) with offices all over the country. These responsibilities fell to the Internal Revenue Service until the ATF was created in 1972. Also under the Treasury's umbrella is the Internal Revenue Service, which accounts for most of the Treasury Department's annual regulatory activity. In 2002, the ATF was divided between the Justice and Treasury Departments, a result of homeland security issues.

Some agencies regulate more than others. Data kept by the General Accounting Office since the passage of the Congressional Review Act in 1996 provide a detailed picture of the annual output of major rules and minor rules by each federal department, the agencies within that department, and independent agencies. Those figures, gathered by GAO since 1997 through the end of 2000, show in table 1.1 that the regulatory heavyweights are the Transportation Department, the Environmental Protection Agency, the Treasury Department, the Commerce Department, the Agriculture Department, and the Federal Communications Commission. But, like counting *Federal Register* pages, the raw numbers the GAO has compiled can be misleading.

The Transportation Department accounted for 1,522 rules in 2000. Closer scrutiny of that number shows that some 1,519 of those rules were considered minor. The other three were major rules that had an impact on the economy of $100 million or more annually. One was a rule issued by the National Highway Traffic Safety Administration setting the standard for how protective air bags must be; one was setting the fuel economy for light trucks; and the third was issued by the Federal Railroad Administration concerning railroad rehabilitation.

Most of the other 1,519 rules that were issued that year by the Transportation Department came from the U.S. Coast Guard (600) and likely were routine notices such as raising drawbridges, restricting marine traffic during fireworks displays, and giving permission for regattas on waterways. The Federal Aviation Administration was the second largest issuer in the Transportation Department (841); on a daily basis, the agency issues several "airworthiness directives," which often require aircraft manufacturers to inspect or make changes to various models of aircraft.

In the Agriculture Department, routine marketing orders are issued almost daily, adjusting the volume of shipments and the grade of the commodity depending on demand in the market and the size of the crop. Avocados,

TABLE 1.1. **Federal Rules Received by the General Accounting Office: 1997–2000**

Agencies	1997	1998	1999	2000
President of the United States[a]				
Major	0	0	0	0
Minor	2	1	2	4
Total	2	1	2	4
Department of Agriculture				
Major	7	5	5	12
Minor	246	314	230	263
Total	253	319	235	275
Department of Commerce				
Major	0	1	7	0
Minor	273	314	335	314
Total	273	315	342	314
Department of Health and Human Services				
Major	6	18	7	13
Minor	165	176	136	150
Total	171	194	143	163
Department of Housing and Urban Development				
Major	2	0	1	2
Minor	23	35	54	50
Total	25	35	55	52
Department of the Interior				
Major	6	7	6	9
Minor	110	112	116	103
Total	116	119	122	112
Department of Justice				
Major	2	1	0	0
Minor	60	45	42	39
Total	62	46	42	39
Department of Labor				
Major	2	2	0	5
Minor	24	36	15	32
Total	26	38	15	37
Department of State				
Major	0	0	0	0
Minor	9	27	12	14
Total	9	27	12	14

Agencies	1997	1998	1999	2000
Department of Transportation				
Major	2	1	4	3
Minor	1,380	1,805	1,520	1,519
Total	1,382	1,806	1,524	1,522
Department of the Treasury				
Major	2	1	0	0
Minor	340	369	326	336
Total	342	370	326	336
Department of Energy				
Major	2	0	0	3
Minor	32	55	83	87
Total	34	55	83	90
Department of Education				
Major	0	0	1	0
Minor	34	22	46	34
Total	34	22	47	34
Department of Veterans Affairs				
Major	0	0	0	0
Minor	44	24	29	25
Total	44	24	29	25
Independent Agencies[b]				
Major	29	42	17	26
Minor	1,176	1,372	1,459	1,327
Total	1,205	1,414	1,476	1,353
Department of Defense				
Major	0	0	1	0
Minor	64	63	72	68
Total	64	63	73	68
Department of Defense–Army[c]				
Major	0	0	1	0
Minor	4	2	80	5
Total	4	2	81	5
Total	4,046	4,850	4,534	4,443
Major	60	78	49	73
Minor	3,986	4,772	4,485	4,370

Source: General Accounting Office (GAO). Reprinted with permission.

[a] Includes Office of Management and Budget Office of the U.S. Trade Representative.

[b] Includes agencies such as Social Security Administration, Environmental Protection Agency, Securities and Exchange Commission, Federal Communications Commission, Consumer Product Safety Commission, and others.

[c] Includes other branches of the service.

oranges, wintergreen oil, and prunes fall in this category with dozens of other crops. The following column is an example of the hundreds of regulatory actions that the Agriculture Department takes annually to make adjustments in the markets—and prices—of various commodities. This one involves the lowly, wrinkled prune.

U.S. Gives Puny Plums the Heave-Ho

The Washington Post, July 10, 2001—It's not a good thing to be an undersized prune: The U.S. Department of Agriculture is taking you out of the mix.

At the request of prune growers and handlers, USDA regulators decided last month to continue a program that allows the industry to remove from the market "the smallest, least desirable of the marketable size dried prunes" grown in California.

The lucky recipients of the dwarf prunes will be livestock: The department decided growers could dispose of them by grinding them into animal feed. Feedlots pay $35 to $40 a ton for the discarded prunes.

Weeding out the undersized prunes will go on through July 31, 2002, with an estimated 3,400 tons of the little guys hitting the feedlot, never to be pulverized into prune juice or dehydrated into prune snacks. As a result, the department and the prune growers hope prices for prunes will increase slightly—though not enough to produce a "significant impact" on retail prices for consumers.

Prune growers and handlers are allowed to get together and make decisions such as these under the terms of a 1949 "marketing order" that Agriculture oversees. The department manages 36 marketing orders that cover a variety of fruits and vegetables, including cranberries, hazelnuts, melons, tomatoes, olives and papaya.

Set up as industry self-help programs, the orders allow appointed boards to decide issues such as quality, volume, research priorities and, in some cases, promotion campaigns. The programs are funded by industry assessments; the prune board's budget will be $8 million this year, more than half of it spent on promotion and advertising.

The 21 handlers and 1,250 growers in California—who produce 98 percent of the nation's prunes, most of them in the Sacramento and San Joaquin valleys—take direction from the Sacramento-based California Dried Plum Board, which has 22 members. The board used to be the California Prune Board, but more on that later.

Last November, the board surveyed the supply-and-demand situation and decided it would be best to get rid of prunes smaller than 24/32 of an inch in diameter because they were money losers. The board has been making recommendations on the "undersized prune regulation" since similar oversupply problems arose in the 1970s.

The small prunes are weeded out by passing them through a vibrating screen. The final rule the Department issued increased the size of the screen holes from 23/32 to 24/32 of an inch in diameter—meaning a few more prunes will fall through the screen and be shipped to feedlots to help constipated cows.

Regulators noted that they received no comments on the rule. "Prunes eliminated through the implementation of this rule have very little value," they wrote in explaining the decision. They added that the situation is "quite bleak" for producers of small prunes.

It costs farmers more than $300 a ton to produce the small prunes, most of that the cost of drying them—which has increased as energy prices have soared in California. (Prunes are created by exposing plums to hot, circulating air to wring about 80 percent of the moisture out of them. It takes three pounds of fresh plums to make one pound of prunes.)

Prune growers and handlers also have faced declining sales during the past decade and a general oversupply of prunes domestically and worldwide. And consumers who snack on prunes prefer larger pitted prunes that are riper and have better flavor.

At the same time, supply has increased because of abundant new prune plantings that produce higher yields. The result is that this year's harvest is expected to yield 215,000 tons, up from 171,754 tons last year. Prices per ton, about $892 on average last year, have been decreasing since 1995.

Though prunes are respected by older Americans for their laxative properties and $100 million worth are consumed annually, the industry found it was having a hard time attracting new and younger consumers.

Cognizant that prunes have a bathroom reputation, the Prune Board embarked on an ambitious name-change program, banishing the word "prune" from its labeling and replacing it with "dried plum"—a makeover that the Food and Drug Administration approved last year. The Prune Board then became the Dried Plum Board.

"We're trying to put a more positive light on the product," said Richard Peterson, executive director of the Dried Plum Board in Sacramento. "Too many people don't get beyond the stereotypical image. For people in their thirties and forties . . . we want them to think of dried plums as a healthful snack."

The board also has aggressively promoted and underwritten research to prove the antioxidant properties of prunes and the possibility that they kill bacteria in food.

Sunsweet, a grower cooperative, is pushing prune juice for its high potassium content. And the industry is advertising everything from pruneburgers—hamburgers with a dash of prune puree for moistness and added fiber—to prune puree to cut fat in baking.

To get those kinds of results, the growers and handlers are assessed a fee of $50 per ton by the board—growers contribute $30 and handlers $20.

Part of that money goes to help Daniel Haley, the board's Washington lobbyist (who also handles figs and walnuts), persuade the federal government to buy more prunes. This year the federal government bought 10 million pounds of prunes for subsidized feeding programs—a huge jump from the 360,000 pounds it bought last year.

There also is a whole firmament of independent agencies and commissions that are active regulators. The GAO data show that in the year 2000 there were thirty-seven independent agencies that issued 1,353 rules, and twenty-six of those were major. The Environmental Protection Agency, which is not a cabinet-level agency, issued 710 rules, and four of those were significant enough to cost more than $100 million; the Federal Communications Commission accounted for 223, and seven were major; and agencies such as the Securities and Exchange Commission, the Nuclear Regulatory Commission, and the National Aeronautics and Space Administration also contributed.

The Rise and Fall of the Regulators

Another constant is that regulators come and go, affecting the total output of regulation. The regulations' creation may have been linked to a special war effort or may be the result of a certain policy initiative of the administration in power. "Throughout the modern era of administrative regulation, which began approximately a century ago, the government's response to a public demand for action has often been to establish a new agency, or to grant new powers to an existing bureaucracy," say Gellhorn and Levin.[10]

The U.S. Government Manual keeps a running list dating to March 4, 1933, detailing which agencies have gone out of business, which is a backward way to look at what had been created. Considering there are hundreds of deceased agencies, their demise illustrates how organic the so-called fourth branch of government is and how variable the output of rules might be at any one time in history, particularly wartime. Some agencies also began as committees or boards that were dissolved but then reemerged as full-fledged agencies.

The predecessor to the National Aeronautics and Space Administration, for instance, was the National Advisory Committee for Aeronautics, which was established in 1915, terminated in 1958, and transferred to what is now NASA. The Agricultural Research Service was established by the secretary of Agriculture in 1953. Then it was consolidated into the Science and Education Administration in 1978. In 1981, it was reestablished as the Agricultural Research Service, and it remains today as part of the Department of Agriculture.

How Far Can They Go?

For however long they exist, these agencies are filled with professionals who are skilled in proposing and finalizing regulations. Many of them are career federal employees, and they take their marching orders from politically appointed regulators who, in turn, execute the public policy preferences of the White House.

The mandate for many of the rules that are promulgated annually comes from Congress. The Clean Air Act was but a skeleton without flesh until the Environmental Protection Agency issued rules to go with the statute. Agencies also take the initiative to regulate on their own, depending on how activist the administration in power happens to be.

The Office of Management and Budget also plays a major role in whether rules actually come to fruition; the Reagan and the first Bush administrations came under scrutiny from the press and public interest groups that accused them of holding up rules and never issuing others. The second Bush administration has been involved in reviewing rules and returning them with critiques. It also has written "prompt letters" to agencies suggesting rules that they might issue. The Office of Information and Regulatory Affairs at the Office of Management and Budget has issued six prompt letters since September 2001 asking that the agencies take a regulatory action. For example, OIRA suggested to the Department of Health and Human Services and the Food and Drug

Administration that they give higher priority to developing a rule that would include in the labeling of food the amount of trans-fatty acid in it. The department had proposed such a rule in 1999.

The regulatory output of an agency is also linked to its budget and the amount of oversight it receives from Congress. Many Republican members of Congress voted several times to delay, or stop, the Clinton administration from issuing a controversial rule to regulate ergonomics in the workplace. Legislative devices called "riders" to the budget appropriations process can be used to direct an agency to stop a rulemaking activity by cutting off the money for it.

Conversely, Congress moved rapidly to pass the Transportation Recall Enhancement, Accountability and Documentation Act when the problems with Bridgestone/Firestone and Ford Motor Co. were escalating. That legislation handed the National Highway Traffic Safety Administration a heavy regulatory workload with a tight deadline. Congress was prescriptive in the legislation and directed the agency to issue rules that set up an "early warning system" to detect more quickly safety hazards in tires and vehicles that might warrant an investigation or a recall. The act, and the rules issued under it, changed the regulatory landscape for manufacturers of vehicles and tires. The following column examines the effect the auto safety legislation will have on the NHTSA, which has the job of churning out the new rules.

At NHTSA, Firestone Fallout:
A Race to Rewrite Safety Rules

The Washington Post, November 14, 2000—The rule writers and the lawyers are going to be very busy at the National Highway Traffic Safety Administration in coming months.

Not since the agency was created in 1966 have there been more new rules expected in so short a time—thanks to the recent passage of safety reform legislation triggered by failures in Firestone tires implicated in more than 100 traffic deaths.

Over the next two years, NHTSA has more than a dozen new regulations to write and three major studies to complete. All could change the way the federal government spots safety defects in vehicles and tires and orders recalls. Many of the new rules have deadlines that call for proposals by next spring.

The recall, and the problems surrounding it, prompted lawmakers to require the agency to update its tire standard, change how it collects information from auto and tire manufacturers, and beef up the civil and criminal penalties the agency can impose.

The legislation also accelerated work the agency already was doing on a rollover standard to test the stability of cars and trucks. And it calls for major changes in how the agency tests child safety restraints and gives consumers information on the safety of infant and child safety seats.

NHTSA will receive an extra $9 million in its $404 million budget for more testing, updating computer databases, and hiring new staff members.

Robert Shelton, the agency's executive director, said it's all a huge workload for NHTSA's 620 employees to undertake. He said NHTSA will begin hiring soon for 30 new positions, and other resources at the agency will have to be moved around to get the job done. Research and testing will be contracted out.

"We are locking in time frames to meet the statutory deadlines," Sue Bailey, NHTSA's administrator, said in an interview.

The agency plans to spend $2.5 million of its new money to upgrade and integrate its consumer and investigative databases to allow it to spot safety trends. NHTSA didn't have that capability in the years and months before the Firestone investigation.

It also hopes to put some of its files on vehicle defects on the Internet—something it now has a very limited ability to do. "It's essential that we have a database system that will work for us," Bailey said.

She added that one important rulemaking that will have to be carefully crafted is the one covering new reporting requirements placed on tire and vehicle manufacturers. The objective is for the agency to get data on claims and lawsuits that already has been analyzed, and flags a problem.

Automakers want to make sure they don't have to file every scrap of paper on incidents they don't consider serious; the agency wants to make sure the industry doesn't underfile or file reports that are meaningless. An indiscriminate data dump from companies would make the agency's job even harder than it is now, Bailey said.

Meaningful data was "what we didn't have in Firestone," the NHTSA boss added. "It would have allowed us to start an investigation sooner and save lives." She said there were thousands of Firestone claims about failed tires that the company was not obligated to provide the agency.

The new rules also will require manufacturers to report foreign recalls.

The auto industry realizes that the rules have the potential for changing the relationship it has with the agency and its customers.

"Certainly the world has changed," said Robert Strassburger, vice president for the Alliance for Automobile Manufacturers. "There is a heck of a lot of work that has to be tackled. We hope to play a very constructive role in the rulemaking process, especially the rules mandating new reporting requirements."

Strassburger said the tight deadlines may do everyone some good.

He said the industry and the agency have been trying to devise a rule on testing and rating for rollover potential for two decades. The legislation calls for one in two years. "Maybe that deadline will help us make compromises and come to consensus," he said.

What safety advocates want to see are strong rules that prevent a recurrence of the Firestone fiasco.

"The question is who will these rules protect: the public, or will they protect the industry from regulation while helping it defend itself from product-liability lawsuits?" said Clarence Ditlow, executive director of the Center for Auto Safety. "There's no doubt this agency has been given a big challenge," he said.

Ditlow likens the planning and early execution of these new rules to the first mile of a marathon. "The next job is the 25 miles which tell us whether NHTSA set good standards. You don't want Swiss-cheese standards that you can run big trucks and rollover-prone SUVs through," he said.

There are a few rule writers at the agency who remember this kind of workload because it's much like what they went through to get the new NHTSA up and running back in the '60s. The challenge then was to get out quickly a few dozen standards that govern the basic safety operations of vehicles—from how windshield defogging and defrosting systems must work to the now-famous Standard 109—which determines how the agency tests tires—until the new one is written.

The Reinvention Phase

The fortunes of agencies and their ability to regulate also wax and wane as political winds shift. In the early part of the Clinton administration, when conservatives held power in Congress and antiregulatory sentiment was running high, the administration opted for what it called "Reinventing Government." This drive for "reinvention" included eliminating unnecessary rules and negotiating new ones with business and other "stakeholders" such as labor or public interest groups. It was a period when the administration sensed that too much straightforward regulating would result in Congress cutting the budgets of agencies or trying to eliminate them outright. The administration also signaled that it would pay more attention to the management of federal regulation and try to avoid duplication and red tape. A new Office of Reinvention was created to dream up ways to regulate more effectively and reward agencies that made positive changes to their regulatory cultures. New approaches to regulation, like the ones examined in the following column, were tried by the Clinton administration.

Rule Reinvention:
Wrenching Change or Minor Tinkering?

The Washington Post, September 20, 1996—The Clinton administration is releasing today its third annual report on reinventing the federal government, a brag book of untold stories in which procurement rules have been cut, regulations have been revised and businesses have benefited from partnerships with federal agencies.

Called "The Best Kept Secrets in Government," the book is a retrospective sprinkled with anecdotes about the progress the administration has made in downsizing the government and making it run more efficiently. One recurring theme is the experimentation among federal agencies with new ways of regulating—creating partnerships with business, eliminating needless regulations and figuring out more efficient ways to regulate.

Some of the Clinton–Gore changes are big ones, like the government's overhaul of meat and poultry inspection or its rewrite of pension rules. Even the toughest critics of reform would agree these are noteworthy and beneficial changes.

"I want the agencies to do more," said Sally Katzen, administrator of the Office of Management and Budget's Office of Information and Regulatory Affairs. "But I look at the end-of-the-year results and I think it's very impressive."

The real lesson may be that reinvention of government will take much longer than an election cycle. At some agencies, the administration is learning that cultural change is necessary before the rule-cutting can begin.

Take the Environmental Protection Agency, where top officials have promised to cut bureaucracy and produce high-impact results. Two of the most promising initiatives are "Project XL," which allows companies to pursue nontraditional strategies to control pollution, and the "Common Sense Initiative," a proposal to change the regulatory structure for six major industry groups. Both offer the carrot of flexibility in exchange for corporate commitments to more stringent pollution control.

With XL, the struggle has been to move agreements forward with individual companies. One that was about to be struck with Minnesota Mining and Manufacturing Co. for its manufacturing facility in Hutchinson, Minn., unraveled recently, after the EPA asked 3M for more specific assurances on pollution abatement. Other XL proposals chug along; one small initiative has been approved for a juice company in Florida.

"Can we get it done in this millennium?" asked one participant in a Common Sense project, only half-jokingly. Industry, agency and environmentalist participants in the various regulatory experiments agree it has taken more than a year merely to establish trust among the participants.

Participants said it is difficult to get agreement between career bureaucrats and administration appointees who want to throw away the rule book on how to give companies more regulatory flexibility while holding them to higher standards of performance.

To address some of these issues, top EPA officials recently held a meeting in New York to urge consistency between regions on how reinvention projects are handled and to give them priority. A new deputy assistant administrator for Project XL has been named at EPA headquarters.

Considering what the EPA is trying to accomplish in less than two years, officials say they are satisfied with the progress of the programs.

The agency's congressional overseers are less pleased. The EPA was criticized this week in a report released by the water resources and environment subcommittee of the House Transportation and Infrastructure Committee.

The congressional report, billed as the "first detailed analysis of EPA's reinvention initiatives outside the agency," concluded that EPA's initiatives are failing. It said the Common Sense initiative has failed to produce results because each "stakeholder" has a veto over suggested reforms; it suggested that EPA fell back on the old "command-and-control" approach to regulation in the XL project involving 3M.

EPA officials view the report as partisan dart-throwing in an election year.

During the latter years of the Clinton administration, the experimental regulating proceeded apace. But there also was plenty of traditional rulemaking that incensed the business community and drew criticism from antiregulatory foes in Congress. The Environmental Protection Agency, the Food and Drug Administration, and the Labor Department issued controversial rulemakings that resulted in litigation, congressional intervention, and spectacular lobbying battles. The administration also was accused of using the Office of the President to make sweeping administrative changes through executive orders rather than rulemaking.

The Ergonomics Rule: Going Too Far?

Businesses often complain loudest about regulation as a burden when they are in the midst of fighting a single, major regulatory battle like a mandate to install ergonomic equipment in the workplace or a dramatic change in how pollution will be controlled. The now-dead ergonomics rule was considered the ultimate in the reach of the regulators, which is why it is worth examining in some detail. It is also among the lengthiest rules written and took more than a decade to produce. It had the potential to affect an unusually large number of average Americans—anyone working in the industries and companies that would have been covered by the rule. Potentially, it could have affected the design of office furniture and computer keyboards, how groceries are scanned at checkout counters, and how much a factory worker could lift. It may not be as sexy as the attempt to regulate nicotine as a drug, but the basics of how the ergonomics rule almost came to be cannot be overlooked in the study of contemporary federal regulation.

The ergonomics rule was such an irritant to business that it became the poster child for everything that was wrong with the Clinton administration regulatory agenda. Any of the intent of the Clinton administration to make regulating more palatable was lost on those who potentially would be subject to a new ergonomics rule.

A look at the history of the rule shows that what it exemplifies is a traditional, extremely complex rulemaking; it had a Byzantine nature, with its many twists and turns over many years and several administrations. Setting a new federal standard is a painstaking undertaking that can take experienced federal bureaucrats years to finish. Administrations often come and go, starting and stopping the same rule as priorities change or political opposition comes into play. Figure 1.1 graphically describes the process of regulation,

FIGURE 1.1. **The Regulatory Process**

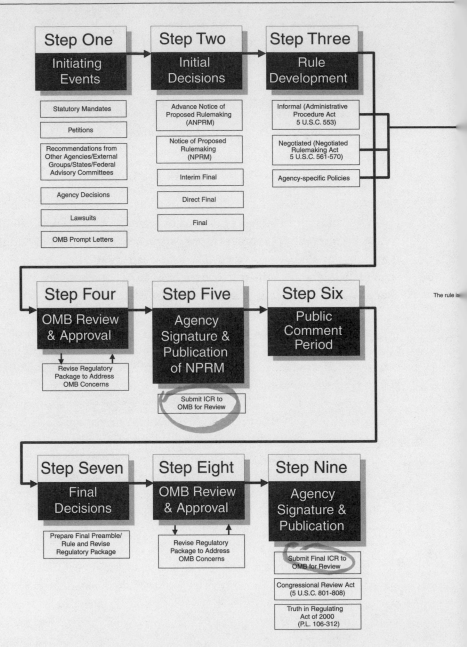

Source: ICF Consulting. Reprinted with permission.

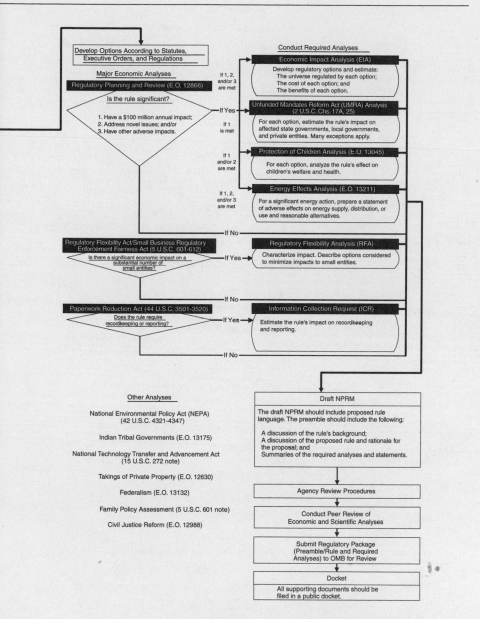

Develop Options According to Statutes, Executive Orders, and Regulations

Major Economic Analyses

Regulatory Planning and Review (E.O. 12866)

Is the rule significant?

1. Have a $100 million annual impact;
2. Address novel issues; and/or
3. Have other adverse impacts.

If 1, 2, and/or 3 are met — If Yes

If 1 is met

If 1 and/or 2 are met

If 1, 2, and/or 3 are met

— If No —

Regulatory Flexibility Act/Small Business Regulatory Enforcement Fairness Act (5 U.S.C. 601-612)

Is there a significant economic impact on a substantial number of small entities? — If Yes →

— If No —

Paperwork Reduction Act (44 U.S.C. 3501-3520)

Does the rule require recordkeeping or reporting? — If Yes →

— If No —

Conduct Required Analyses

Economic Impact Analysis (EIA)

Develop regulatory options and estimate:
The universe regulated by each option;
The cost of each option; and
The benefits of each option.

Unfunded Mandates Reform Act (UMRA) Analysis (2 U.S.C. Chs. 17A, 25)

For each option, estimate the rule's impact on affected state governments, local governments, and private entities. Many exceptions apply.

Protection of Children Analysis (E.O. 13045)

For each option, analyze the rule's effect on children's welfare and health.

Energy Effects Analysis (E.O. 13211)

For a significant energy action, prepare a statement of adverse effects on energy supply, distribution, or use and reasonable alternatives.

Regulatory Flexibility Analysis (RFA)

Characterize impact. Describe options considered to minimize impacts to small entities.

Information Collection Request (ICR)

Estimate the rule's impact on recordkeeping and reporting.

Other Analyses

National Environmental Policy Act (NEPA) (42 U.S.C. 4321-4347)

Indian Tribal Governments (E.O. 13175)

National Technology Transfer and Advancement Act (15 U.S.C. 272 note)

Takings of Private Property (E.O. 12630)

Federalism (E.O. 13132)

Family Policy Assessment (5 U.S.C. 601 note)

Civil Justice Reform (E.O. 12988)

Draft NPRM

The draft NPRM should include proposed rule language. The preamble should include the following:

A discussion of the rule's background;
A discussion of the proposed rule and rationale for the proposal; and
Summaries of the required analyses and statements.

Agency Review Procedures

Conduct Peer Review of Economic and Scientific Analyses

Submit Regulatory Package (Preamble/Rule and Required Analyses) to OMB for Review

Docket

All supporting documents should be filed in a public docket.

Copyright © February 2002 by ICF Incorporated.
All rights reserved. This document may not be reproduced in any form without permission.

which applies to any rule, from passing a law calling for rules to printing the final version in the *Federal Register.* It is a long and winding road.

The ergonomics rule, which was issued by the Clinton administration and rescinded through a special congressional process in the second Bush administration, actually got its start under the administration of President George Bush when Elizabeth Dole was secretary of Labor in 1990. Dole created the Office of Ergonomics Support; Lynn Martin, her successor, who also was a Republican, issued the first stage of an ergonomics rulemaking in 1992. Over the course of a decade, the proposal to regulate ergonomics and the final rule caused a hailstorm of opposition by the business community that intensified during the Clinton administration. Its fear was that the rule would be the ultimate in overreaching by federal regulators as virtually every workplace would be affected.

The following, a partial chronology prepared by the Department of Labor, sets out the tortured path of the ergonomics rule. It is a compelling example of the intricacies of the regulatory process, the effect of politics and lobbying on it, and the persistence of proponents and opponents of the rule in advancing their positions:

- 1979   First ergonomist joins the Occupational Safety and Health Administration, which is part of the Department of Labor
- early 1980s   OSHA begins discussing ergonomic issues with labor, trade associations, and professional organizations
- May 16, 1986   OSHA begins a pilot program to reduce back injuries
- April 21, 1987   OSHA asks for information on reducing back injuries in all industries
- 1990s   OSHA signs corporate-wide settlement agreements with industries including automakers
- August 3, 1992   Advance Notice of Proposed Rulemaking on ergonomics published in *Federal Register*
- March 1995   OSHA discusses outline of draft standard with stakeholders
- July 1995   Congress prohibits use of fiscal year 1995 funds from OSHA budget to issue a proposed or final standard or guidelines

- October 1995   Congress prohibits use of fiscal year 1996
                      funds to work on standard
- October 1997   Congress says OSHA can work on the rule
                      but not issue a standard or guideline and
                      promises that this will be the last time the
                      rule will be held up
- 1998   OSHA holds stakeholder meetings around
                      the country on a rulemaking
- November 23, 1999   OSHA publishes proposed ergonomics stan-
                      dard for comment
- November 14, 2000   OSHA issues final ergonomics standard
                      to become effective on January 16, 2001
- March 20, 2001   President George W. Bush signs into law
                      S.J. Res. 6, which repealed the ergonomics
                      standard[11]

The following is the official press statement issued by the White House, explaining its reasoning:

For Immediate Release
Office of the Press Secretary
March 21, 2001

Statement by the President

Today I have signed into law S.J. Res. 6, a measure that repeals an unduly burdensome and overly broad regulation dealing with ergonomics. This is the first time the Congressional Review Act has been put to use. This resolution is a good and proper use of the Act because the different branches of our Government need to be held accountable.

There needs to be a balance between and an understanding of the costs and benefits associated with Federal regulations. In this instance, though, in exchange for uncertain benefits, the ergonomics rule would have cost both large and small employers billions of dollars and presented employers with overwhelming compliance challenges. Also, the rule would have applied a bureaucratic one-size-fits-all solution to a broad range of employers and workers—not good government at work.

The safety and health of our Nation's workforce is a priority for my Administration. Together we will pursue a comprehensive approach to ergonomics that addresses the concerns surrounding the ergonomics rule repealed today. We will work with the Congress, the business community, and our Nation's workers to address this important issue.

> GEORGE W. BUSH
> THE WHITE HOUSE,
> March 20, 2001.[12]

The business community was almost united in its delight over Congress and the president's repudiation of what probably is the most sweeping rule any administration ever tried to put into place. The rule epitomized to them the overreaching of the regulatory establishment—especially at the Labor Department's Occupational Safety and Health Administration—and the Clinton administration's disregard for their viewpoint. Business sued the government before the rule was even officially released.

One of the primary objections was the cost of the rule. The Clinton administration said that it would cost $4.5 billion annually for the business community to make necessary changes to the physical contours of workplaces to comply with the rule. Business did its own math and said that it was more in the neighborhood of $100 billion. Business also disagreed with the case that organized labor had made for the rule, namely, that ergonomic injuries on the job such as repetitive stress and hand and back ailments were increasing. Companies thought that voluntary efforts to control the injuries were working and a mandatory standard was not necessary.

Powerful business groups headquartered in Washington such as the National Association of Manufacturers and the U.S. Chamber of Commerce devoted millions of dollars to the successful defeat of the rule through a never-used legislative maneuver called the Congressional Review Act. More broadly, these groups viewed the demise of the rule as a strike against the Clinton administration's regulatory philosophy, the scope of federal regulation, and the increasing cost of regulation—a growing federal obligation that in their minds was no different than a hidden tax.

Looking at Costs

For some business interests, the only way to measure the impact of regulation and its growth is to use the bottom-line approach. How much does it cost?

That is a difficult calculation, fraught with almost as many pitfalls as counting pages of the *Federal Register*. How can the cost of a rule be established when its benefit might be cleaner air and fewer cases of asthma in children or the prevention of a strangulation death in the guardrails of a bunk bed? Because of these uncertainties, there are no reliable numbers from previous years to compare regulatory costs. At best, there have been broad-ranging guesses by regulatory scholars and estimates by analysts in the federal government.

The Office of Management and Budget, under orders from Congress, now makes an annual attempt to gauge the cost of regulation. The most current report, issued in 2002, estimates that the total cost of all rules falls between $520 and $620 billion annually, which is close to the federal government's total discretionary budget authority in fiscal year 2001.[13] Other estimates have put costs as high as $843 billion annually.[14] The government also tries to capture what the benefits are from those expenditures and came up with $2 trillion at the high end of its estimate—an estimate it called "highly uncertain."

A more specific way to analyze the cost of regulation is to examine a smaller universe of rules that were issued more recently. The Office of Management and Budget estimates in that same report that major federal rules issued between April 1, 1995, and September 30, 2001, cost up to $54 billion; the benefits from those rules ranged from $49 to $68 billion.

What business is even more concerned about is who bears the brunt of the costs. A study prepared by the Small Business Administration found that small businesses, which account for 90 percent of the firms in the United States, shoulder most of the regulatory burden, especially in environmental and tax compliance: They pay almost $7,000 per employee per year. Firms with 500 or more employees pay $4,500.[15]

These numbers are of great interest to business concerns and the Bush administration. The dollars and cents of regulation have become a paramount consideration; the second Bush administration has emphasized the use of analytical tools such as cost-benefit analysis and risk assessment to determine if a regulation is worthwhile, a trend that started to take hold two decades ago. The Office of Management and Budget has issued guidance on how agencies should uniformly do their calculations "to standardize the measures of benefits and costs of federal regulations." This approach, arguably, could rein in the reach of regulators if new rules do not pass the cost-benefit test, and it has been the subject of much criticism from public interest groups that fear that dollars and cents will drive important regulatory decisions.

The prevailing philosophy is, as President Bush stated on October 15, 2001, in front of a gathering of federal employees, that the reach of the regulators not get too long: "We must resist pressure to unwisely expand government. We need to affirm a few important principles, that the government should be limited, but effective; should do a few things and do them well. It should welcome market-based competition whenever possible. It should respect the role and authority of state and local governments, which are closest to the people." In chapter 2, we meet some of the regulators and examine some of their decisions—some of them highly controversial. The regulatory bureaucracy, how it was built, and who is part of it are important factors in understanding the growth of federal regulation and its effect on American society.

 ## Summary

This chapter gives you a broad overview of many of the issues that are connected with the growth of the regulatory state, how business has responded to this growth, and how business interests manage their affairs in Washington. Two major rulemakings have been discussed—the auto safety rules growing out of new auto safety legislation and the ergonomics rule—to illustrate the breadth and complexity of routine regulating. The chapter also offers a glimpse of the everyday minutia of the regulatory state—the attempt to regulate everything from the size of holes in Swiss cheese to the serving size of breath mints. It is an introduction to the history of the regulatory bureaucracy and the creation of agencies, commissions, and panels. It discusses the various ways that measurements can be taken to assess the size and scope of the regulatory landscape, from the number of pages in the *Federal Register* to the cost of rules.

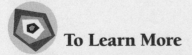 ## To Learn More

There are many excellent Internet websites that give the status of federal regulations (where they are in the pipeline), detailed information about their content, their costs and benefits, when they will be published, and political commentary. Among the best are www.access.gpo.gov/nara, which will allow you to view the *Federal Register* electronically; www.archives.gov/federal_register; www.reginfo.gov; www.gao.gov; www.ombwatch.org; www.regradar.org; www.regulation.org; www.cato.org; and www.thecre.com. The nongovernmental sites all give the flavor of the kind of debate that arises around most major rules. Some federal agencies also have put their regulatory dockets online, so you can search for proposals, final rules, and the comments on them. Among the best is the electronic docket at the Department of Transportation, www.dot.gov. And the fastest way to find a department, agency, board, commission, or other governmental entity that regulates is to go to www.lib.lsu.edu/govdocs and then click on "Federal Sources."

Want to file an obscenity complaint with Federal Communications Commission regulators? The FCC website has all the background on obscenity in broadcasting, including an explanation of the law, the rules that were issued by the FCC governing how to spot obscenity (context is everything, the FCC says), what complaints must be based on, and how to file a complaint. The site also lists the enforcement actions taken by the FCC since 1999 and the fines meted out. Go to www.fcc.gov and find your way to "Broadcast and Cable." Click on "How to File a Complaint" and subsequent links to get a firsthand look at one of the most interesting and subjective regulatory jobs in Washington.

There is nothing like examining the fine print of a rule yourself. The Swiss cheese rule issued by the Department of Agriculture on July 20, 2000, can be found in the *Federal Register,* vol. 65, no. 140, pages 45018–32 (47CFR part 73). You can search for the full text of the rule by using the electronic address for the *Federal Register,* www.access.gpo.gov/nara, to find it by date and agency, which is the Agricultural Marketing Service.

Notes

1. Morton Rosenberg, "Regulatory Management at OMB," in *Office of Management and Budget: Evolving Roles and Future Issues,* prepared for the Committee on Governmental Affairs, U.S. Senate, by Congressional Research Service (February 1986), 187.

2. James. Q. Wilson, *The Politics of Regulation* (New York: Basic Books, 1980), 391.

3. Michael Schroeder and Cassell Bryan-Low, "Enron Collapse Has Congress Backing Off Deregulation," *Wall Street Journal,* January 29, 2002: A22.

4. Grant McConnell, *Private Power and American Democracy* (New York: Alfred A. Knopf, 1966), 295.

5. Cornelius M. Kerwin, *Rulemaking: How Government Agencies Write Law and Make Policy* (Washington, D.C.: CQ Press, 1994), 292.

6. Ernest Gellhorn and Ronald M. Levin, *Administrative Law and Process in a Nutshell* (St. Paul, Minn.: West Publishing, 1990), 179.

7. Michael White, "The *Federal Register*: A Link to Democratic Values," *The Record* (internal newsletter for the National Archives) (1996).

8. Executive Office of the President, Office of Management and Budget, "Report on Executive Order No. 12866, Regulatory Planning and Review, Part VI," *Federal Register* 59 (May 10, 1994): 24278.

9. The President's Committee on Administrative Management, *Report of the Committee with Studies of Administrative Management in the Federal Government* (January 8, 1937): 313.

10. Gellhorn and Levin, *Administrative Law and Process in a Nutshell*, 1.

11. From U.S. Department of Labor, Occupational Safety and Health Administration, "OSHA Ergonomics Chronology," April 2002, at www.osha.gov/ergonomics/ergonomicschronology02.html (accessed October 16, 2001).

12. George W. Bush, "Statement by the President," March 20, 2001, at www.whitehouse.gov/news/releases/2001/03/20010321.html.

13. Office of Management and Budget, Office of Information and Regulatory Affairs, "Draft Report to Congress on the Costs and Benefits of Federal Regulations," *Federal Register* 67 (March 28, 2002): 15014.

14. Thomas D. Hopkins, *Regulatory Accounting: Costs and Benefits of Federal Regulations,* prepared for the Subcommittee on Energy Policy, Natural Resources and Regulatory Affairs, House Government Reform Committee (105th Cong., 2d sess., March 12, 2002).

15. U.S. Small Business Administration, *The Impact of Regulatory Costs on Small Firms,* prepared by W. Mark Crain and Thomas D. Hopkins (October 2001), 3.

The Regulators: Who Makes the Rules, and How Much Power Do They Have?

The Cup Board Isn't Bare Yet; Apparently the FDA's Tea Tasters Will Get Federal Funding Again

The Washington Post, August 9, 1995—In these days of raucous budget fights, appropriations battles and veto threats, there are government programs—modest though they may be—that are unsinkable.

Consider, for example, the Food and Drug Administration's Board of Tea Experts, which yet again has managed to sniff at its critics politely, pour itself another cup of oolong and beat Washington budget-cutters.

It may be just a drop in the teapot, but taxpayers will likely pick up about 60 percent of the board's $200,000 tab in the next spending year so they can be guaranteed that imported tea is up to certain standards of "purity and wholesomeness."

Since 1897, the Import Tea Act, which created the board, has governed the flow of tea into the United States, keeping out inferior and adulterated batches. Beginning in 1940, importers paid 3.5 cents per hundredweight of tea imported. Congress raised the fee in 1993 to 10 cents, a move that importers supported to continue getting the government's inspection services. The government collects about $80,000 from the industry in fees each year, partly offsetting the taxpayers' cost.

"It's difficult for industry to do this alone—set standards," said Joseph P. Simrany, president of the Tea Association of the U.S.A. "It's the first line of defense relative to keeping bad tea out of the country."

The board rejects about 1 percent of the 209 million pounds of tea imported each year.

The seven-member board meets once a year for two days without compensation. The members lost their $50 per diem and travel expenses, which totaled about $7,000 a meeting, two years ago. Six of the members are from private industry, appointed to four-year terms by the Health and Human Services secretary. Chief tea examiner Robert H. Dick is an FDA employee and tastes tea full time; his salary is $68,622.

The board meets in a special tea-tasting room at the FDA's Brooklyn office. It's nothing fancy, FDA officials are quick to point out—no silver service or scones and clotted cream.

When this year's budget battle was gaining steam, it looked possible that the board might be among the 63 commissions that House budget-cutters would wipe out. House Budget Committee Chairman John R. Kasich (R-Ohio) initially proposed killing the board, but his panel didn't follow through. Its funding is included in the House version of the spending bill covering the FDA; the Senate hasn't acted yet.

The Clinton administration tried to dump the board last year, including it in the Advisory Committee Termination Act. Sen. John Glenn (D-Ohio) introduced the legislation last fall that would have wiped out 31 statutory committees, including the board. But as the Office of Management and Budget said, "It did not advance."

(However, the administration has managed to get rid of the Advisory Committee on Swine Health Protection, whose duties have been assumed by the Agriculture Department's Advisory Committee on Foreign Animal and Poultry Diseases.)

The OMB is working on another proposal. "These committees have outlived their purposes," an OMB official said. "It's not huge sums of money, but there are important principles in not wasting the taxpayers' money."

Yet FDA officials point out that as long as the Import Tea Act is on the books, someone has to set standards for the tea that comes into the country.

Dick, 76, has spent his entire 56-year government career tasting tea and is probably one of few Americans who can distinguish green, black and oolong by aroma. He knows, for example, that "a good Formosa oolong never fails to bring expressions of delight at its pleasing and penetrating aroma from the tea drinker lucky enough to taste it," as he wrote in an article in a FDA publication. He adds that it's pretty boring to taste hundreds of so-so teas every day.

In the article, Dick described the teataster's routine: "He sits by a large rotating table . . . on which handleless cups of approximately 5-ounce capacity are placed along with the corresponding sample in a bag or tin. He weighs a uniform amount of tea in each cup (usually 35 grains), pours on boiling water, and smells the aroma of the hot wet leaves, which he removes with a spoon. . . . He sucks a spoonful into his mouth with a 'swoosh' that sends an atomized spray onto his palate and the aroma up his nose."

After rolling it in his mouth, he spits it into an oversized cuspidor.

Ahhhh.

It's Dick's job to taste samples daily as they are sent to two FDA locations by importers. Last year, some 31,604 imported tea samples were turned over to the FDA for examination. To spread the tasting around a bit, five other FDA employees play a part-time role in examining, tasting and setting standards for tea. Dick's health recently forced him to cut back, but his assistant, Faith Lim, has slowly been learning the job, which includes being executive secretary of the board and helping appoint its members.

Simrany of the tea trade group said he thinks the board and the tasting process are wonderful examples of industry–government partnership. If the fees the industry pays do not cover the cost of the program, the government should raise them, he said.

But that kind of cooperative attitude has not done much to keep the board out of the line of fire.

Presidents Richard M. Nixon and Jimmy Carter tried and failed to get rid of the board. Its closest brush with death came in 1993, when Sen. Harry M. Reid (D-Nev.) called for dumping the board overboard in a "congressional tea party." "Why should there be one penny of taxpayer money involved in tea tasting?" he asked. Noting that he bought a bad watermelon, he asked: "Should we have a watermelon tasting board?"

Congress spared the board but killed its members' travel expenses and raised the industry's fees to cover more of its costs.

If the board goes up in steam but the Import Tea Act remains, the government likely would have to hire the same people to do the job at higher consultant pay rates.

And that might be tough to swallow.

Who Are the Regulators?

Among the regulators is Robert H. Dick, who spent more than fifty years tasting tea for the federal government, before he died in 1996 at the age of eighty-two. The position of chief tea taster and the Board of Tea Experts were voted out of existence by Congress that same year, putting an end to that esoteric regulatory specialty.

The tea taster had an unusual skill set. He was part of an elite corps of bureaucrats who constitute their own power center in Washington. It is a semi-cloistered cadre of technical specialists, public policy experts, lawyers, longtime career federal employees, and political appointees who are responsible for billions of dollars in regulatory expenditures annually. They have the power to enforce rules as well as to create them. They regulate informally—that is, by giving notice, taking comment, and deciding—and formally, using legal procedures such as a hearing. They also issue settlements, hand out benefits and licenses, inspect and ban products, supervise recalls, monitor ongoing business practices, render advisory opinions, award grants and contracts, give guidance, sanction rule breakers, and adjudicate disputes. It is a broad portfolio. They are what President Franklin Roosevelt's Committee on Administrative Management called a "headless 'fourth branch'" of government. Many refer to the extensive regulatory regime in Washington as a shadow government.

Not many Americans realize that the Food and Drug Administration had someone like Dick, with superior olfactory skills, on the government payroll. The board itself was an even more bizarre example of how an anonymous but powerful regulatory clique can have influence. (During the board's existence, the agency was reluctant to give reporters much access to Dick for fear Congress would swoop in and try to eliminate the position.) But tea is not the only consumer product subject to testers. The Consumer Product Safety Commission has a toy tester whose job it is to crush, pound, drop, and measure the openings of juvenile playthings to see if they meet the commission's standards.

The Federal Communications Commission has the ears of a specialist expertly tuned to detect obscenity in radio broadcasts, listening for the seven objectionable words it classifies as prohibited for the airwaves. This function of the commission has caused countless lawsuits, fines, and objections from recording artists and disc jockeys who use bad language over the airwaves. The following column showcases the job of a career regulator whose job was to get an earful and help decide whether major broadcasting companies should be fined.

Minding the Airwaves:
One FCC Lawyer Is Always Getting a Stern Talking-To

The Washington Post, November 16, 1993—Howard Stern, meet your regulator. Or at least one of them.

Long before Stern's hotly controversial radio show burns the ears of the chairman and commissioners of the Federal Communications Commission, Robert Ratcliffe has his portable Sony Cassette Corder TC 140 tape player plugged in, its wheels whirring, his office door closed.

He is listening to the juiciest—some would say the most offensive—selections of Howard Stern sent in by outraged listeners. Ratcliffe is, as Stern once said, part of the "thought police. Burp."

Ratcliffe may be one of the cops on the Howard Stern beat, but he hardly comes across as a prude. As Ratcliffe put it: "I'm not a pure-minded stick-in-the-mud." But he is the classic understated government lawyer who has spent his entire 18-year career buried at the FCC. He is a married man with two children, a guy who had an amateur radio license as a kid and someone who admits freely that administrative law fascinates him.

As the FCC's assistant chief for law in the Mass Media Bureau, he has seen and heard it all—couch dancing on the "Jane Wallace Live" show (don't even ask what that is); "ultrasound sex" on the "Donahue" show; and Michael Jackson holding his crotch while he sings. And, as the rules are written, lots of these things are perfectly legal.

If the material doesn't pass Ratcliffe's legal test, it eventually finds its way to the commission, which makes the ultimate decision.

Though his job involves more than listening to Stern's greatest hits, he says the questionable material flowing into his office is becoming overwhelming as TV and radio stations push the envelope on what is permissible and what is not.

Infinity Broadcasting Corp., which is the licensee for the Howard Stern show, has been hit with several "notices of apparent liability" (that's FCC-ese for fines) because of Stern's language that add up to more than $1 million.

So far, Infinity has not paid a penny. The company has played regulatory Ping-Pong with the agency for years, insisting that it's not guilty and delaying enforcement.

As Stern has said on the air, "I don't care what the FCC says. . . ."

———————————

At the Federal Trade Commission, there are regulators like Elaine Kolish, associate director of its Bureau of Consumer Protection, who can recite chapter and verse the hundreds of regulatory actions the commission takes every year. As I noted in one column published in 1995, Kolish has the labeling rule for plumbing down cold: 1.6 gallons per flush for residential toilets, 3.5 gallons for commercial, and 1 gallon for urinals. She can tell you, chapter and verse, anything you want to know about how clothes have to be labeled by manufacturers so consumers can care for garments in their washing machines or at the dry cleaners.

Dick's judgments about the quality and flavor of imported tea had a direct impact on a miniscule amount of tea. But other regulators' judgments are controlling factors in major business deals, often making or breaking them. Decisions made by antitrust regulators are in this category. They have a direct influence on consumers' choices and their pocketbooks, as well as on the structure of what often are large conglomerates. In November 2001, for example, the Justice Department approved Proctor & Gamble's purchase of Clairol hair care products from Bristol-Myers Squibb Co. As a result, Proctor & Gamble, already a powerhouse in hair care products like shampoo, would control more shampoo brands and add hair-coloring products to its portfolio. Earlier in 2001, the staff of the Federal Trade Commission recommended disapproval of the $13.4 billion purchase of Quaker Oats by PepsiCo, but the commissioners, who are free to ignore the staff's suggestions, let the deal go forward. The decision allowed PepsiCo to gain control of the Gatorade sports drink, eliminating a competitor to its own brand and opening the possibility of price increases. And, of course, the government's antitrust case against Microsoft would have determined the course and profitability of that company for years to come if the company had lost the case. Think of the result of the federal government's antitrust case against the old Bell Co., which created seven regional phone companies; they, in turn, helped spawn much of the revolution in telecommunications over the past thirty years.

Labeling is a powerful regulatory function. Several agencies and their experts in label claims have the power to decide what should be on the label of a product or a bottle, giving them a central role in the marketing of a product. The Food and Drug Administration is a major arbiter of labeling content, and its permissiveness is the last word on whether a drug goes to market and may change the positioning of a product already on the market. For example, the FDA sent a batch of letters to natural food companies suggesting that they are offering misleading information to consumers in saying that their products are free of genetically modified organisms (GMOs). The FDA is preparing guidance on the issue, which will set the boundaries for what companies can and cannot say. In the meantime, the agency is concerned about the labeling because it has declared the technology safe. One company, after receiving the letter, said it probably would drop the claim on its natural baby food. "We have a natural philosophy, so we avoid GMOs," said Richard Presto, who runs Healthy Times Inc. "But we aren't big enough to fight the FDA."[1]

The Treasury Department's Bureau of Alcohol, Tobacco and Firearms has the power to decide whether a label accurately reflects what is inside a wine bottle, a decision that can have broad marketing and financial implications for vintners. The following column is about the squabble over what constitutes a real Riesling, a question that roiled the domestic wine industry.

In a Ferment over Labeling:
Another Grape Moment in History for the ATF

The Washington Post, January 29, 1999—It was a fine wine while it lasted.

The wine industry is pleading with the Treasury Department's Bureau of Alcohol, Tobacco and Firearms to allow domestic wine companies to continue calling wine made from White Riesling grapes Johannisberg Riesling, at least until Jan. 1, 2006. The bureau eliminated the designation on Jan. 1 of this year.

Seems like a simple enough request, but in the world of federal wine and spirits regulation, there is no detail that is overlooked, or not reviewed at length. Some of ATF's rulings are as complex as the fermentation of the wines that are being considered. Many are influenced by complicated trade decisions.

In this case, the ATF decided in 1996 that, after a three-year phaseout, it would no longer allow the designation "Johannisberg" on Rieslings even though the name had appeared on 95 percent of domestic Rieslings for almost a century. The change was part of ATF's decision to eliminate misleading references in labeling.

The name comes from a grape grown for more than a thousand years in a district of the Rheinegau region of Germany. In the United States, the name has been used to distinguish the premium White Riesling, which is a medium-dry, highly complex wine, from other varieties that are not true Rieslings and considered inferior, wine experts said.

"We looked at all the Riesling names and phased out as many as we could," said an ATF official. For example, it was found that the correct variety of grape for Grey Riesling was not related to the Riesling grape and was misnamed; it was finally identified as the variety Trousseau gris and that became its name.

Johannisberg, also known as J.R., is the top-selling Riesling in America, with 36 million bottles sold annually, according to Stimson Lane Vineyards & Estates in Woodinville, Wash.

The ATF decided that "Johannisberg" would be dropped as a "prime grape name" or as a synonym for one, and it could be used for advertising and labeling only until Jan. 1, 1999. Wine bottled after that would be

called "Riesling" or "White Riesling." The change, the ATF said, was to clar-
ify wine labels for consumers and make them more accurate.

The decision was like throwing a glass of Riesling in the eye of
American vintners, who guessed that German vintners wanted the
name back.

"Johannisberg Riesling is a category brand, not a corporate brand, but
no less valuable. It would be as though Coca-Cola reclaimed the exclu-
sive rights to the term 'cola,'" said Allen Shoup, president and chief executive of Stimson Lane.

After ATF's decision, the wineries turned to the law firm of Buchman
& O'Brien, which specializes in issues concerning alcoholic beverages, in
hopes of reversing the decision, arguing that the ATF did not give them
proper notice that the name was being eliminated.

"If ATF's notices on this particular topic were truly adequate, it is fright-
ening to imagine what other decisions that ATF might have made on the
topic of 'Grape Variety Names for American Wines.' ATF could have used
the same arguments to delist, at the eleventh hour, Chardonnay or any
other grape name . . . and the arguments would be just as specious," said
the request on behalf of the wineries.

The firm cited two prior rule-makings on grape variety names for
domestic wines and a decision by a special committee that led wineries
to believe that "Johannisberg" would be preserved as a name.

"You don't just take it away from the industry after years of believing
the name would be preserved," said E. Vincent O'Brien, a partner of
Buchman & O'Brien. "We were stunned."

Last July, American wineries came back with a modified proposal that
asked that the "Johannisberg" designation be kept for seven more years
so winemakers could educate consumers.

Domestic producers of Johannisberg Riesling were worried that U.S.
Rieslings would lose significant market share to imported Rieslings if the
name was suddenly dropped. Wineries estimated expenditures up to millions of dollars to educate Johannisberg Riesling purists about the apparent disappearance of the wine.

Steve Burns, executive director of the Washington Wine Commission
in Seattle, said the decision is an important one for his state, which has
2,080 acres planted in grapes that end up as Johannisberg Riesling.

"You don't just market things overnight," said Burns. "This isn't beer.
You don't make it every week." He explained that if vintners were going to

switch the grapes they grew, "it takes four to five years before a vine hits its stride."

ATF said in retrospect it probably should have allowed more time to phase out the name. The bureau will take comments until March 8 on extending its use.

Not surprisingly, the Germans have views on the "Riesling Issues," as the Deutscher Weinfonds, a quasi-governmental authority, put it in correspondence with the ATF in 1993. This entity supported the use of Riesling as the prime name and White Riesling as an alternative name. It does not want to see the word "Johannisberg" used on U.S. wines.

Another group, the Deutsches Weininstitut, said in a recent letter to the ATF it agreed with the proposed extension and would go along with it to avoid any litigation over the issue.

But Robert Maxwell, president of the National Association of Beverage Importers, said American wineries already have had three years to prepare for the change and should be given only a "reasonable amount of time" to finish making the label transition.

Sounds like it isn't too soon to stock the wine cellar—if your guests are the sort who read the label.

Regulators and Their Qualifications

Some regulators are highly qualified to make those kinds of competitive decisions—be it wine or Gatorade. But others come to top jobs with no particular qualifications other than political connections or a desire to serve in a public capacity. Early in the lives of many independent commissions, there were complaints that commissioners were corrupt or inept.

"Partly as a result of its ambiguous statute, the Federal Trade Commission got off to a rocky start. In no one's eyes did it represent a distinguished regulatory body," writes Thomas K. McCraw in *Prophets of Regulation*, an examination of four men who played seminal roles in the early development of federal regulatory policy. McCraw continues, "Of the original five appointees, two were businessmen, one a career politician, one a lawyer–politician, and one . . . a practicing lawyer. None had administrative talents of the first rank. By 1918, only three years after the commission's first meeting, not a single one of these first five members remained in office." The assessment of Louis D. Brandeis, a Boston lawyer who was involved in the creation of the Federal Trade Commission and was President Woodrow Wilson's chief economic adviser, is as follows: "It was a stupid administration."[2]

That charge, in most cases, does not hold today: The chairman of the Federal Trade Commission in the Clinton administration, Robert Pitofsky, brought to the job extensive government and legal experience and was an expert in antitrust issues and trade regulation. He raised the profile of the agency and was well respected. Similarly, the George W. Bush administration chose as chairman Timothy J. Muris, who held three previous top staff positions at the commission as well as with the Office of Management and Budget. An expert in antitrust issues, he also worked in private practice and academia. Many appointees in commission positions now work to stay as long as they can, rather than leave their posts for law suites or lobby offices. The following column found a real career civil servant in John Truesdale. He tried to leave his job at the National Labor Relations Board but could not.

A Veteran Member Comes Out of Retirement

The Washington Post, December 25, 1998—The National Labor Relations Board has its own John Glenn: John C. Truesdale, 77, has begun serving his fifth term on the panel, which settles labor and management disputes under the National Labor Relations Act.

Truesdale was quietly appointed to serve as chairman on Dec. 4, and his term will last until Congress recesses next fall. His predecessor, William Gould, who was controversial, opinionated and estranged from some of his fellow board members, departed Aug. 27.

The White House called Truesdale in August and asked if he would be agreeable to coming back to the board. "I was very conflicted about it," Truesdale said. "But I worked for the NLRB for almost 50 years. How can you say no?"

Until his latest appointment, Truesdale had been in retirement since 1996. Before that, he had served four terms as a board member—one for just 38 days—and two terms as executive secretary over a span of 20 years.

"He's incredibly well respected, and a very nice, distinguished guy," said NLRB member Sara Fox, a Democrat, who tangled frequently with the previous chairman. Fox said the four members "get along famously well and John fits right into that."

Things weren't quite that calm in the previous administration.

Gould, who has a sharp intellect, a distinguished background in labor law and is a prolific speechmaker, argued with fellow board members over their productivity, battled with Congress, and fought with members of the management bar, some of whom took a dislike to him. His critics considered him combative and more favorable to labor's point of view than management's. Gould is a rabid baseball fan who never missed a game in the city he was in for business, a habit that some found inappropriate.

"He came through here like a meteor," a source at the board said. One lawyer said Gould left, "Riding out of town, shooting behind his back."

Gould, reached in California, where he is a professor at Stanford Law School, said he enjoyed his time at the board. "I feel very proud of our accomplishments," he said, referring to an increase in the board's productivity and resolution of major policy issues. He said progress slowed in the last year or so "in the face of a hostile political environment in Congress."

Sources in the labor law community said the Clinton administration had no choice but to make a recess appointment, which does not require Senate confirmation, because Republicans were unlikely to approve any new Democratic members. The Republican seats are currently filled.

None of this bothers Truesdale, who considers himself a utility infielder. "He gives new meaning to hitting the ground running," an NLRB employee said.

Before getting the call from the White House for his next mission, Truesdale was busy cultivating a part-time career as a labor arbitrator while doing some reading, gardening and traveling. He said he doesn't have any grand scheme for his time at the board.

"I spent my entire career trying to expedite the issuance of cases. I come in with no preconceived notions of policy but to reduce the amount of time it takes to issue decisions," Truesdale said. The board has a backlog of about 700 cases.

That wasn't the style of his predecessor, Gould, who had outspoken views on the law and stressed the promotion of collective bargaining for workers.

Gould now is writing a book on his NLRB tenure, based on the diary he kept since March 1994, when he became chairman. Many of his former colleagues are awaiting it with a mixture of anticipation and dread.

"We figure there will be an index party when the book gets released," said Daniel Yager, vice president and general counsel for LPA Inc., a

Washington-based association that represents management on labor issues.

The LPA, which was highly critical of Gould, said it has "nothing but nice things to say about Truesdale."

A Close-Knit Group

Unlike elected members of Congress who hear from their constituents when a controversial issue arises, these regulators are often known only to lobbyists, consultants, contractors, and corporate government representatives who are as specialized as they are. Among themselves, they speak a kind of "regulatese" that is laden with acronyms and legal phraseology. "Curiously, although we have been told a very great deal about regulation, we remain relatively ignorant about the regulators themselves," McCraw writes.[3] Anthony Downs, in his book *Inside Bureaucracy,* works at defining the nature of the bureaucrat and comes up with characters such as climbers, conservers (keep what you have attained), zealots, advocates, and statesmen. The agencies and departments they work at, which he calls bureaus, are characterized by large size, the people within them have a serious commitment to their jobs, there is no outside evaluation of employee performance, and hiring and promotions are dependent on performance in an organizational role.

Once a new administration comes to power, there is a period during which the top appointments are widely publicized, especially if they are controversial. But only the closest government watchers take note of the routine press releases that are issued by the agencies and commissions when the second- and third-tier jobs are filled—though these often are the appointments that are key to crafting and executing important regulatory policy. They also provide a blueprint for understanding the political sensibilities of an administration and its approach to regulation.

For example, at the Interior Department and the Environmental Protection Agency, many of the top jobs in the George W. Bush administration went to appointees who had interests in the industries they are now regulating. They held top jobs in the automotive industry, the oil and gas industries, and the mining industry. At the Department of Transportation, the first head of the Federal Motor Carrier Association, which regulates the trucking industry, came from one of the country's biggest trucking companies. A key post in the Agriculture Department's Forest Service went to a seasoned timber industry lobbyist. The second in command at the Occupational Safety and Health Administration had extensive Capitol Hill experience, serving House members who opposed much of what the agency was trying to accomplish during the Clinton administration. At the Department of Transportation, the deputy assistant secretary for governmental affairs managed the lobbying operation at American Airlines. The former chief regulator at the Securities and Exchange Commission, Harvey Pitt, represented the major accounting firms he later was in charge of overseeing—an arrangement that many Democrats decried as a glaring conflict of interest that made him ineffectual in his job. Sen. John McCain (R-Ariz.) called for the resignation of Pitt, saying that he was an obstacle to reform because of his close ties to the accounting industry. Democrats joined the refrain to remove Pitt, who resigned on Election Day in 2002.

Whatever their political leanings, modern-day regulators take their direction from Congress and from the administration in power through the appointments process, oversight hearings, and the budget, as well as statutory directives. The courts also play a role in checking how much authority is vested in the rulemaking bureaucracy. For example, opponents of regulations that allow Mexican trucks to enter the United States went to federal court to try and stop the regulations from being implemented. Similarly, in spring 2002, a major environmental rule that would lessen pollution from diesel trucks was upheld by a federal appeals court after industry challenged the rule. The Supreme Court also gets involved in setting the ground rules for agencies. In the case of the Food and Drug Administration, the Court ruled that the agency did not have the authority from Congress to regulate tobacco, putting an end to a major Clinton administration initiative.

But, to some extent, regulators have license to follow their own instincts, and their work can be highly interpretive. Indeed, they have considerable latitude and independence. The constraints they do have come from Congress, which controls the purse strings of agencies and oversees them; the White House, which has regulatory policy objectives and controls the review of rules; and, depending on the nature of the issue, the people they regulate. In more unusual times, such as the aftermath of the terrorist attacks on September 11, 2001, the public also becomes part of the jury, judging how effective top regulators are and whether they are exercising their power appropriately. Agencies such as the Environmental Protection Agency, the Department of Transportation, the Justice Department, the Centers for Disease Control, and the Labor Department's Occupational Safety and

Health Administration instantly took on added importance after the attacks on the World Trade Center and the Pentagon, as well as in handling the anthrax scare that swept the nation. Many of the agencies, which in the past had been criticized for their failings or for too much regulating, became the first line of defense in beefing up the nation's security, safety, and preparedness. Indeed, the public's trust in government and the work of civil servants surged after the bombings to its highest levels since the 1960s. A Brookings Institution survey done in July 2001 showed that only 29 percent of Americans trusted government to do what is right always or most of the time; by October, the number jumped to 65 percent.[4] Several polls showed that public trust in government rose to levels not reached since the early Vietnam era. The public did not object to the idea of creating a whole new federal bureaucracy to oversee airport security in the aftermath of the attacks or to a new Office of Homeland Security.

The Proliferation of Rulemakers

Even before the unusual events of fall 2001, when more spending and staffing were expected, the size of the regulatory bureaucracy was increasing. In fact, one study suggests that the number of regulators and regulatory spending spread across fifty-four agencies now is at an all-time high, though the total number of federal workers has been decreasing. At the end of 2001, there were 131,983 full-time staff carrying out regulatory responsibilities at the agencies. This growth began in 1992 after eleven years of declining numbers. Overall, there was dramatic growth in staffing in the 1970s when new consumer-related and social agencies were being created: staffing went from 69,946 in 1970 to 121,791 a decade later. A 12 percent drop followed in the 1980s as the first effects of deregulation of major industries like the airlines were felt and President Ronald Reagan put a damper on new rules in general.

By the 1990s, however, growth resumed. Data in table 2.1, prepared by the Center for the Study of American Business at Washington University, predicts that "if this growth trend is extrapolated to the rest of the decade, federal regulatory employees will increase by 25 percent."[5]

Unlike the other branches of government, where voting among the Supreme Court justices or the lawmakers in Congress determines the outcome of an issue, this part of the federal government is filled with powerful public servants whose influence is more subtle and less public. Regulators have statutory obligations that often are quite explicit, but they have broad

TABLE 2.1. **Staffing of Federal Regulatory Agencies (Fiscal Years, Full-Time Equivalent Employment)**

Year	Social Regulation	Economic Regulation	Total
1970	52,693	17,253	69,946
1971	61,788	17,940	79,728
1972	68,117	18,248	86,365
1973	75,305	18,877	94,182
1974	75,522	19,972	95,494
1975	80,523	21,720	102,243
1976	84,999	22,835	107,834
1977	85,454	23,334	108,788
1978	89,955	25,077	115,032
1979	94,322	25,478	119,800
1980	95,533	26,258	121,791
1981	91,909	25,300	117,209
1982	82,627	23,788	106,415
1983	78,396	22,907	101,303
1984	78,804	23,043	101,847
1985	79,293	22,899	102,192
1986	78,447	23,486	101,933
1987	78,660	23,144	101,804
1988	80,537	23,875	104,412
1989	83,019	23,998	107,017
1990	87,395	27,289	114,684
1991	91,176	27,349	118,525
1992	96,257	29,581	125,838
1993	98,322	31,338	129,660
1994	97,332	31,578	128,910
1995	98,179	31,864	130,043
1996	96,573	29,727	126,300
1997	95,120	28,928	124,048
1998	96,136	28,994	125,130
1999	96,409	29,318	125,727
2000*	99,080	30,735	129,815
2001*	100,583	31,400	131,983

Source: Center for the Study of American Business, Washington University. Derived from the *Budget of the United States Government* and related documents, various fiscal years. Reprinted with permission.

*Estimates

mandates as well that allow them to act as quasi-legislative, -executive, and -judicial entities in their own right. Agencies are not official branches of the federal government, but the individuals who write the rules do have the force of law behind them.

"Administrative officials enjoy considerable lawmaking responsibility. . . . Legislatures have granted to administrators considerable discretion to decide questions of law and policy within more or less generous statutory constraints and guidelines," write Stephen G. Breyer and Richard B. Stewart. "The lawmaking output of administrative agencies far exceeds that of legislatures and courts in quantity, if not always in importance."[6]

Rules for the Regulators

As the importance of federal regulation grew during the New Deal and the number of agencies proliferated, there was growing concern over the influence of the regulators and whether there needed to be an institutional check on their power. Lawyers, in particular, worried that Congress had delegated too much power to the agencies and that there was no general standard for rulemaking. "The specter of unelected and essentially invisible bureaucrats writing, in near secrecy, laws that had the direct or indirect effects of curtailing freedom and confiscating property was a compelling, if somewhat melodramatic, argument for reforming the administrative process," writes Cornelius M. Kerwin.[7]

President Franklin Delano Roosevelt worried that a proposal to let federal courts do the regulating would imperil the authority and flexibility of the agencies that the New Deal created. To address the problem, Roosevelt created the Attorney General's Committee on Administrative Procedure, and its report, completed in 1941, became the basis for the Administrative Procedure Act of 1946.

The act became the legal template for agency procedures, though there still was plenty of wiggle room for agencies to modify their own rulemaking and adjudicatory procedures. Basically, the new law laid out what Kerwin calls the "core elements" of rulemaking: information or public notice about the fact that a rule is under way and when it becomes final, public participation through written comments or other forms of communication, and accountability in the form of judicial review of rules. These were supposed to be practical limits for how regulators conducted themselves, while also giving the public a role in the regulatory process. Over the years, as the number of rules has increased exponentially, the simple requirements of the APA have been overtaken by two other trends. One is the passage of laws adding many new requirements to the regulatory process. The other is the tendency of rulemakers to comply creatively with the requirements of the APA.

Besides creating minimums for the procedures that regulators had to follow, the APA also defined what a rule is: "The whole or part of an agency statement of general or particular applicability and future effect designed to implement, interpret or prescribe law or policy." In other words, it was up to the people at agencies to write the rules that derived from a particular statute. Anything other than a rulemaking the APA classified as an adjudication, which generally is a proceeding between an agency and a private party. These encounters might settle a dispute over a rule or a determination by an agency.

That may sound like a license to regulate, but, over time, Congress and presidents have made it more difficult to regulate with impunity. Executive orders, issued by the president, have a major impact on the latitude of regulators. Since the Nixon years, there has been a series of orders that have directed agencies to take into consideration costs, benefits, alternatives to the rule at hand, effects on the states, and the submission of rules to the Office of Management and Budget for review. Each president has had the authority to revoke previous orders and issue ones of his own.

Some regulators have worked at a particular agency for almost as long as it has existed, and they know the system well. They are aware that Congress can meddle legislatively in their work, that the White House can issue orders and memos telling them what to do, and that special interest groups can take their pleadings to the public. All of this is in the job description of a top-notch regulator whose interest in the job is not usually diminished by these procedural hurdles. In fact, the most facile regulators are able to issue rules despite these considerations (or can stymie a rulemaking, if that is what is called for). Others come and go, gaining experience and moving back into the private sector. Top-ranking regulators who are politically appointed and head agencies like the Environmental Protection Agency do not have terms, but they are confirmed by the Senate and generally serve for the length of the presidential administration. The chairs and commissioners of independent agencies also are nominated and confirmed but have set terms, and the majority reflects the party in power.

The Fight for Power

Top regulatory posts are coveted in Washington. These are important jobs, often prompting nasty confirmation rows in the Senate over the president's nominees. Special interest groups have strong views on the president's picks, and they often make them known during the nomination and confirmation process. The press plays a role, editorializing about controversial candidates or examining their personal and professional backgrounds, business relationships, and political views. Some nominees do not make it though the confirmation process after their political positions, past statements, or writings about future plans for an agency are scrutinized. Others are delayed interminably by the process, which is often laced with political rivalry and hoary claims of congressional prerogative. The following column lays out the political tangle involving two regulatory appointments.

Filling These Jobs Means Moving Heaven and Helms

The Washington Post, August 5, 1994—Mary Schapiro wants to be chairman of the Commodity Futures Trading Commission. Sheila Bair may be interested in a job at the Securities and Exchange Commission and would like her term extended at the CFTC. Karl Mertz would like his job back as an equal employment opportunity officer at the Department of Agriculture in Athens, Ga.

These are all frustrated public servants that have one thing in common: Their jobs are in the hands of Sen. Jesse Helms (R-N.C.).

For weeks now, several high-level regulatory appointments have been tangled in a values-laden dispute between Helms and Agriculture Secretary Mike Espy. Their disagreement is over policies (and proposed policies) at Agriculture regarding gay employees.

Mertz was taken out of his equal employment opportunity job and transferred to another at Agriculture after he said in a television interview on a Biloxi, Miss., station that he opposed policies that might offer taxpayer-funded benefits to partners of gay employees. He said the department should be moving toward "Camelot, not Sodom and Gomorrah."

Mertz, who'd been in the EEO position since 1987, said he opposes a gay lifestyle on moral grounds, but believes gays have the right to a job. A master at parliamentary blockades, Helms asked Espy in a letter he sent

Wednesday to "give the man his job back" and he'll let the Schapiro nomination go to the Senate floor for a vote.

"I've said before to you, and I now reiterate, you're too nice a guy to allow yourself to be dragged into this," Helms said in the letter.

And a mess it is.

While Espy stands firm on his position that Mertz can no longer carry out the duties of his job, careers are stalled, industry groups are fuming, a bipartisan public interest law firm defending religious liberty is threatening to sue Espy on behalf of Mertz and Democratic senators are vowing to hold up Bair's nomination (she is Republican) until Schapiro's is released.

The net effect of the feud is that the CFTC has not had a permanent chairman for 19 months and Schapiro, who currently is in overtime as a commissioner at the SEC, is waiting impatiently for her transfer to the CFTC.

"This is really ridiculous. You'd think six months after my confirmation hearing I'd be getting started at the CFTC," Schapiro said.

"This creates gridlock in the industry," said William Brodsky, chairman of the Chicago Mercantile Exchange, which is regulated by the CFTC. "Schapiro can hit the ground running but they won't let her put her sneakers on."

It's also hard to plan ahead.

Bair, who is waiting for the Senate to vote on a one-year extension of her CFTC term, also has her eye on Schapiro's job at the SEC. Sources said Bair has been campaigning for the seat, figuring the all-male SEC could use an experienced Republican woman.

And, just to drive his point home a little harder, Helms won enough votes for an amendment to the Agriculture appropriations bill, which, if passed, would give Mertz his job back.

At least someone would be happy.

Each of these posts at various agencies, and the rivalry for them, illustrates how coveted regulatory jobs are in Washington. These episodes—dealing with candidates who were poised to run the confirmation gauntlet in the Senate—illuminate the role that the Senate plays in advancing or delaying regulatory nominations. Richard Strout, writing almost a half century ago in *The New Republic*, calls the federal regulatory commissions "seemingly dull faceless agencies that protect the consumer."[8] That is still true. Yet, whenever a new administration comes to power, the jockeying for top spots is intense despite the prospect of an increasingly tough confirmation process.

Similarly, the careerists at agencies, who remain in place as bosses come and go, face changes in fortune with each new administration.

Case Studies: Gall and Scalia

Two nominations in the George W. Bush administration illustrate the intense politics of regulation in Washington and the import attached to regulatory jobs. Let us look at the experience of Mary Sheila Gall, a commissioner at the Consumer Product Safety Commission who was nominated by President George W. Bush to be chair of the three-person commission, and Eugene Scalia, an attorney who is the son of Supreme Court Justice Antonin Scalia, nominated to be solicitor of the Department of Labor.

Gall and the CPSC

Mary Sheila Gall was a member of the CPSC for ten years before being nominated by George W. Bush to be chair of the independent agency. In fact, she was originally nominated for the agency by George W. Bush's father and was renominated by President Bill Clinton. Gall, a Republican, was confirmed by the Senate both times. Before being nominated to be chair of the CPSC, she was an outspoken negative minority view on many safety issues.

Meanwhile, the consumer agency became a high-profile, aggressive regulator in the Clinton administration. This followed after years of diminishing budgets and staff, when the agency's influence was ebbing and influential voices favored eliminating it altogether. But under Clinton administration appointee Ann Brown, the agency was revitalized. A professional consumer advocate, Brown used media savvy and the bully pulpit of her post to pressure industries into recalling products. Brown managed to execute "voluntary" recalls by persuading companies that it was better to get positive publicity for a recall than negative press for being recalcitrant. During her tenure, which lasted from 1994 to 2001, Brown pressed the agency to address safety problems in Daisy air rifles, Whirlpool microwave ovens, household products such as suntan oil that contain hydrocarbons, mattresses that were flammable, bunk beds, baby bath seats, baby walkers, children's car seats, gun locks, scooters, and dive sticks that were dangerous—to name only a few. The agency also addressed what it thought was a problem with asbestos in crayons, leading crayon manufacturers to reformulate their products—one of the biggest safety initiatives undertaken by the agency. The following column shows how the CPSC under Brown took a high-profile approach to a problem with bunk beds.

Safety Agency Wants Bunk Beds to Measure Up

The Washington Post, March 19, 1999—Kids love bunk beds, and the top bunk in particular is prime nocturnal real estate.

But as much fun as it might be to sleep on the top tier, it also can be a dangerous place if the bed is not designed with special safety features.

Lynn Starks, a mother in Oklahoma City, found this out when her 3-year-old daughter, Whitney, died after becoming entrapped between the guardrail and the bed frame. Starks began a crusade that led to passage in Oklahoma of a law mandating bunk-bed safety features.

Now Starks and the Consumer Product Safety Commission want a national safety standard that would determine the dimensions of the beds as well as allow the agency to fine companies that don't comply with the rule.

"Bunk beds should be a safe and happy childhood experience—not a parent's worst nightmare," said Ann Brown, the commission's chairwoman.

Over the past eight years, at least 89 children have died of strangulation and thousands of others have been injured. Most of the deaths are from entrapment under the guardrail, within the end structures of the beds or between the bed and the wall. Most of the victims are children under age 3, and most of the accidents occur in the top bunk.

The problem has not gone unnoticed or unattended by either government regulators or the furniture industry. For 20 years, there have been voluntary safety guidelines that provide warnings, information on manufacturers and recommended design perimeters.

The voluntary standard calls for guardrails on both sides of the top bunk, but they do not have to run the entire length of the bed, which means they often leave a gap where many accidents occur. Openings in the rails should not be wider than 3 1/2 inches. The CPSC proposal would add new requirements: A continuous guardrail on the wall side of the bed, so the rail would meet both ends of the bed, and changes to the end structures below the top bunk.

The CPSC also has ordered recalls—there have been nine since 1994, involving 46 manufacturers and 547,500 beds.

But the existence of small companies, mom-and-pop operations, and a growing number of importers that don't know about or don't comply with the voluntary standard have continued to cause problems. The American Furniture Manufacturers Association said that of the 89 fatal accidents, four involved beds that were made by its members.

Russell Batson, the association's director of congressional and regulatory affairs, said the industry has addressed bunk beds' hazards as they have arisen, and the voluntary rule has been changed several times.

But changes in design often inadvertently create a new problem. For example, one manufacturer put a curved arm between the top and bottom beds and a child became stuck and died in a small corner where the arm met the top of the bed. Parents also persist in putting children under age 6 on top bunks, despite warnings not to. In two recent fatal accidents, an 18-month-old baby and a 4-year-old became entrapped on the top bunk.

Batson estimated that about 10 million bunk beds are in use and most don't cause a problem, and he noted that fatalities also happen in regular beds. From 1990 to 1997, 326 children aged 2 years and under died in accidents in adult beds.

Bunk beds "aren't problematic in and of themselves," Batson said. "But kids use them, and the challenge is to design them so they can be used safely."

But the persistence of fatalities—accidents on bunk beds kill an average of 10 people a year—has prompted the CPSC to abandon the voluntary effort and propose a mandatory standard that would allow it to assess civil penalties of up to $1.5 million against offenders and give U.S. customs inspectors the authority to inspect imports.

"A mandatory standard is the one remaining tool we have to stop all these deaths," Brown said. "We went the voluntary route and it isn't working. Kids are dying."

Ron Medford, CPSC assistant executive director for hazard identification and reduction, said one problem is that some companies ignore the voluntary standard.

Overall, 160 makers of bunk beds are known to the CPSC, which believes 40 of those are responsible for 75 percent of sales.

The number of companies that conform to the voluntary standard is high—probably 90 percent. But the other 10 percent are problematic and account for everything from parents banging together a bunk bed in their garage to an upscale company making $2,500 beds that look great but aren't built according to the standard. Some manufacturers are repeat violators.

"These companies would have made sure their beds complied if there was a mandatory standard," said Alan Schoem, assistant executive director of CPSC's Office of Compliance.

The agency will vote this summer on whether to put a mandatory rule on the books.

It can't come soon enough for Starks, who thinks bunk beds should be in the same league as child safety seats, toys and cribs. "We have all these laws for other things for kids, but they have left out the bunk beds," she said.

When Brown resigned, the agency used a press release that recapped her accomplishments, and interviews that she gave late in her tenure at the agency emphasized the advocacy role that she thought the chair of the agency should play in protecting consumers and children from harmful or unsafe products. Bunk bed regulation is only one among many issues she pursued and publicized.

Consumer groups loved Brown's emphasis on safety and her tenacity. They admired her for rehabilitating the image and importance of the CPSC in the firmament of agencies in Washington. They realized that, under Brown, the CPSC went from becoming an imperiled agency to being one that maximized its resources and actually won an increase in its budget.

The companies regulated by the CPSC were far less enthusiastic. They complained that they often learned of agency actions by tuning into a morning television news show on which Brown was appearing. They complained that they were being regulated by press release. "One of her problems, particularly in the last couple of years, has been that her goal has been to promote issues in the media, and due process has suffered as a result," said Frederick Locker, general counsel to the Juvenile Product Manufacturers Association.[9]

Gall's views about bunk beds, which became subject to a safety standard, and other children's products were decidedly different than Brown's. On the topic of bunk beds, and other controversial children's items such as baby bath rings and baby walkers, Gall thought caregivers and parents should be the first line of defense. She said parents should not leave children unattended in bath tubs, expecting bath rings to keep them sitting up in the water; gates should be put up and doors closed so that children in baby walkers would not fall down stairs; and, to avoid entrapment, parents should not put infants and young children in top bunks. She said that the risk of gas-fired water heaters igniting flammable vapors is a problem of consumer behavior rather than any defect in the product. In these cases, Gall often dissented from majority votes of the panel and defended her views in separate written statements.

Gall and another commissioner voted against regulating baby seats in 1994. Explaining her opposition to a rulemaking in a written statement after the vote, Gall said,

> It is clear that the irresponsible actions of those entrusted with caring for these children have, almost without exception, caused their deaths. If the commission fails to address this issue, we will have failed in exercising our responsibility to alert consumers to the primary cause of these tragedies. Parents and caregivers must use these products as labeled and never leave a baby unattended in a bathtub.

Seven years later, Gall reversed her position. In her statement on May 30, 2001, Gall said that neglect still plays a role in some infant drownings. She said, however, that the voluntary standard was not working because children in bath rings died even when caregivers were present and there were technical issues that needed to be addressed such as stability and the size of leg-hole openings. Chairwoman Brown, who was the only commissioner in 1994 who voted for a formal rulemaking, said she was "haunted" by the deaths of sixty-five babies since the 1994 vote. She said, "The behavior of the parents or caregivers is not what is at issue."

Gall's views, including the switch in her position on baby bath seats, came to haunt her during her confirmation hearing in summer 2001. The opposition was led by Sen. Hillary Rodham Clinton (D-N.Y.), who charged that giving Gall the top job was "like hiring a lifeguard who doesn't like to swim." Democrats staunchly opposed Gall and blocked her nomination from coming to a full vote in the Senate. Methodically, Gall's record was picked apart by the Senate Commerce Committee even though she did support a number of important regulatory initiatives. The final vote was twelve–eleven against her, with Democrats voting as a block opposing her confirmation. A month later, Gall asked to withdraw her nomination; she said she would serve out her term as a commissioner until 2005. It was the first nomination defeat for a regulatory post in the Bush administration. It was not until spring 2002 that the administration came up with another nominee: Harold D. Stratton, a former attorney general in New Mexico who finally was confirmed by the Senate in July 2002.

Gall did get support from industry. Many businesses welcomed the prospect of her taking over after seven years of Brown's leadership. They hoped for more restraint from the agency and more emphasis on voluntary standards.

But the battle for what had become a high-profile job was over. It was determined by a change in party in the Senate from Republican to Democrat. The Bush administration had assumed that Gall would be a shoo-in with a Republican-controlled committee that wanted to see less regulation; instead, the Gall vote reflected the power Democrats in the Senate had over regulatory appointments and their insistence that nominees not be overly conservative in their views. It is a case study of the rough-and-tumble politics that go hand in hand with many regulatory appointments and the intense battles that often erupt over them. In the case of the CPSC, Ann Brown elevated the role of the chair to the point that she knew it was pointless to stay on as a commissioner in the Bush administration when all the power at the agency rests with the chair. Senate Democrats felt the same, which is why they blocked Gall.

Scalia at the Labor Department

An equally fractious fight preceded the attempt to confirm Eugene Scalia as solicitor for the Department of Labor. Scalia was a favorite with the business community but was viewed as too conservative by labor unions and consumer groups. The following column lays out the battle that erupted when the Bush administration picked Scalia for the top legal job at Labor. Scalia, who had publicly aired his views opposing an ergonomics regulation, found that his statements were being used against him. This column recounts the controversy.

Scalia the Younger vs. "Questionable Science": Labor Choice Decried Ergonomics Rule

The Washington Post, June 12, 2001—Labor Secretary Elaine L. Chao won't show her hand until September about whether she will propose a new rule on repetitive-motion injuries in the workplace, but one of her chief lieutenants-to-be has played his card publicly about the hot-button issue.

As Eugene Scalia, a labor lawyer at Gibson, Dunn & Crutcher, awaits a confirmation hearing by the Senate on his nomination to be solicitor at Labor—the top legal perch in the department—his views precede him. His opinions have raised concern with labor officials who have been watching the nomination warily.

In the *Wall Street Journal* in January 2000, he wrote that the then-proposed ergonomics rule was "a major concession to union leaders, who know that ergonomic regulation will force companies to give more rest periods, slow the pace of work, and then hire more workers (read: dues-paying members)."

In a Cato Institute article in May of last year, he wrote: "One need not wade into the debate between ergonomists and their critics to appreciate the inappropriateness of the ergonomic regulation—one need only examine OSHA's dreadful performance in the ergonomics cases it litigated to judgment."

And in another Cato piece last June, he wrote: "OSHA wants to entrench the questionable science of ergonomics in a permanent rule. But no agency should be permitted to impose on the entire American economy a costly rule premised on a 'science' so mysterious that the agency itself cannot fathom it."

At the time, the 37-year-old Scalia, son of Supreme Court Justice Antonin Scalia, represented the most strident opponents of a federal ergonomics rule—the National Coalition on Ergonomics, United Parcel Service Inc. and Anheuser-Busch Cos. He also participated in efforts to block ergonomics standards in California and Washington State.

Scalia declined to be interviewed, citing his pending nomination.

Eric Frumin, health and safety director for the Union of Needletrades, Industrial and Textile Employees, calls Scalia an "extremist." He said Scalia has "a 10-year history of trying to deny the obvious reality that ergonomic hazards injure millions of American workers."

Peg Seminario, safety and health director for the AFL-CIO, said: "We haven't taken a final position. But we are quite concerned based on what we know about him."

Bush administration sources said his views on ergonomics became mainstream when a majority of the Congress voted to kill the Clinton administration's ergonomics rule.

Supporters say Scalia was a forceful advocate for his clients in opposing an ergonomics rule. But William Kilberg, who was Labor solicitor under presidents Richard M. Nixon and Gerald R. Ford and a Scalia mentor at Gibson, Dunn & Crutcher, said: "There's no reason to believe that Eugene Scalia would do anything but carry out the law . . . or wouldn't be fully committed to carry out the mission of the Labor Department to further the interest of working men and women."

As solicitor, Scalia would have jurisdiction over a wide range of legal and regulatory issues, ranging from mine safety and job training, to migrant workers and pension rights.

Kilberg said Scalia's writings on sexual harassment and labor unions show that he is neither liberal nor conservative. "People who think he's ideological are off base," he said. "He's not a wing nut. If you read what he's written, it's thoughtful and you can't put it in ideological terms."

For example, he has written that the federal government should give more recognition to labor unions, even to the point of letting them take over some regulatory responsibilities.

Baruch Fellner, another colleague at Gibson, Dunn & Crutcher on the ergonomics cases, said of Scalia: "His intellect is incandescent. The Department of Labor is so damned lucky to have a person of his ability at the helm of their legal department."

J. Davitt McAteer, Labor solicitor during part of the Clinton administration, said the job requires upholding laws and rules that Scalia has expressed opposition to. "It will be a real challenge not to have his strongly held ideology interfere with his obligations as chief law enforcement officer at Labor," he said. "It's not to say it can't be done, but it will be harder to carry out."

The Senate Committee on Health, Education, Labor and Pensions is expected to hold a hearing on the nomination in July. The committee is now headed by Sen. Edward M. Kennedy (D-Mass.), who supported the Clinton ergonomics rule.

If Scalia is confirmed, he will be the third top-level appointee at Labor with ties to Antonin Scalia. D. Cameron Findlay, the new deputy secretary, and Howard Radzely, the new deputy solicitor, were both law clerks for the Supreme Court justice.

As solicitor, Scalia would not argue cases before his father—the Justice Department does that. But he would have influence on cases, and his name may appear on legal briefs at the high court. He has never argued a case before the court and his firm kept any income from Supreme Court cases segregated so it didn't figure into Scalia's pay, law partners said.

The Scalia vote, when it got to the Senate Health, Education and Labor Committee in October 2001, was as contentious as the column had predicted. Democrats on the committee, led by Chairman Sen. Edward M. Kennedy (D-Mass.), opposed Scalia based on his highly publicized views about worker safety and ergonomics and his career as a labor lawyer representing the interests of management. They feared that Scalia, as head of five hundred lawyers at the Labor Department, would block or hold up any significant regulation that had to do with ergonomics in the workplace or other worker initiatives from pension rights to mine safety.

Like Gall, Scalia tried to soften some of his previous hard-line, conservative rhetoric when he appeared before the committee. He said that ergonomics injuries do exist but that the rule that the Clinton administration had in mind as a fix was too extreme. The vote was eleven–ten in favor of Scalia along party lines, with Sen. Jim Jeffords, the Independent from Vermont, giving Scalia the margin of victory. The vote from the full Senate stalled for weeks after the hearing, probably because of political considerations but also the result of unfortunate timing. The Senate after September 11, 2001, became immersed in issues dealing with terrorism, anthrax in Senate buildings, and passing an economic stimulus package. So, for months, Scalia worked at the Labor Department as a "consultant," where he could examine and review documents and cases but not make any legal decisions or recommendations. It is a kind of nominee limbo—some might say purgatory—that many regulators-to-be fall into if their appointments are controversial. In his place, Howard M. Radzely, who did not have to weather the confirmation process, acted as solicitor and eventually became Scalia's deputy.

The political infighting over ergonomics and the slights Scalia got about his pedigree did not leave him any less eager to have the third most important job in the department. While his confirmation was pending, Scalia kept a low profile, saying little about his published views. The *Wall Street Journal* came to his defense in an editorial that strongly hinted that Democrats were trying to punish the son for the sins of the father: Supreme Court Justice Antonin Scalia was one of the five justices who voted to put George W. Bush in the White House, the capstone to one of the nation's most fractious presidential elections. Democrats also believe to this day that the elder Scalia was the principal force within the Court to determine the ultimate outcome of the contested 2000 election.

"Since their substantive complaints are so flimsy, it's fair to wonder if what Democrats aren't playing here is a game of payback. Justice Scalia has lifetime tenure and can't be touched. But his son's career can be mauled and his reputation tarnished," said a *Wall Street Journal* editorial on October 10, 2001. But while the conservative editorial page of the *Wall Street Journal* was defending

Scalia as a stellar selection for the Labor Department job, liberal voices were calling attention to the importance of the post and the influence that Scalia would have on sensitive rulemakings when he was finally confirmed. The solicitor job at the Labor Department holds sway over the enforcement of some two hundred labor laws.

"Scalia is now a familiar type in the Bush administration: a policy assassin who's built a career fighting a specific set of regulations and finds himself appointed to a top position in the very agency he's long opposed," charged an article in *The American Prospect*.[10] Those views were echoed by the labor unions that opposed Scalia. They researched Scalia's professional past thoroughly, hoping that what they dredged up—mostly his negative views on the Clinton administration ergonomics rule—would put pressure on Senate members to oppose him.

In the end, there was no vote, and the Bush administration appointed him during a congressional break, a procedure called a recess appointment, which allows the president to make appointments when the Senate is not in session. This maneuver typically is used when an administration realizes that a vote in the Senate would not support the nominee. When the Senate returned to Republication control in November 2002, the Bush administration renominated him for the post, assuming Scalia would be easily confirmed.

Where the Regulators Come From

These kinds of battles do not erupt with every nomination. In fact, regulatory posts often get filled with little notice. Appointments in the George W. Bush administration reflected the tenor and philosophy of the administration: his appointees were comfortable with close alliances with business, and regulation is often a last resort for them. In previous administrations, appointees may have been plucked from the ranks of labor unions, environmental groups, or liberal-leaning special interest groups. The Senate generally goes out of its way to let an administration pick its own team.

Many of Bush's appointees left private industry to return to government, sometimes after serving in his father's administration or the Reagan administration. It was the revolving door swinging the opposite way. For example, at the Department of Housing and Urban Development, six out of nine appointees served in Bush's father's administration. Ann M. Veneman, secretary of the Department of Agriculture, held positions in both the Reagan administration and the first Bush administration.

A *National Journal* analysis in June 2001 of 300 Bush appointees at the White House, cabinet-level departments, independent agencies, boards, and commissions showed that Bush appointees were real insiders: Almost 75 percent had worked in the federal government previous to their appointment. Forty-four percent working in executive branch agencies worked for George W. Bush's father. Another 38 percent were business executives. "The son of a President, George W. Bush has created a 'son of' administration," the magazine said.

The survey produced a profile of the appointees (not all of whom are regulators and not all of whom were confirmed by the Senate) that showed they were predominantly male, white, married, and had worked in government previously. Their average age was forty-eight. Table 2.2 is a look at the modern regulator.

TABLE 2.2. **Regulators in the George W. Bush Administration: Where They Worked and Went to School**

Top Places Where They Worked in 2000	Percentage
Washington, D.C.	44
Texas	11
Virginia	8
California	7
Indiana	3

Top Undergraduate Schools	Number of Graduates
Yale University	12
Harvard University	11
University of Texas	11
U.S. Naval Academy	10
Georgetown University	9

Top Graduate Schools	Number of Graduates
Harvard University	40
Georgetown University	9
George Washington University	9
Indiana University	8
University of Chicago	8
University of Virginia	8

Source: National Journal (June 2001). Reprinted with permission.

The Presidential Appointee Initiative at the Brookings Institution in Washington did a study of appointees in the George W. Bush administration and found that Senate-confirmed nominees for the top jobs in the first year were more often male and more often white than appointees in the Clinton administration. The study showed that 74 percent were male, compared with 54 percent in the previous administration. There were more Hispanic appointees but fewer African Americans in the Bush administration. Like the *National Journal* survey, the Brookings data showed that more than half of the top appointees were from the Washington, D.C., area, meaning they were already established in some part of official Washington. Almost 60 percent of Bush's picks have master's degrees or Ph.D.s, and 35 percent have law degrees. Their professional backgrounds are top-heavy with experience in the federal government, law, business, and consulting, as figure 2.1 shows.

The kind of hierarchy that an administration builds at departments and agencies has consequences for regulatory policy and for how regulators perform in their jobs. The experience and professional backgrounds that regulators bring to their jobs determine the tone of the agency, its enforcement policy, its aggressiveness as a regulator, and its relationship with the community it regulates. During the Clinton administration, the top appointee at the Labor Department's Occupational Safety and Health Administration was Charles N. Jeffress. His entire professional life had been spent as a regulator; he had been director of North Carolina's occupational safety and health program, a career that began in 1977 with various positions in the state's Department of Labor. He championed implementing what would have been one of the federal government's most expansive and controversial new regulations, an ergonomics rule. His replacement in the George W. Bush administration was John L. Henshaw, who came from the other side of the regulatory equation. His career was spent at chemical companies, helping them comply with health and safety regulations. Respected by business and labor, Henshaw's agenda stresses cooperation and helping companies follow Occupational Safety and Health Administration rules and guidelines so they avoid violating them. Under his leadership, the department issued guidelines, instead of rules, to urge companies to fix ergonomics problems in their workplaces.

Arthur Levitt Jr. and Harvey L. Pitt

The Securities and Exchange Commission is another example that illustrates how the power of an agency emanates from the top leadership position

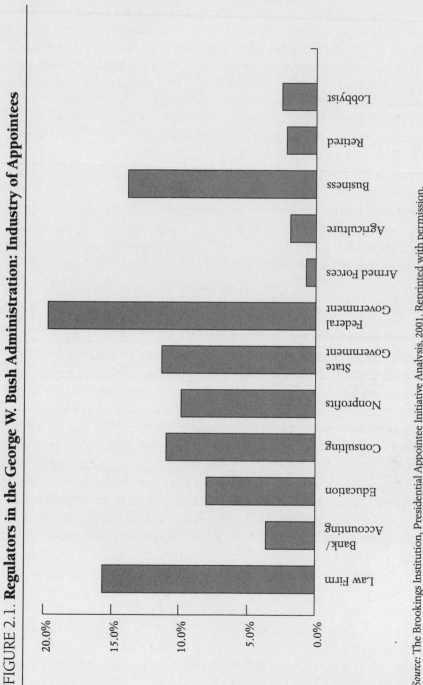

FIGURE 2.1. **Regulators in the George W. Bush Administration: Industry of Appointees**

Source: The Brookings Institution, Presidential Appointee Initiative Analysis, 2001. Reprinted with permission.

and the regulatory philosophy of the party in power. During the Clinton administration, the SEC was led by Arthur Levitt, who challenged powerful interests in the securities and accounting industries and defended the individual investor. His opponents thought that he had a heavy hand when it came to regulation, and they disagreed with his populist view that the small investor is as entitled to as much information and protection as the big investor is. He held forty-three town hall meetings for investors during his eight-year chairmanship, which raised his profile and the profile of the agency. In his years at the SEC, Levitt extended the regulatory reach of the commission, going after municipal bond underwriters, the securities exchanges, and the accounting profession. Some members of Congress and highly influential players in the securities industry often battled him (remember, the collapse of Enron and its accounting problems was yet to come). This column shows Levitt's attempt to regulate more fully the murky world of financial derivatives, how he tried to flex the muscles of the agency, and the resistance he got to those efforts.

On the Hill, Moves to Stamp Out Derivatives Disclosure

The Washington Post, April 4, 1997—Three years ago, financial regulators in Washington were being criticized for not having a regulatory apparatus in place to oversee a complicated array of financial instruments called derivatives that companies, municipalities and banks were using to hedge against possible losses, or to make money, in a variety of markets.

Derivatives-related disasters that resulted in multimillion-dollar losses for Procter & Gamble Co. and Gibson Greetings Inc. and multibillion-dollar losses for Orange County in California, made derivatives the subject of great regulatory debate. Derivatives are financial contracts whose value is linked to, or "derived from" an underlying asset such as commodities, stocks and bonds.

Recognizing that the value of derivatives contracts in 1995 was an astounding $24 trillion, the Securities and Exchange Commission got to work on a rule to tell investors more about how companies use derivatives.

Despite a chorus of opposition from regulated companies and money managers who sell derivatives to their clients, the SEC issued the rule in February after it surveyed about 500 companies and their disclosure practices on derivatives. The commission did not pass judgment on the use of derivatives—not all of which are mind-numbingly complex or particularly risky—but it did express concern that disclosure could be better.

At the time the rule was being issued, SEC Chairman Arthur Levitt Jr. summed it up: "Derivatives are like electricity—dangerous if mishandled, but also capable of doing enormous good."

The commission decided that companies would have to lay out in their annual reports what derivative deals they were engaged in and choose one of three ways to quantify the value—or risk—of those deals.

At the same time, the Financial Accounting Standards Board, the independent body that sets the accounting rules that companies live by, is working on a proposal of its own that may require companies to account for their derivatives activity on their balance sheets, a prospect dreaded by many companies.

In fact, the FASB rule is of more concern to many companies and dealers in derivatives than the SEC rule because it would force a financial accounting of the derivatives deals—some of which are so complex that chief executives confess they can't understand them. As one financial regulator put it: The SEC rule is merely the warm-up for the real ballgame that starts when FASB issues its rule.

Nevertheless, the SEC disclosure rule is being picked apart in Congress.

Several weeks ago, Sen. Phil Gramm (R-Tex.), chairman of the Senate Banking subcommittee on securities, held a hearing looking at the effects of the SEC rule and the FASB proposal. Gramm, who is predisposed to let markets regulate themselves, is concerned that the SEC did not do enough cost-benefit analysis.

His wife, Wendy Gramm, who is a former chairman of the Commodity Futures Trading Commission and who refused to regulate certain kinds of derivative deals, said rules such as the SEC's may stifle the market's ability to come up with ways to measure risk.

"It's seductive to say it's just disclosure. There are side effects you have to consider. The market is working. They are devising all kinds of methods to manage and disclose risk," said Wendy Gramm, who has been a kind of outside expert on the issue.

Rep. Michael G. Oxley (R-Ohio), a member of the House Commerce Committee, also has asked the SEC for its analysis on what the rule would cost companies—competitively and financially.

Even more disconcerting to the SEC, Capitol Hill sources said, is the prospect that the rule might become a candidate for one of the first in-depth reviews done under the auspices of the newly minted Congressional Review Act.

The act sets out procedures that can be used by members to review a rule, send it back to an agency or, if need be, reject it. Politically, the derivatives rule might be a relatively easy target for CRA scrutiny, since the issue is so complicated and there is little likelihood of the kind of public outcry that has resulted from Republican attacks on environmental, health and safety rules.

The author of the CRA, Rep. David M. McIntosh (R-Ind.), who is chairman of the House subcommittee on oversight and investigation, signaled to the SEC in two letters that he thinks the quantitative element of the rule may have a "counterproductive effect," that there are "procedural irregularities" in the writing of the rule and that the agency's chief economist raised objections to the rule.

Despite these correspondences and the hearing, the subcommittees are not prepared to recommend a "resolution of disapproval" under the CRA, though the prospect of it has hung over discussions the agency is having with congressional staff members like thick cigar smoke.

The SEC said it hasn't heard much protest from companies about the final rule.

But the International Swaps and Derivatives Association as well as other groups with an interest in the rule have been pointing out the shortcomings of the regulation on Capitol Hill.

"The objective here is to improve the rule and there are many ways to do that," said Mark Brickell, a member of ISDA's board and managing director of J. P. Morgan & Co.

For its part, the SEC said it bent over backward to give companies flexibility in reporting on derivatives activity. It phased in the rule, exempted small businesses, and promised to review it in three years. As for the chief economist's comments, they are considered part of the rule-making process that allows for differing viewpoints.

SEC Commissioner Steven M. H. Wallman, who testified at the Gramm hearing, stands by the rule. "Something like this is an improvement and will be quite beneficial," he said.

Going after derivatives was only the beginning. Levitt later targeted accounting fraud and "accounting gimmicks" that he said were used to "manage" the financial results of clients and sometimes cleverly obscure the truth. In a speech called "The Numbers Game" that he delivered in 1998 to the New York University Center for Law and Business, Levitt said,

Many in corporate America are just as frustrated and concerned about this trend as we, at the SEC, are. They know how difficult it is to hold the line on good practices when their competitors operate in the gray area between legitimacy and outright fraud. A gray area where the accounting is being perverted; where managers are cutting corners; and where earnings reports reflect the desires of management rather than the underlying financial performance of the company.

This campaign against the accounting industry went on for several years and resulted in a truce, at best. Levitt reveled in that crusade and others like it that he embarked on during his tenure.

Levitt's background was an eclectic one, and he came to the commission with varied life experiences. Along with being chairman of the American Stock Exchange, he was a publisher of a newspaper that covers Capitol Hill, and he worked on Wall Street for sixteen years. He was comfortable on Wall Street and in Washington.

Enter Harvey L. Pitt, Levitt's successor in the Bush administration, who was forced out of the job by his own conflicts. Pitt barely had time to redecorate the chairman's office before he announced a kinder, gentler approach to regulation—a philosophical standing typical of other Bush appointees. The regulatory approach had gone from vigilant enforcement on a shoestring budget to cooperation and more voluntary compliance. Companies that reported the error of their ways themselves often could depend on lighter punishment if any rules or laws had been broken.

In fall 2001, Pitt delivered a speech that reversed the regulatory thrust of Levitt's long tenure at the agency. "Somewhere along the way, accountants became afraid to talk to the SEC, and the SEC appeared to be unwilling to listen to the profession. Those days are ended. I speak for the entire commission when I say that we want to have a continuing dialogue, and partnership, with the accounting profession, and we will do everything in our power to evidence a new era of respect and cooperation," Pitt told the American Institute of Certified Public Accountants. "At the Commission, we view the accounting profession as our partner in maintaining and developing a financial reporting system that serves as the bedrock of our financial markets." The comfort level rose even higher when one of Pitt's lieutenants was plucked directly from the accounting industry: Robert K. Herdman, the new chief accountant at the SEC, is formerly vice chairman of Ernest & Young, one of the nation's top corporate accounting firms.

Pitt's professional background helps explain his regulatory style and philosophy. Regarded as one of the nation's most brilliant minds in securities law, Pitt represented in private practice the very interests he would be regulating—a prior professional relationship that became troublesome during the investigation into the collapse of the Enron Corp. in late 2001 and with other companies. During the time he practiced at the high-profile firm of Fried Frank Harris Shriver & Jacobson, his clients included the Investment Company Institute, which lobbies for the mutual fund industry, Morgan Stanley Dean Witter, and Merrill Lynch. For twenty years, he represented the American Institute of Certified Public Accountants, the group that fought Levitt's new rules and reforms of the profession, and the Big Five accounting firms. Pitt also had extensive experience as a regulator: He spent ten years of his career at the SEC in various high-level staff positions—including general counsel—before he left for private practice.

Not surprisingly, the accounting group was one of Pitt's supporters when he was under consideration for the chairmanship. The group praised Pitt as "someone we could work very closely and cooperatively with."[11]

A day after the October 2001 speech, the SEC put some regulatory teeth into Pitt's promises to the accountants. The agency issued new enforcement guidelines that allowed companies to confess their sins and offer to do better before they would be officially sanctioned. Many agencies use this carrot-and-stick approach to discipline rule breakers, but many of them quietly apply the policy on a case-by-case basis without public press releases.

In this case, the commission announced that it would gauge a company's cooperation by whether it policed itself to find infractions, whether it reported the problem to the public and regulators, whether it took action to fix the problem, and whether it cooperated with law enforcement authorities. "Credit for cooperative behavior may range from the extraordinary step of taking no enforcement action at all to bringing reduced charges, seeking lighter sanctions, or including mitigating language in documents the Commission uses to announce and resolve enforcement actions," the SEC announced, reversing eight years of regulatory policy.

Pitt may have wished he had never been quite so explicit and enthusiastic in his defense of the accounting profession. His light touch became cannon fodder for Democrats on congressional committees who were looking into the role of professional accountants in the downfall of the Enron Corp., whose balance sheet was riddled with accounting improprieties. Despite growing criticism of his approach, Pitt's answer to the problem was to continue to resist formal government regulation of the accounting profession. That approach later was overtaken by events and legislation that called for tougher oversight of corporate wrongdoers that included sending them to jail.

Who the regulators are can be a deciding factor in how an administration sets and follows a regulatory course; equally as important are the special interests that influence the outcome of the regulatory process for their own benefit. This is the dynamic explored in chapter 3.

 ## Summary

Chapter 2 looks at some of the more interesting characters who are regulators in the federal government and their jobs, as well as the influence they have on the regulated community. The chapter explores why these jobs are important, who covets them, and the battles that can ensue among the nominee, Congress, and the White House over appointments to regulatory posts. There are two case studies at the Consumer Product Safety Commission and the Labor Department to show how the political appointment process works and why the personal and professional backgrounds of the nominees are so important. Finally, the chapter focuses on the different approaches taken by two top regulators at the Securities and Exchange Commission.

 ## To Learn More

For more reading on the Administrative Procedure Act, consult:

William F. Fox, *Understanding Administrative Law,* 4th ed. (Lexis Publishing, 2000).
Ernest Gellhorn and Ronald Levin, *Administrative Law and Process in a Nutshell,* 4th ed. (West Nutshell Series, 1997).
Jeffrey S. Lubbers, *A Guide to Federal Agency Rulemaking,* 3d ed. (ABA Book Publishing, 1998).

An excellent website that has links to federal agencies, discussion groups, journals, texts of important regulatory policy documents, and state and international sources of regulatory information is www.law.fsu.edu/library/admin/.

For insight into a group of men who were regulatory pioneers, in that they either created agencies, served in them, or helped to bring an end to them, consult *Prophets of Regulation* by Thomas K. McCraw (Belknap Press, Harvard University Press, 1984). The chapters on Louis D. Brandeis, one of the architects of the Federal Trade Commission (as the book puts it), and James M. Landis, regulatory theoretician and designer of the Securities and Exchange Commission, are excellent reference points for comparing the leaders of those agencies in the early 1900s to those who currently hold those perches at the FTC and SEC.

For an ongoing look at the appointment process, the Brookings Institution has a project called the Presidential Appointee Initiative. It not only keeps a running tally of the status of appointees—nominations, number confirmed, recess appointments—but gives insight into the difficulty of getting confirmed by the Senate for top jobs in the federal government, many of which are regulatory posts. The site includes the forms that nominees must fill out to be considered; this would be a good exercise to go through to experience the complexity of the process firsthand.

Notes

1. Scott Kilman, "FDA Warns of Misleading Labels on Genetic Modification in Foods," *Wall Street Journal*, December 20, 2001: B9.

2. Thomas K. McCraw, *Prophets of Regulation: Charles Francis Adams, Louis D. Brandeis, James M. Landis, Alfred Kahn* (Cambridge, Mass.: Belknap Press, Harvard University Press, 1984), 125–26.

3. McCraw, *Prophets of Regulation*, viii.

4. Paul L. Light, "To Restore and Renew: Now Is the Time to Rebuild the Federal Public Service," *Government Executive* 33, no. 14 (2001): 32–47.

5. Center for the Study of American Business, Washington University, St. Louis, Mo., *2001 Annual Regulatory Budget Report*, Regulatory Budget Report 23 (June 2000), 5.

6. Stephen G. Breyer and Richard B. Stewart, *Administrative Law and Regulatory Policy: Problems, Text, and Cases* (Boston: Little, Brown, 1985), 1.

7. Cornelius M. Kerwin, *Rulemaking: How Government Agencies Write Law and Make Policy* (Washington, D.C.: CQ Press, 1994), 48–49.

8. Richard Strout, "TRB: Regulatory Agencies," *The New Republic* (1957): 128.

9. Caroline Mayer, "Safety Agency Chief Going Out with Gusto," *Washington Post*, October 30, 2001: E1.

10. Joshua Green, "Ergonomic Enemy; After a Career of Bashing Workers' Rights, Eugene Scalia May Soon Control Them," *The American Prospect* 12, no. 16 (2001): 6.

11. David S. Hilzenrath, "SEC Chief: 'Gentler' Agency," *Washington Post*, October 23, 2001: E1.

Special Interests: Bending the Will of the Regulators

GOP Plans Attack on Workplace Rule; Congressional Maneuver Could Kill New Ergonomics Regulation

The Washington Post, March 3, 2001—Senate Republican leaders are planning to use a little-known legislative weapon next week to try to kill the Clinton administration's regulation to prevent injuries on the job, the most sweeping and costly workplace change government has ever ordered.

Business groups have long opposed the ergonomics rule, which was first suggested when Elizabeth Dole was secretary of labor in 1990, because of its scope and compliance costs. They already have filed suit to block it, but corporate lobbyists say a special congressional resolution would be faster and the outcome more certain.

Issued in November and scheduled to take effect Oct. 14, the ergonomics regulation would cover about 100 million workers in 6 million workplaces. Estimates of its cost range from $4.5 billion to $100 billion annually. It would pay workers disabled by their injuries, in some cases more and longer than under state workers' compensation laws. It also would require employers to redesign jobs that involve typing, lifting and other types of work if employees report problems.

Four GOP senators, led by Assistant Majority Leader Don Nickles (R-Okla.), introduced a "resolution of disapproval" late Thursday under the Congressional Review Act. If the resolution is approved by a simple majority in each house and is signed by President Bush, the ergonomics rule will be rescinded.

The vote, the first time Congress has taken on a regulation published in the final months of the Clinton administration, could come as early as Tuesday. Under the law, no amendments are allowed and debate is limited to 10 hours in the Senate, though Democrats may try to filibuster the motion to take up the resolution.

Leadership aides in both parties said yesterday the prospects for rejecting the rule are good, even with the Senate split 50–50 along party lines.

Labor unions have passionately supported the ergonomics rule as the way to address the 600,000 repetitive stress injuries, such as carpal tunnel syndrome, tendinitis and back pain, that result in lost work every year.

The unions and their Democratic allies are lobbying furiously to defeat the GOP effort. The AFL-CIO launched a campaign called "Hands Off the Ergo Standard" this week. Union members picketed a National Association of Manufacturers meeting on Wednesday where Vice President Cheney spoke; they also introduced injured workers at a press briefing yesterday. "This is the number one job safety issue in America," said Lynn Rhinehart, the AFL-CIO's associate general counsel.

The law allowing Congress to initiate a "resolution of disapproval" was passed by the Republican-controlled Congress in 1996. It has not been used on a major rule before and isn't likely to be used again anytime soon, GOP aides said.

Bush's action on the resolution would send a strong signal about the new administration's attitude toward late Clinton rules. White House spokesman Scott McClellan yesterday said, "We need to continue to protect the health and safety of workers, but there is a concern about burdensome regulations that may have a negative impact on our economy."

Sources said Bush reacted favorably in a meeting Monday with House and Senate Republicans when Nickles told him about plans to try to kill the ergonomics rule.

White House Chief of Staff Andrew Card issued a memo the first day in office telling agencies to delay the effective date of Clinton rules so new appointees could decide how they wanted to handle key regulatory issues. But some business lobbyists were shaken when the Agriculture Department recently approved a Clinton proposal to test for listeria bacteria in processed meats and the Environmental Protection Agency permitted final release of a Clinton regulation cutting the levels of sulfur in diesel fuel.

Sen. Christopher S. Bond (R-Mo.) said in a statement that "Congress has no choice but to head off the devastating side effects of the Clinton ergo rule by dismantling it. This menacing regulation's days are numbered."

Rep. Roy Blunt (R-Mo.), a deputy whip who has been lining up House votes to eliminate the rule, said in an interview, "The ergonomics regulation is the perfect target for the first effective use of the Congressional Review Act." A spokesman for House Speaker J. Dennis Hastert (R-Ill.) said, "We're going to await Senate action before deciding how to proceed."

Sen. Edward M. Kennedy (D-Mass.) accused the Republicans of mounting a stealth attack on the regulation. "Republicans intend to sound the death knell for protections from ergonomic injuries—the most significant safety and health problem that workers face today," he said. "No friend of America's workers could welcome such a result."

Democrats argued that a key provision of the congressional review law makes it doubtful, if not impossible, for strong ergonomics rules to be implemented in the future.

The law bars reissuing any revoked rule, or any new rule "that is substantially the same" as the old rule, unless it is specifically authorized by Congress. It's an "all or nothing proposition," Kennedy and 22 other Democrats argued Thursday in a "Dear Colleague" letter.

Nickles spokesman Brook Simmons disagreed. "All it [overturning the rule] means is not this regulation. It doesn't prevent the administration from readdressing this issue in a more workable and less intrusive regulation," he said.

Business groups have also been lobbying the issue heavily. They note that many workplaces already have ergonomic programs, and complain that there is no evidence that work alone causes the most commonly cited problems. They have had their members in Washington for face-to-face visits on the issue, and fax machines have been in overdrive, sending "alerts" to members on the importance of killing the rule.

"It's like rolling thunder," said Randy Johnson, vice president for labor and employee benefits at the U.S. Chamber of Commerce, of his group's lobbying effort.

———————————

As the column predicted, the Congressional Review Act was used to nullify the ergonomics regulation, one of the most far-reaching federal rules ever put on the books. The defeat of the ergonomics rule in spring 2001 was special interest opposition warfare at its best and a textbook case of how the regulatory and legislative process is influenced by outside forces. For the business community, the defeat of the rule, which was issued in its final form late in the Clinton administration, was a sweet, spectacular victory and a broadside against one of the most significant regulatory initiatives of the last decade. A newsletter issued after the vote by the National Association of Manufacturers, one of the nation's biggest business lobbying groups, summarized success this way: "We won because manufacturers large and small understood the importance of this vote and made their voices heard. When they did, it moved the earth. The vast and overreaching ergonomics rule is dead. We have sent OSHA back to the drawing board." For labor, which supported the rule and worked for it tirelessly, it was a breathtaking setback and the first harbinger of how the Bush administration would handle regulatory affairs and factor in the views of the business community.

The defeat of the ergonomics rule is a way to look at the dramatic power of special interest groups in Washington and how they can influence regulatory outcomes. In this case, two powerhouses in the business community—the U.S. Chamber of Commerce and the National Association of

Manufacturers—and the AFL-CIO, representing labor, played the key roles in both the development and the demise of the rule. Staffed with professionals who know the technical and political sides of regulatory issues, these three groups, along with thousands of other organizations, hold sway in Washington. Some work for trade associations and corporations that pay them six figures, while others live on more modest salaries paid by nonprofit groups that have an interest in regulation.

The practical effect of the lobbying on the ergonomics rule was that it defeated an experienced cadre of regulators within the Clinton administration, removing what the business community considered a highly troublesome, costly rule. Using the Congressional Review Act to squash the rule also sent a signal to regulators that there was now a way to defeat unpopular rules outside of court—the more traditional and, often, unsuccessful route.

Though the ergonomics rule already was being challenged in court by business, this was a quicker, more definitive death, one that left the regulators who created it no choice but to abandon it completely. In fact, the legislation includes a provision forbidding the Occupational Safety and Health Administration from coming up with anything similar to the old rule. Put another way, the lightening-fast vote in Congress against the rule was the equivalent of a lethal injection, repudiating the goals of regulators in the Clinton administration who insisted that the rule was necessary to stop debilitating workplace injuries.

It was also a test of the effectiveness of the Congressional Review Act, a little-known legislative device specifically created in 1996 to give Congress the authority to overturn final rules. Until the defeat of the ergonomics rule, many members of Congress were not fully aware of the power of the device; those who were cognizant of it were hesitant to use it, fearing that they would not have the votes to overturn a rule and would thus suffer political embarrassment. But as soon as there was a president in the White House who would sign legislation negating the final rule, business lobbyists pulled out all the stops to educate members of Congress on how the law worked— and to encourage them to use it.

In the broadest sense, the demise of the ergonomics rule is a case study of how powerful special interests can get their way in Washington—particularly if all the stars in the political firmament line up correctly. The ergonomics rule—and the success the business community had in defeating it—is likely to be considered as interesting and as important as some of the intense regulatory battles fought over the years by the tobacco industry over labeling and nicotine content.

The Battle Plan

The lobbying against the rule began in earnest in January 2001, when the balance of power shifted toward the business community with the election of a Republican president. If former Vice President Al Gore, Bush's rival, had been elected president, the rule would have stood. Gore would have vetoed any legislation that changed or eliminated a rule that was so significant and so central a part of the Clinton administration regulatory agenda.

The business community also counted on Elaine Chao, the Bush administration's new secretary of the Department of Labor, to help abolish the Clinton rule by assuring members of Congress who were wavering in their opposition that the administration would revisit the issue and come up with a plan of its own. In fact, the day before the vote in the Senate, Chao sent a letter to senators that assured them that voting against the Clinton rule was not a vote against an ergonomics rule but, rather, a vote against a Clinton administration rule. For business, this was a crucial message to get out to some members of Congress who were worried about alienating their labor constituencies.

Within a few months, business had a lock-tight plan in place and felt it could swing the votes to kill the rule. There were no cracks in the enamel, no splintering among various business groups. There was no disagreement about the approach. Everyone hung together with representatives from the biggest and best bankrolled of the business groups as well as thousands of unnamed smaller businesses traveling to Washington to tell members of Congress how the rule would hurt their companies. Funeral directors, builders and contractors, food distributors, truckers, convenience stores, insurers, and others all put their lobbyists to work. 7-Eleven Inc., FedEx Corp., Ryder Systems Inc., and other big companies all signed on to work to eliminate the rule. Their job was to convince members that the rule was too costly and regulation run amuck.

In the week before the vote, every day at 6 p.m. sharp, business lobbyists met in the office of Representative Tom Delay of Texas, then the House majority whip, to discuss strategy, talk with key lawmakers, hand out lobbying assignments, and count votes. They set up a "war room" in the Longworth House Office Building where, if they got there early enough, they could munch on Krispy Kreme doughnuts, Hostess chocolate cupcakes and Ho Hos, and Entenmann's cookies supplied by the members of the American Bakers Association, one of the leading opponents of the rule. One lobbyist said: "We are moving heaven and earth."

One of the lobbying techniques was unusually creative. Another opponent of the rule, the Food Marketing Institute, which represents 22,000 grocery stores, delivered twenty-two frozen turkeys to House members who had yet to make up their minds about the ergonomics vote. All of the birds weighed more than 15 pounds each, over the limit that OSHA had suggested is safe for filling shopping bags. The institute wanted to make the point that you could not stuff a 20-pound turkey into a 15-pound grocery bag, hoping it would make the rule seem foolish to members of Congress who were on the delivery list. All six Democrats in the Senate who voted against the rule were turkey recipients.

The American Hotel & Motel Association took a different approach. It sent to members "Do Not Disturb" signs in the shape of door hangers like those used in hotels. The message was "do not disturb the interests of your constituents."

Before the vote in the Senate on March 6, 2001, the National Association of Manufacturers fired up its so-called Member Involvement Network, asking members to contact thirteen Senate offices and blast twenty-five faxes to them or make twenty-five calls. The NAM supplied a sample letter that businesspeople could send to Congress, talking points, and a list of "priority senators" to contact. Lobbyists pounded away at calculators to arrive at dramatic estimates of how much it would cost to comply with the rule. Lobbyists used their personal contacts. David Rehr, president of the National Beer Wholesalers Association and a key Washington insider, wrote notes to all the Republicans he has known and cultivated relationships with over many years.

On another front, the Ergonomics Coalition, which was made up of companies that opposed the rule, began mailing position papers to the Bush administration transition team and buttonholed anyone who would listen in the new administration. As an added bonus, some of the same businesses working to kill the rule had their executives on the presidential transition team, giving them a pipeline into top policy makers in the White House.

Business groups watched closely what their labor rivals were doing to protect the rule, especially as the vote moved to the House. Pro-labor Democrats held press conferences pointing out the injustice of repealing the rule and how it would hurt workers. The AFL-CIO pressed affiliates into service, providing them with flyers with toll-free numbers so workers could call Capitol Hill on their breaks to express their outrage. Then cell phones were delivered to work sites so the calls could be made. Some 8,497 faxes went to Capitol Hill from workers. At AFL-CIO headquarters in Washington, a website was set up with a counter that tallied how many musculoskeletal injuries were happening on the job every day. The unions started a campaign called "Stop the Pain. Start the Healing: Hands Off the Ergo Standard." It included fact sheets, demonstrations, rallies, briefings with reporters and editorial writers, and bringing injured workers to Capitol Hill to tell their stories. It was a level of effort usually reserved for lobbying Congress on major legislation such as tax packages and health and education initiatives. Labor stressed that the defeat of the rule would put an end to any meaningful regulation governing such workplace injuries.

With the balance of power sharply tilted toward the business community, it became clear that momentum had built to kill the rule and labor's efforts would be fruitless. Once the legislation was scheduled for consideration in the Senate, it took just two days to get the job done. With minimal debate, the mammoth rule, which would have affected virtually every business in America, was gone. The following is an account of how the voting went.

House Scraps Ergonomics Regulation; New Alignment Nets Big Win for Business

The Washington Post, March 8, 2001—Rarely has American business been as united in a cause as it was in trying to scuttle a stringent Clinton administration regulation to prevent workplace injuries, and rarely has it worked more closely with congressional Republicans to get what it wanted.

As a result of this confluence of interests and a new political alignment in Washington, the House yesterday followed the lead taken by the Senate less than 24 hours earlier and voted, 223 to 206, to kill the rule, which is aimed at curbing repetitive-motion injuries on the job. The measure now goes to President Bush, who has indicated he will sign it.

The swift action to overturn 10 years of work on the regulation underscores that, no matter how close the November election was, the balance of power has shifted dramatically in Washington. There is no longer a Democrat in the White House to veto Republican bills. There is a Republican president to sign them. So for groups such as business, there is new incentive to try what might have been impossible only a few months ago.

With this in mind, business organizations and GOP leaders seized the opportunity and mounted a surprise attack to get rid of the ergonomics rule, which President Bill Clinton endorsed last year despite business claims that it is unworkable and could cost $100 billion to implement. As lawmakers dusted off a little-used procedure to speed passage of a resolution revoking the rule, business groups mobilized—with phone calls, e-mails and personal visits—to bring pressure on lawmakers from both parties.

Organized labor fought hard, too, but with less impact. An aide to one Democratic senator who voted against the rule reported receiving 10 phone calls from business people for each call he received from labor.

In a blitzkrieg that lasted less than a week, corporate America scored one of its biggest victories in years, and organized labor, despite its increased clout in political campaigns over recent years, suffered a major defeat.

Despite Democratic gains that produced a 50–50 split in the Senate and a narrower margin of GOP control in the House, Republicans demonstrated that they still control Congress, at least when they are more disciplined and united than Democrats. In the Senate, instead of a close vote Tuesday night reflecting the even party split, six Democrats bolted to join all 50 Republicans, producing a 56 to 44 victory for the GOP and its business allies. In the House yesterday evening, 16 Democrats, mostly from the South, joined 207 Republicans in voting for the measure.

All six Democratic senators who voted in favor of repeal are from states carried by Bush. Three of them, Sens. John Breaux (La.), Blanche Lincoln (Ark.) and Ernest F. Hollings (S.C.), had voted last year for a proposal to cut off funding for finalizing the rule. Of the other three, two—Mary Landrieu (La.) and Max Baucus (Mont.)—are up for reelection next year in conservative-leaning states where business has more clout than unions. The sixth, Sen. Zell Miller (Ga.), has lined up with Republicans on many major issues.

The White House declared its support for the Republican move, warning that the Clinton regulation "would cost employers, large and small, billions of dollars annually while providing uncertain new benefits."

Labor Secretary Elaine L. Chao pledged other action to combat ergonomic injuries, which an estimated 1.8 million American workers suffer from. She said she will seek a more "comprehensive approach to ergonomics, which may include new rulemaking" that will "provide employers with achievable measures that protect their employees before injuries occur." Several Republicans said they would welcome a new rule-making effort.

Business leaders hailed the vote. "The Senate has done the right thing in terms of reining in an agency [that] has gone beyond the original intent of Congress," said Bruce Josten, executive vice president of the U.S. Chamber of Commerce.

"Business groups were emboldened by a Republican president in the White House, and this was the first chance they had to flex their muscles in Congress," said Jim Manley, a spokesman for Sen. Edward M. Kennedy (D-Mass.).

"I can't think of another issue that was so important to business in so many states, and senators had to be cognizant that how they voted on this issue would be remembered for a long time," said a Senate Republican leadership aide. On many other issues, ranging from taxes to health care, corporate America often divides. But workplace rules "cut across all the lines in the business world," the aide said.

Labor groups condemned it. "'Dishonest' and 'disgraceful' are not strong enough words to describe the Senate vote against injured workers," AFL-CIO President John Sweeney said.

The ergonomics regulation, which was issued last November and would have taken effect in October, would cover 102 million workers at more than 6 million work sites, according to the Occupational Safety and Health Administration. OSHA estimated the compliance cost at $4.5 billion, far less than many business groups.

The rule would require employers to provide workers with information about possible injuries and risk factors, review complaints, redesign workplaces if they were found to cause problems, ensure access to medical care, and provide compensation for disabilities. In some cases, employers would have to pay disabled workers more, and for longer periods of time, than would be the case under state workers' compensation laws.

Business lobbyists and Republican leaders began gearing up shortly after Bush emerged as the winner in the November election.

House and Senate leaders began planning to use the Congressional Review Act to overturn the rule, orchestrating just how the votes would proceed. The legislative device, which was coauthored last year by Assistant Senate Majority Leader Don Nickles (R-Okla.) and then-Rep. David M. McIntosh (R-Ind.), gave Republicans a means to eliminate the rule, which was finalized in November by the Clinton administration and was set to go into effect in October.

As early as last week, Republican leaders in both chambers were quietly getting ready to launch the attack, planning a quick, successive vote that would leave little time for lobbying or second-guessing. "This was a two-way thing from the get-go, and we realized we couldn't win without the Senate voting first. We thought it was the best strategy if the Senate went first," said an aide in the House leadership office.

Meanwhile, business lobbyists went into high gear, realizing that labor had lost the clout it possessed during the Clinton administration and that a mechanism was now at hand—the review law—to get rid of the workplace rule that unions had worked so hard to get.

The Persistence of the Business Lobby

Even before the lobbying against the rule became a contact sport on Capitol Hill, the business community was laying the groundwork to defeat it. Over the years, high-profile lawyers were hired to challenge the Labor Department every step of the way as the rule wound its way through the regulatory process. Congressional opponents of the rule cut funding for it several times over the years at the behest of business groups. A barrage of lawsuits was filed the minute the Clinton administration issued the final rule in fall 2000, shortly before it lost the election. The U.S. Chamber of Commerce and the National Association of Manufacturers led the charge, keeping the rule in their crosshairs over many sessions of Congress. The following column lays out the legal strategy that the business community used to fight the rule at the courthouse and within the Clinton administration, long before Congress got involved.

Repetitive-Lawsuit Syndrome: Ergonomics
Rule Puts Court System to Work

The Washington Post, November 28, 2000—There is something for almost everyone to hate in the Clinton administration's ergonomics rule.

In the two weeks since the Labor Department issued the final regulation, business and labor groups have rushed to courthouses around the country with complaints about the government decision ordering companies to take steps to ease the pain and strain of injuries incurred on the job. Many corporations, including insurers, the steel industry and trucking companies, think the regulations are too onerous and are filing separate court challenges; unions think they are too weak.

Companies are so outraged about the rule, which they must begin complying with next October, that they have been packing strategy meetings of the National Coalition on Ergonomics, a group of some 60 companies. Said one source: "There were 50 lawyers in the room and 20 on the phone." They think the rule is vague, not grounded in sound science, and unnecessary, officials said.

The coalition's petition for review, filed in the U.S. Court of Appeals for the District of Columbia, represents the views of the Air Conditioning Contractors of America, the Automotive Oil Change Association, Federal Express Corp., Anheuser-Busch Cos., the National Turkey Federation and the Manufacturing Jewelers and Suppliers of America—to name a few. "All of the industry groups are meeting and working together," said Stephen Bokat, general counsel for the U.S. Chamber of Commerce. "It's practically every association in town."

Charles Jeffress, the assistant secretary of labor in charge of the Occupational Safety and Health Administration, was unmoved by the flurry of legal action. "Prior to OSHA's publication of the ergonomics rule, business associations said they would challenge whatever we adopted, so we were not surprised by the suits," he said in an interview. "We believe our rule is reasonable and will be effective in reducing the injuries that thousands of American workers are suffering each year."

Corporate lawyers say they are astonished by the breadth of the rule.

"I think this is the biggest regulation in the history of the republic," said Baruch Fellner, a lawyer with Gibson, Dunn and Crutcher who filed a challenge on behalf of the National Association of Manufacturers and the ergonomics coalition. "This deals with sitting, the angle of your neck and whether you can lift 10 pounds. What doesn't it deal with?"

Insurers, who have brought a separate legal challenge to the rule, oppose the standard because of its compensation provisions. Under the rule, workers suffering ergonomic injuries will be entitled to 90 percent of their after-tax pay for 90 days. Insurers say that would be a disadvantage to workers with other types of injuries, who are limited to collecting workers' compensation, which, though also nontaxable, provides only two-thirds of gross pay.

More fundamentally, Bruce C. Wood of the American Insurance Association, which is coordinating a lawsuit for dozens of insurers, said OSHA doesn't have the legal authority to mandate compensation payments. Wood said the law mandates that OSHA prevent injuries and that the states handle compensation for them.

The American Trucking Associations says the rule is inequitable because it does not cover workers in the maritime and railroad industries.

The American College of Occupational and Environmental Medicine withdrew its support for the rule the day it was announced. It said the final rule lacks the requirement that a firm medical diagnosis be made and that a worker's symptoms be definitively linked to the job being performed.

The rule says a health-care professional must determine whether an employee's symptoms are related to the ergonomic design of the workplace, but it does not specify that the professional be a doctor, nurse practitioner or physician's assistant skilled in spotting such injuries.

The college, which represents 7,000 physicians, whose specialty is in occupational medicine, is mulling what legal action it might take, probably on the business side, said Greg Barranco, spokesman for the doctors.

The chamber's Bokat said a special judicial panel would decide by lottery which circuit court will handle the challenge. Each group has filed its petition for review in the court where it thinks it will get the most favorable hearing, hoping it "wins" the lottery.

It could be 15 months from now before there is any decision on the validity of the rule, Bokat said. In the meantime, it will go into effect as scheduled next fall.

Taking these kinds of disputes to court is a familiar outcome for the agency and the constituencies that it regulates. Almost every major rule that OSHA issued in its 30-year history has landed in court.

One common scenario is that labor groups petition for a stronger rule than the one finalized by the agency. Sometimes the court sends OSHA back to the drawing board to make the regulations more protective of workers.

"It's just part of the rulemaking," said Peg Seminario, director of health and safety for the AFL-CIO. Seminario said the courts not only

upheld OSHA's asbestos exposure rule and its standard requiring employees be informed of workplace hazards but also told the agency to
broaden and strengthen them.

In the ergonomics case, the AFL-CIO, the International Brotherhood
of Teamsters, textile workers and steelworkers have asked for review of
the rule in various courts. Their main objection is that the worker safeguards and medical treatment are not triggered until there is an injury. The
unions believe an employer should have to act when it knows a hazardous situation exists, without waiting until a worker is hurt.

"We do typically win most of these suits," said Susan Fleming, an
OSHA spokeswoman. The one challenge the agency did lose was setting
permissible exposure limits for hundreds of chemicals at one time. The
court said the agency would have to do detailed risk assessments for each
substance—a job it hasn't gotten around to doing.

"Years from now, when ergonomic programs are an accepted and
successful part of the American workplace, people will be celebrating the
substantial benefits achieved," Jeffress said.

Not every rulemaking is as spectacular as the ergonomics standard, which
attracted attention for many reasons. Its cost, the idea that the government
would play a role in how employers design their workplaces, the breadth of
the rule, and the relentless intensity of the opposition distinguished it from
the lobbying directed at other rulemakings. Seldom do business groups display such unanimity in their opposition to a rule. In many cases, business
lobbyists reflect the priorities and self-interest of their own clients, and the
outcome may disadvantage other companies. In addition, most rules are targeted toward a sector of the economy, a single industry, or an individual
company. But in the case of the ergonomics rule, almost everyone would be
affected, and almost everyone in the business community tried to play a role
to defeat the rule. Hence, the eagerness to get on the bandwagon to the
courthouse to challenge the rule.

Delaying Tactics

Over the span of a decade, while the rule was in various stages of development, one of the most effective ways of blocking its progress was to choke
off funding the development of the rule by having Congress prohibit OSHA

from spending any federal money on it. Over the course of four nonconsecutive years, Congress prohibited funds to be spent on developing or issuing an ergonomic standard three times. This is a tactic that Congress often favors when it wants to quietly stop the progress of a regulation.

Another delaying tactic, which business lobbied strenuously for, was to pass legislation ordering extensive government-funded research on the science that would support such a rule. Over the years, numerous studies were done on the nature of repetitive stress injuries such as tendinitis, carpal tunnel syndrome, and lower back pain, which delayed the rule. When the agency would come close to actually proposing a rule, Congress stepped in to ask for more study. This created more delay for the rule and successive, smaller victories for business that wanted to keep the rule at bay. The following column took a snapshot of one of the efforts that opponents made to call for more study of the ergonomics issue.

Business Groups Strain to Stop Ergonomic Rule

The Washington Post, June 25, 1999—Since the Occupational Safety and Health Administration took the first steps in February toward issuing a federal ergonomics rule, the battle between proponents and opponents of such a rule has centered on fighting science with science.

The disagreement over whose science knows best came to a head on Wednesday when the House Education and the Workforce Committee approved legislation to block OSHA from proposing an ergonomics rule until completion of a study now being conducted by the National Academy of Sciences—a two-year delay.

It was the fifth time Republicans have acted to stop the agency from addressing ergonomics, the science of fitting the job physically to the worker, for example by altering chairs, adjusting the speed of an assembly line or using special braces to ease back strain from lifting heavy loads.

Some businesses have acted on their own to guard workers against disabilities such as tendinitis, carpal tunnel syndrome, and joint and muscle injuries, but the Clinton administration wants to require employers with ergonomic problems to come up with programs to fix them.

The committee's legislation, strongly supported by business groups, was introduced by Rep. Roy Blunt (R-Mo.) shortly after OSHA issued its ergonomics proposal. The committee approved the bill 23 to 18, with only one member crossing the party line.

OSHA envisions a standard that would cover jobs in general industry such as in bakeries, supermarkets and offices. Firms whose workers suffer injuries would have to establish reporting systems and offer medical care and time off to the injured.

The rule has been eight years in the making and may still take years to become final. But the business community isn't taking any chances.

Defeating an ergonomic initiative is a priority for the U.S. Chamber of Commerce, the lead player in the National Coalition on Ergonomics, which has as its members many other powerful business groups.

They insist, as do many conservative Republicans, that there is no consensus in the medical community over what causes ergonomic injuries or the best way to address them.

Randy Johnson, the Chamber's vice president of labor, said the legislation to block an ergonomics rule was "highly reasonable" because OSHA "should postpone any important rulemaking until they have enough science to know what they are doing."

Democrats and labor groups insist that the problem has been studied to death, and a majority in the scientific and medical community agrees there is a link between certain jobs and workplace injuries. Nurses, for example, are at risk for back injury from handling and transferring patients, according to the American Nurses Association.

Supporters of a rule point out that the National Institute of Occupational Safety and Health and the National Academy of Sciences, in earlier studies and reports, cited "strong evidence" of a link between musculoskeletal disorders and physical factors at work.

Rep. George Miller (D-Calif.), a member of the committee, charged Republicans with being insensitive to the needs of workers. "Maybe the Republicans would understand this if we related one of the injuries to tennis," he jabbed.

Republican Vernon Ehlers of Michigan said he's very sensitive to ergonomic issues because of problems he has with his own back. But Ehlers said "these are very complex issues" and a rule "has to be done right or it doesn't work."

The day before the committee vote, Democrats mustered their best scientific arguments at an event sponsored by Rep. Nancy Pelosi (D-Calif.), who assembled a battalion of doctors, scientists and occupational experts who vouched for the adequacy of the science supporting a rule.

Pelosi sponsored a successful amendment in 1996 that allowed OSHA to work on the rulemaking. Democrats said her intervention may be needed again if the Blunt bill goes to the floor. There also is a companion bill in the Senate.

Some Democrats on the panel suggested that waiting for another study was not an attempt to clear up scientific uncertainty but an effort to put off any action in hopes that a new administration might be opposed to an ergonomics rule.

"It's an inexcusable delay tactic," said Rep. Lynn C. Woolsey (D-Calif.).

Charles Jeffress, OSHA administrator, said he doubts the new National Academy of Sciences study will turn up much new: "We know enough to act now."

Another strategy the business community used was to build a case that OSHA was committing procedural errors in developing the rule. The following column looks at how opponents of the rule and conservatives in Congress found fault with the agency's use of expert witnesses during hearings on the proposed rule. There was a lively back-and-forth, with all the attendant filings, between the agency and critics in the business community as well as Republican members of Congress who thought OSHA had acted improperly. Much of the background for this column came from extended correspondence between a House regulatory affairs subcommittee staff member and the Department of Labor.

Protection Racket? Repetitive Stress Surrounds Ergonomics Rule

The Washington Post, August 8, 2000—Paid witnesses. Coaching. Hushing up contractors.

Republicans in Congress and industry groups are making it sound as if the mob is running the ergonomic rulemaking at the Occupational Safety and Health Administration. The National Association of Manufacturers has gone so far as to joke that the agency is putting on its own episode of "The Sopranos" and tampering with witnesses at its hearings on the controversial rulemaking.

This name calling is the latest nasty skirmish between the agency, its critics in Congress and industry groups that oppose regulating ergonomics—the science of fitting the worker to the physical demands of the job.

The ergonomics proposal is a big target for the business community. It's among the most far-reaching rules the agency has ever advanced. And it is opposed by most of the millions of companies that would have to comply with it. Under the plan, they would have to identify and correct problems and compensate workers for injuries related to the design of the workplace.

There are wildly varying estimates on what it would cost to comply with the rule. OSHA estimates it at $5 billion annually; some business groups say it's more like $18 billion.

OSHA supporters point out that the closer the agency comes to issuing the rule at the end of the year, the more intense the opposition. The House and Senate both included provisions in the Labor Department's appropriation to stop work on the rule—a move that has prompted a veto threat from the White House.

In the House, Rep. David M. McIntosh (R-Ind.), chairman of a House subcommittee that oversees regulations, has been peppering OSHA with questions on why it hired 28 expert witnesses and didn't disclose that they were paid about $1.8 million, and perhaps more.

In a flurry of correspondence demanding reams of documentation from OSHA, McIntosh alleges that the agency's use of paid witnesses and other contractors—including doctors, ergonomists and insurance specialists—is improper and taints the impartiality of the rule-making.

Sen. Fred D. Thompson (R-Tenn.), chairman of the Committee on Governmental Affairs, has asked the General Accounting Office to investigate the practice of agencies paying witnesses, the standards for public disclosure and whether OSHA coached its witnesses.

Supporters of the rule say the attack on OSHA for its use of contractors is the latest strategy for blocking the rule, which has been in the making for a decade.

They also believe the purpose of the contract investigation is for business to gain access to information that it otherwise would not be privy to, so it can see how OSHA crafted the rule and better challenge it in court when it's made final.

"Every government agency uses contractors in regulatory proceedings," said Peg Seminario, director of the AFL-CIO Department of

Occupational Safety and Health. "It's just another tactic to throw hurdles and roadblocks in front of the standard. Every year, it's a different tack."

In the past, industry charged that there was no scientific basis for the rule and that not enough research has been done into what causes back and neck problems and repetitive-strain injury—common ailments of the modern workplace.

"OSHA's goal is to protect workers," Charles Jeffress, the assistant secretary of labor in charge of the agency, said in a statement. "An ergonomics rule will benefit employers and employees alike. There are some who have a different agenda, who want to derail an opportunity to save hundreds of thousands of employees from needless suffering and billions in unnecessary medical and insurance costs every year. It is hard to understand why."

OSHA told McIntosh it is not illegal or unusual for it to pay people to help build the rationale for a new rule. In this case, the agency acknowledged that it did not expressly disclose that witnesses were paid. But officials said OSHA has a long-standing practice of compensating people who spend two to three weeks preparing testimony and attending a hearing.

In a June 28 letter to McIntosh, Jeffress said the use of expert witnesses is authorized by law, has been sanctioned by the courts, is authorized by federal regulations and has been reviewed by the GAO.

OSHA has used experts to testify in at least seven rule-makings. Their number has varied from one to 46, depending on the rule, officials said. Other agencies use experts in similar ways, but OSHA proceedings call for cross-examination of witnesses, making the expert's presence at the hearing necessary.

Business opposition to the rule, which was proposed last November, has been well organized and hard-edged. While the NAM handles grass-roots opposition, the U.S. Chamber of Commerce, the National Coalition on Ergonomics and companies such as United Parcel Service have hired legal help of their own to fight the rule.

"Those involved in the rule-making feel there have been an enormous amount of procedural irregularities and we regard the contractor example as another irregularity," said Eugene Scalia, partner with Gibson, Dunn & Crutcher, who represents several large companies and the National Coalition on Ergonomics. The chamber has hired Willis Goldsmith, a partner at Jones, Day, Reavis & Pogue, who has successfully argued ergonomics cases against OSHA.

Said one source who supports the rule-making: "How much did industry pay their witnesses?"

The Nuts and Bolts of Defeating the Rule: All Hands on Deck

It was a broad-based, patient effort that worked. All of the tactics employed by the business community over many years eventually led to an erosion of confidence in the rule, and the regulators, that encouraged Republicans and enough Democrats to vote against it.

The success that special interest groups had in finally ridding themselves of the ergonomics rule stemmed from many factors. Powerful, well-bankrolled business groups put their best Washington lobbyists on the case. Influential business groups such as the U.S. Chamber of Commerce, an organization that has thousands of members all over the country and an experienced lineup of Washington-based operatives, and the National Association of Manufacturers called on their grassroots constituencies to rally their opposition. They faxed letters to members of Congress, called Capitol Hill, ran national advertising campaigns, participated financially in broad-based coalitions of companies, made personal visits to influential members of Congress, commented negatively on the rule and testified against it in hearings held by OSHA, threatened to withhold contributions from incumbents who supported the rule, and hired the best legal talent. All of these tactics and more were used.

Opponents of the rule also found—and hired—influential voices of opposition such as former regulators, medical professionals, and legal experts. Eugene Scalia, who was appointed solicitor for the Department of Labor in the George W. Bush administration over many voices of opposition, was then a partner with Gibson, Dunn & Crutcher, a law firm in Washington. As noted previously, Scalia was an outspoken opponent of the rule and the son of a Supreme Court justice.

The rule attracted an extraordinarily high rate of interest group participation—on both the management and the labor sides of the issue—but a middle ground was never achieved between the two groups. In other words, there was never a grudging consensus on the need for a rule. The data submitted by both sides of the argument had no commonality. In other cases, even a contentious rule eventually becomes accepted if the rule is altered enough to reflect both sides of the argument—a common phenomenon in rulemaking. Cornelius Kerwin has observed that healthy and robust participation enhances a rule. But, he explains, if "the participation is hampered by hostility, intransigence, secrecy, or incompetence on the part of the agency, the rule will be deprived of information that is crucial in establishing its authority with the affected community. In other words, stupid rules do not beget respect."[1]

Ergonomics: What Lies Ahead

After the rule was nullified, the Department of Labor was prodded by a few members of Congress, such as Republican Senator Arlen Specter of Pennsylvania, to start working on a new approach to address ergonomic injuries. After the hearing took place, the terror attacks of September 2001 diverted the Labor Department and OSHA's resources and attention to issues related to terrorism. The hearing, however, did give a glimpse of the preliminary ergonomics agenda the Bush administration was planning to pursue, one that business groups said they could live with. This column captures the tension between members of Congress who voted to abolish the rule—expecting a new one—and the new top manager of the Department of Labor.

Chao, Senators Clash on Ergonomics Rules

The Washington Post, April 27, 2001—Labor Secretary Elaine Chao received a chilly reception at a Senate hearing yesterday when she refused to commit the Bush administration to a deadline for producing a new ergonomics standard intended to reduce repetitive stress injuries.

In front of a packed audience that included injured workers brought in by labor unions, and 25 others, Sen. Arlen Specter (R-Pa.) curtly told Chao to summarize her testimony and pressed her to set a timetable for replacing the controversial workplace rule Congress killed last month. Business groups had lobbied hard to overturn the regulation, issued late in the Clinton administration after a decade of study.

Chao told Specter that setting a date would be irresponsible without more study. "One of the problems in the past was there was no consensus," she said. "If we were to proceed again without due consideration of all the groups, we wouldn't be able to craft something that was sustainable and long-standing. That's not what I want. I want to do the right thing."

"If you can get consensus, that's wonderful," Specter shot back. "But you'll have to make a decision as secretary of labor, and we'll review that."

"I guess what I'm hearing is that this is just going to dribble on for 10 years, five years, two years," Sen. Tom Harkin (D-Iowa) told Chao, who was making her first appearance before Congress since her confirmation hearing.

Specter is chairman and Harkin is the senior Democrat on the Appropriations subcommittee that controls the Labor Department's budget.

Chao's unread testimony hinted about the Bush administration's general philosophy toward handling workplace regulation. She said the department had limited resources and favored preventing injury through compliance and cooperation with businesses rather than "relying on command and control regulation."

On the ergonomics issues, Chao said the department would focus its efforts on high-risk occupations and would consider having an independent entity review estimates of the cost of the legislation to business. She also indicated that any new program would not include a federal mandate that workers be paid for their injuries.

The rule repealed by Congress would have covered 102 million workers. The Clinton administration estimated it would cost $4.5 billion annually to implement, but businesses said the cost could approach $100 billion. The rule required employers to correct conditions in their workplaces that might cause injuries such as back and neck pain, tendinitis and carpal tunnel syndrome, and to compensate workers for their injuries—sometimes more than what state programs currently pay.

Specter was among those who voted to overturn the Clinton rule. He said at the time that he would call hearings to examine the issue in detail. Yesterday's hearing lasted three hours, as a parade of experts from business, labor and academic circles summarized their views on the workplace standard.

The AFL-CIO and other labor groups petitioned the Labor Department yesterday, asking that a new rule be issued "without further delay."

Specter said in an interview after the hearing that he wasn't hostile to Chao but asked her to summarize her statement because he had to stick to a tight timetable so all the other witnesses could be heard.

He said he was surprised he could not get commitment on when a new rule would be completed, or even when its drafting would begin.

"This . . . process can take an interminable amount of time and we're entitled to a deadline or a target," he said.

———————————

The postscript to the revocation of the ergonomics rule was a long time coming. It was not until spring 2002 that the Bush administration announced that it would prepare voluntary guidelines, instead of a mandatory rule, to address injuries such as carpal tunnel syndrome, tendinitis, and bursitis in the workplace. The administration said the guidelines would be targeted toward industries with high ergonomic hazard rates and that enforcement would go after "bad actors" who would be prosecuted if they did not meet their "general duty" to protect their workers. The administration said it would develop the first guidelines for the nursing home industry to address back injuries and ergonomic problems and also issue guidelines for poultry processing and grocery stores. Sen. John Breaux (D-La.), who voted against the Clinton rule, said he still preferred a rule to guidelines. He introduced legislation in spring 2002 requiring the Department of Labor to reissue a rule within two years, but it would not cover disorders not related to work. "I believe a federal regulation is not only warranted, but it is the only way to ensure our nation's ergonomics problems are addressed," said Breaux when he introduced the bill.

Unions, which had fought for more than a decade for a rule, dismissed the guidelines as meaningless and window dressing on the part of the administration. For business, despite the threat of enforcement actions, it was a victory.

A Culture of Bending the Rules

Washington is filled with skilled legal practitioners, lobbyists, and consultants who understand how to use the regulatory system to their clients' best advantage. At any given time, Washington regulators hear from environmentalists, snowmobile proponents, defenders of animals, highly specialized industries such as those that burn waste in cement kilns, peanut growers, water conservationists, makers of children's pajamas, telecommunications conglomerates, drug makers, auto companies, organic farmers, chemical companies, milk producers, funeral homes, sheep growers, importers of retail goods, truckers, nuclear plant owners, and those who covet space on the nation's airwaves. They all have made appearances in Washington. As James Deakin writes in *The Lobbyists*: "Washington swarms with lobbyists."[2]

The case study presented here of how the ergonomics rule came and went is only one of hundreds of examples of how professionals skilled in regulatory warfare interact with each other and various Washington political institutions. I would define lobbying as it concerns regulation in the broadest sense: It attracts professional lobbyists who have to register who their sponsors are and what they spend on influence. But regulators are influenced equally by the constant interplay among so-called public interest groups, labor, business trade associations, professional groups, think tanks, Congress, the White House, and the press.

The National Federation of Independent Business, for example, is devotedly loyal to the Republican Party and has made great strides in influencing the passage of legislation favorable to its small business members as well as the rules that go with the laws. Since the bankruptcy of Enron, the business lobby, led by the U.S. Chamber of Commerce, was hard at work trying to blunt the reforms that Congress contemplated to rein in corporate wrongdoers and protect shareholders and their pensions and investments. The accounting industry beefed up its ranks and focused on trying to mitigate restraints on its business, such as not allowing auditors to be consultants and more policing of the industry by a new oversight board and the Securities and Exchange Commission. In response, the AFL-CIO and consumer groups held town meetings and lobbied Congress to counteract the business groups' lobbying. In other words, it's everyone into the pool.

"Regulation has served as a versatile tool whose handle has been seized at different times by reformers, business managers, bureaucrats, and lawyers—and manipulated as often for the particular interests of one of these special groups as for the general interest of the American public," says Thomas K. McCraw in *Prophets of Regulation*.[3] As the number of agencies has proliferated since the New Deal and opportunities for participation have increased, special interests of all kinds have become involved in rulemakings, trying to steer the outcome to their best advantage. Some have a one-time interest, and they might hire an experienced Washington regulatory practitioner to make their case; sometimes a party with an interest in a regulatory proceeding relies on grassroots pressure from its home base to influence a decision made at an agency in Washington. Others have a single Washington representative to look after their interests.

Then there are huge institutions on the business and labor side of the regulatory ledger, which have tentacles in a wide variety of regulatory issues. The U.S. Chamber of Commerce, for example, played a cameo role in the defeat of the ergonomics rule, but it also was busy with many other public policy issues. Over the past few years, it played a key role in shaping important auto safety legislation that includes criminal penalties for companies that do not sufficiently inform the federal government of problems with their products. The Chamber was among business groups that sued the Occupational Safety and Health Administration for a program that asked companies to voluntarily comply with rules to lessen chances of being inspected by the government. It won. The Chamber played a major role during the George W. Bush administration transition period, offering suggestions on how to rewrite regulatory executive orders and pushing—successfully—for the defeat of a rule that would have affected how federal contractors do business in Washington. It has the funding, manpower, and experience to wield influence in all these areas by lobbying both Congress and the regulators.

The public interest sector has skilled professionals such as Joan Claybrook, president of Public Citizen, as well as volunteers and young people interested in representing the consumer point of view in contentious regulatory issues such as health care, auto safety, and the environment. Many of these groups have far less manpower, but they provide a unique kind of regulatory oversight: They often prod recalcitrant agencies to regulate, and they watch the development of new rules critically. Public Citizen, for example, played a central role in the outcome of a rule dictating the safety requirements of Mexican trucks coming over the border into the United States. These groups also make liberal use of the Freedom of Information Act to obtain controversial documents associated with agency actions that otherwise might never be made public. They usually are skillful in informing the press of what they find. Some are affiliates of consumer activist Ralph Nader, whereas others may not be under the Nader umbrella but still practice similar interest group politics and lobbying.

All of these professionals, whether they are paid handsomely or are part of a nonprofit organization operating on a shoestring, know the regulatory land mines and the politics surrounding the issues. They also know that often they play a primary role in a rulemaking because they are repositories of the technical information that regulators need to make a decision. All are in the business of influencing regulatory decisions, whether it be by filing comments on a rulemaking, publishing an ad challenging a rule, trying to involve Congress in the process, or challenging a rule in court. Some of the outcomes are seemingly insignificant to anyone but the party involved, whereas others carry multibillion-dollar price tags and have ramifications for whole communities, if not the nation.

For a look at an effort to help out a single small company with an unusual regulatory problem, consider the following column. The company complained to the Department of Agriculture, which claimed that it was following the rule book, and the member of Congress representing the district where the plant was located, to bring pressure on the agency. And despite the unusual nature of the product involved and its limited applicability, there was no shame about pursuing the issue, proving that there is a special interest interested in every rule.

"Denaturing" a Pet Treat for Fido: Inspector's Order Proves the Unkindest Cut of All

The Washington Post, March 1, 1996—This little piggy went to market . . . at least most of him did.

Until a few months ago, one of Oink-Oink Inc.'s best-selling products was a pet treat called Pork Tenderloin. Made from the penises of male hogs, Pork Tenderloin was processed by the Detroit-based company into a doggie delicacy that was sold for $3.99 a piece at specialty pet stores. Dogs loved them.

But sales of Pork Tenderloin were halted last year when the Iowa Packing House, Oink-Oink's supplier, was told by an Agriculture Department inspector that it had to dye the pig penises green, a "denaturing" that characterizes them as not fit for human consumption.

That put an end to the production of Pork Tenderloin because R. Miles Handy, president of Oink-Oink, thought the green dye made the tenderloins look unappealing. Besides, he didn't know how or if the dye would affect pets. So he stopped making the product, losing about $100,000 in sales. "It killed the product," he said.

"It's one more way the government is in our face," Handy grumbled. Or, maybe it's the government sticking its snout in the affairs of small businesses. "We have dog owners going crazy because we're out of this product."

Handy said he got the idea of making pig penises into pet treats around the time of the Lorena Bobbitt trial. He and his staff were sitting around the office, cracking a few jokes, when a light bulb went on. Oink-

Oink was already using ears, hoofs, snouts, hearts, feet and livers of pigs. Cow parts were processed too. Why not pig penises?

After some research and development with his 12-year-old beagle, Heidi, Pork Tenderloin was added to the line of "natural" Oinkers Doggie Snacks, such as Oinker Roll and Lamb Roll, cold cuts for pets, which contain real meat.

Handy, however, avoids the P word when describing the product's ingredients. "You know what it is," he said modestly. "The product is not revolting. It's not disgusting. We made them clean and nice for animals."

Handy, a 30-year-old entrepreneur with an $8 million pet treat business, got so upset over the green penises that he wrote his congressman, Rep. Joe Knollenberg (R-Mich.), who took the whole thing pretty seriously too. He wrote a letter to USDA demanding to know why the penises suddenly were showing up green.

The Agriculture Department said that some animal parts have to be marked with green dye or charcoal powder if they are going to a nonfederally inspected plant to be further processed. It's a sort of green alert.

Daniel Ochylski, president of the Iowa Packing Co., said an inspector at the company's Des Moines plant got snippy over shipments of the product to Oink-Oink and told them to use the dye.

Iowa Packing had been selling "pizzles"—as it prefers to call them—to Oink-Oink for about a year before the Ag Department stepped in. Iowa Packing officials weren't clear on whether those shipments were treated with charcoal dust, another denaturing agent, or whether they went au naturel to Oink-Oink.

Handy said he hopes the government will make an exception for him and let him go back to making Pork Tenderloins. If not, he says, he'll be forced to import foreign pig parts.

"We're looking for products that are healthy, lean and digestible for dogs," he said.

Amazingly, the pressure worked. About a year later, the regulators at the Department of Agriculture decided it would be all right to "denature" the pig penises in charcoal, rather than green dye. This suited Oink-Oink just fine. Rolling the "pizzles" in powered charcoal meant they were washable and useable to be made into doggie treats. Rep. Knollenberg counted it as a victory against senseless regulation. He said it was freeing another "small businessman from the shackles of government regulation."

General Electric Co. Takes on the Regulators

Some rulemakings cost an extraordinary amount of money to fight; others require little more than congressional intervention and the pressure of public opinion. Many of the decisions made about rulemakings have effects on people and communities far from the inside-the-Beltway politics played by professionals in Washington. The case of General Electric Co. fighting the Environmental Protection Agency is one that took many years, many high-priced lobbyists, and many millions of dollars paid by the company.

GE waged a high-priced lobbying campaign to try to persuade the Environmental Protection Agency that dredging the Hudson River to remove decades-old polychlorinated biphenyls, or PCBs, discharged from its plants was the wrong thing to do. It argued that the decision would be costly to communities along the river that would be economically penalized by the dredging, GE would have to pay some $500 million, and the scenic river would suffer environmental setbacks because of the dredging. The company spent an estimated $15 million on its opposition campaign in New York State alone and millions more on Washington lobbying. The following column was written shortly before the EPA made its decision, and it captures the steadfast opposition of the company and the pressure it brought to bear on regulators, state officials, and members of Congress.

A High-Voltage Line of Attack:
GE Ads Zap the EPA Over PCB Cleanup

The Washington Post, July 24, 2001—When big companies want regulatory agencies to see things their way, one approach is to hire high-priced lobbyists and lawyers to do some quiet persuasion. The rules for public disclosure are followed, but the real decision making often is done in private, with few beyond a small inner circle saying much.

General Electric Co. has taken a different tack. After more than a decade of fighting the Environmental Protection Agency over how PCBs, or polychlorinated biphenyls, from its plants should be removed from the Hudson River, the company is shouting from the rooftops that the plan the agency wants to adopt to restore the river—targeted dredging—is the wrong one.

The EPA banned PCBs in 1979, after they were found to cause cancer in animals and probably in humans.

Using a tactic that is usually reserved for putting public pressure on Congress before a big legislative vote on a national issue such as competition in the telecommunications market or health care reform, GE has unleashed ads over the airwaves in Washington that take issue with a complicated regulatory decision.

During the past few weeks, the GE ads in Washington have echoed the very public campaign that the company has been carrying out against the EPA for the last year in New York State. There it has used television, radio, newspapers, an infomercial and a video documentary (free to anyone for the asking) to lobby local communities to oppose the EPA's preliminary decision to dredge the Hudson at a cost of $460 million to GE.

At its recent annual meeting, the company said the cost of the campaign in New York was between $10 million and $15 million.

Timing is key. The agency is expected to make its final decision soon, although it said it isn't finished cataloguing the 72,000 comments it has received on the proposal after it was issued in December.

The ads chastise the agency's deep-dredging proposal and tout GE's own cleanup method—called source control—which, it says, is "nature friendly" and has already restored much of the river.

"With GE's source-control program, PCB levels in fish in the Upper Hudson are projected to reach FDA safety levels years before the EPA dredging would realistically be complete," one ad says. "GE will spend whatever it takes to clean the Hudson right-of-way. And dredging is the wrong way."

The company has an elaborate Web site called HudsonVoice.com that explains its position, criticizes the EPA's stance on dredging the river and offers assistance to people who want to oppose the agency.

A GE spokesman said the ads are a "modest response" to a campaign that environmental groups have been waging against GE in Washington on the Hudson River issue. "Our point is to ensure there is a balanced debate about the future of the Hudson River," he said.

The problem in the Hudson dates to the 1940s, when two of the company's plants were making electrical equipment, using PCBs for their fire-resistant properties. According to the EPA, GE discharged as much as 1.3 million pounds of PCBs.

Since 1983, when a 200-mile stretch of the Hudson was declared a Superfund site, the agency has been studying the problem and trying to figure out the best way to clean up the river.

The EPA plan calls for a five-year targeted dredging project of "hot spots" along a 40-mile stretch of the river below two GE factories.

Departing GE Chairman Jack Welch, who has been involved with the PCB issue for more than 20 years, said at the company's annual meeting that the EPA approach would cause massive damage to the river and would be like "having an offshore drilling platform in your back yard."

Welch called the proposal, made by then-EPA Administrator Carol Browner, "irrational" and said it was a "last-minute rush to please a small group who want to make GE dredge the Hudson as punishment for things they think we did wrong over 40 years ago."

The accusers Welch has in mind are those such as Clean Up GE, a Ralph Nader–inspired group whose Web site has the banner "GE Has Taken Good Things From Our Life"—a parody of the company's slogan. It has been running its own print ads in the *New York Times* and *Roll Call* encouraging the Bush administration to press ahead with the EPA plan.

"This is a good opportunity for the administration to do the right thing, if they want to do something consistent," said Todd Main, project director of Clean Up GE. "They have always said they make these kinds of decisions on sound science. We've studied this puppy for 10 years, and the science is in."

Main and his allies worry that GE's public-relations campaign may pay off. They predict the administration may have the EPA's New York regional office make the final decision on dredging, insulating EPA Administrator Christine Todd Whitman from blame. Or, they fear the EPA may settle for a pilot dredging program, which would delay a full-scale cleanup for years.

Supporters of the EPA plan expect GE to fight on, no matter what decision is made.

In the words of Stephen Ramsey, GE's vice president for corporate environmental programs, after the EPA announced its proposal: "If the EPA thinks the upriver communities want their protection, they're wrong. We're going to fight this with everything we've got."

GE Loses

In the end, despite its expenditures and hope that a new Republican administration might look more favorably on not going forward with a dredging plan, GE lost. In December 2001, the EPA decided that the best course was to clean up the upper Hudson with dredging, removing 2.65 million cubic feet of sediment at the bottom of the river. The plan then is to remove 150,000 pounds of the chemical that was deposited from GE factories in Hudson Falls and Fort Edward, N.Y.

Environmental groups with national and regional scope played an important role in lobbying for the cleanup plan. Though not equipped with as much spending money, they lobbied loudly and very publicly for their point of view. One group, Scenic Hudson, stayed with the issue for years. The group's website is a trove of information on PCBs and the Hudson River, as well as an archive on the scientific work on the removal of PCBs. The group also did its own lobbying, offering supporters form e-mail letters to send to Washington and Albany, as well as alerts every step of the way in the long regulatory process. A larger coalition of anti-GE forces was Friends of the Hudson, which included groups such as the Appalachian Mountain Club, Friends of the Earth, Greenpeace, Riverkeeper, Inc., and the New York Public Interest Research Group.

Congress Is a Special Interest

Some of the most pronounced pressure on regulators comes from the Capitol. Members of Congress, concerned about reelection strategies and pleasing constituents, often get involved in rulemaking or force regulators to act on an issue of concern to them. It is not unheard of for a member to oppose a regulatory initiative that is in the works at an agency—even though there is a statutory mandate to produce the rule. In some cases, the influence of a member is so strong that an entire regulatory proposal goes out the window, such as when Sen. Ernest Hollings (D-S.C.) threatened to cut the budgets of the Federal Trade Commission and the Department of Justice because he opposed a Bush administration plan to change the review process for mergers and acquisitions.

Congress's power over the agencies is formidable because it has staff who are expert in the regulatory process or the workings of a single agency—a specialty that often is honed over many years. Most members of Congress rely on expert legal and administrative advice from staff members, many of whom are as educated about a rule as the regulators themselves. In some cases, the staff member may have written the legislation that is the underpinning of the rulemaking.

Staff direct the congressional oversight hearings of agencies and often set the agenda for what a committee or subcommittee will examine. They can be influential in affecting the budget of an agency. They can initiate long-running investigations of agency programs or rulemakings. In other words, a letter of inquiry or complaint from a member of Congress—usually drafted by a shrewd, knowledgeable staff member—can cause turmoil, consternation, and hours of extra work at an agency. In the years when Rep. John Dingell (D-Mich.) headed the House Commerce Committee, there was nothing an agency feared more than the arrival of what came to be known as "Dingellgrams."

Agencies also pay attention to their congressional overseers because they control the purse strings. Members of appropriations subcommittees have great power over regulators and the programs that get funded at agencies. Partisanship also plays a role: Republican members overseeing agencies in a Democratic administration tend to be critical of zealous regulating and spending on regulatory initiatives. When Republicans had the majority in the Senate, they kept their eye on how the Clinton administration was crafting regulatory policy, especially whether it was weighing the cost of rules. This column previews how the Republican chair of the Senate Governmental Affairs Committee, who was a proponent of reforming the federal regulatory process, would view rulemaking in the Clinton administration and his concerns about the decision making that leads up to a rule.

A Target for Sen. Thompson: Checking on Whether Rule Reinvention Is a Hit or a Miss

The Washington Post, March 7, 1997—The new chairman of the Senate Governmental Affairs Committee, Sen. Fred Thompson (R-Tenn.), wants to make sure the rulemakers are playing by the rules.

Though Thompson's committee is expected to spend much of its time on investigations into Democratic campaign fund-raising efforts in the last election, Thompson's staff promises that plenty of time will be spent overseeing how federal agencies and the Clinton administration are going about the business of regulating business.

An indication of how Thompson plans to proceed are several requests he made to the General Accounting Office over the past few weeks, asking for details on how selected regulatory agencies are doing on several fronts.

Specifically, GAO will be asking:

Did the agency weigh alternatives carefully enough, or consider no rule at all as a possibility? Did it do economically and scientifically sound cost-benefit evaluations of proposals?

How did the rule evolve and what changes may have been made to it by appointees in the Office of Management and Budget's Office of Information and Regulatory Affairs (OIRA)?

Have paper-intensive agencies such as the Environmental Protection Agency and the Occupational Safety and Health Administration cut red tape and paperwork for the companies that they regulate? Are the rules that have been eliminated significant, or meaningless ones?

The GAO investigation suggests that Republicans are monitoring whether the administration is living up to the terms of an executive order it issued in 1993, which called for openness in the regulation process—a practice that Republicans were accused of ignoring in the Reagan and Bush years.

"Many regulations have improved our quality of life, but we can do better," Thompson said. "The public has a right to know why and how agencies reach their decisions. We need to open up our regulatory process. We can make regulations more efficient, more effective and more fair—and should. It's really a matter of common sense."

The administration has stressed that it is trying to "reinvent" the regulatory process, make it more open, and remove or revise rules that don't work.

Republicans like Thompson, sources said, don't believe that the administration is living up to its rhetoric. They worry that OIRA is backing away from requirements to document all changes made to rules; that many rules that had been eliminated didn't really lighten the regulatory "burden" on business; that some agencies were not analyzing the cost of regulation.

Sally Katzen, head of OIRA, views the inquiries as a follow-up to a hearing held last September, when some of these same issues were raised.

Katzen said the administration "has a very good record. We set high standards for ourselves and lived up to them."

Committee aides said the GAO findings will be the foundation for more hearings on the regulatory process. Thompson hopes he can craft a bipartisan bill that would make some of the provisions of the executive order—like openness and cost-benefit analysis of rules—statutory requirements.

"If you do the right thing to begin with, you won't have all this blood, sweat and tears in the end," said a majority staff source, explaining why legislation should focus on how rules are made, rather than on the final proposals.

Congress: Nothing Is Off Limits

Most of the input from Congress involves examining weighty issues such as environmental, financial, workplace, and safety regulation. For example, after the federal government became involved in investigating why Bridgestone/Firestone tires were failing when they were paired with Ford Motor Co. Explorers, House and Senate commerce committees took an active interest in investigating the problem and legislating a solution. In this case, as with the earlier example concerning ergonomics, the full complement of special interests and political alliances came into play as Congress struggled to pass the Transportation Recall Enhancement Accountability and Documentation Act in fall 2000. When the Enron scandal broke in winter 2002, a dozen congressional committees and subcommittees wanted to pick over the carrion of the company and examine the relationships among regulators, auditors, and investment bankers. Similarly, when Enron, Worldcom, Martha Stewart, Arthur Andersen LLP, and the Halliburton Corp., Vice President Cheney's old firm, ran into trouble, Congress jumped into the fray with both feet to determine who was at fault among the corporate hierarchy and the regulators.

But some involvement is pure self-interest. Rep. Joe Knollenberg (R-Mich.) led something of a crusade against a rule that he found personally intolerable. His problem was with so-called low-flow toilets and their performance. He issued press releases, held hearings, and introduced legislation to try to get regulators at the Department of Energy to reconsider how much water should be allowed per flush. The following column highlights how much power members of Congress wield in influencing regulations.

Going against the Flow: One Legislator Isn't Bowled Over by a Conservation Rule

The Washington Post, March 21, 1997—Opponents of low-flow toilets may have a royal flush on their hands.

Responding to a torrent of complaints about backed-up and over-flowing toilets, Rep. Joe Knollenberg (R-Mich.) is leading the march to override a water conservation law that mandates less water per flush in toilet bowls and lighter sprays in shower heads and faucets.

Over the objections of plumbing fixture manufacturers, Knollenberg proposed the Plumbing Standards Improvement Act of 1997, which changes a provision of the Energy Policy and Conservation Act of 1992. The 1992 law set permissible flushing levels at 1.6 gallons a flush, an amount that some users consider a skimpy swish, replacing the old, more robust standard of 3.5 gallons per flush.

Had it not been for some last-minute objections to Knollenberg's gambit, the old law might have been wiped off the books. Instead, his proposal was referred to the Commerce Committee for further consideration.

Flush-reform advocates note that ever since the 3.5-gallon-per-flush toilets were outlawed, there has been something of a black market in the old models. Some owners and plumbers say they flush better, handle more volume and don't back up. Stories abound of frustrated flushers who are unhappy with their 1.6-gallon models, which in theory can cut indoor water usage by as much as 25 percent—except for all the double and triple flushing going on.

"Not to be indelicate, but the standard sometimes does not equate with what a human can produce," said Jim Rooney, a home inspector in Annapolis and a home improvement columnist. "They need to be plunged, and that's not a happy thing for most people."

To make sure consumers don't end up with non-complying toilets, faucets and showerheads, the Department of Energy recently proposed how manufacturers must certify and test their products. Let's just say it gets into the physics of flushing.

In the measurement proposal for faucets, for example, DOE discusses Bernoulli's equation of fluid mechanics, "which states that the ratio of water flow through a fixed orifice at different pressures is equivalent to the square root of the ratio of the pressures."

Knollenberg considers the mandate and the rules that go with it government meddling into people's private affairs. He thinks states and municipalities should be allowed to set their own limits, depending on their water problems.

"Certain communities do have water problems . . . but we don't feel it should be federally mandated," Knollenberg said. "We want to remove the federal lid," he said.

The Plumbing Manufacturers Institute, which lobbied for the standard in the first place, wants the lid to stay right where it is. It fears that manufacturers would have to comply with a multiplicity of state and local ordinances and thereby lose the investment they made in retooling for the 1.6-gallon standard.

"What would happen is that states that need to conserve water would drive the industry standard and it would be a lower volume than it is now. We're on the edge of technology [with 1.6 gallons] with the conventional gravity flush. We can't go lower," said Richard Church, president of the Plumbing Manufacturers Institute.

Edward Pollack, deputy director of the Office of Codes and Standards at the Department of Energy, worries that removing the mandate would interfere with new technologies under development. He said early 1.6-gallon models may not have worked well but those now on the market get the job done.

To change now, he implied, would just be another case of government waste.

Two years later, Rep. Knollenberg was still pushing for the Department of Energy to change the standard or at least to allow the old toilets back on the market. At a hearing of the Commerce Committee's Subcommittee on Energy and Power, which was considering low-flow toilet repeal legislation, Knollenberg confided that he owned two "nonperforming" "slow-flush" toilets in his houses and that he avoided using them. Also bringing pressure on the Department of Energy was Rep. Richard Burr (R-N.C.), who said he came to grips with the regulation when he was in a hotel and there was a sign in the bathroom advising that it might be necessary to flush twice or summon the front desk. He read his statement off a roll of toilet paper.

Rep. Strom Thurmond (R-S.C.) had a different issue with the regulators at the Department of Treasury. He went after the Treasury Department's Bureau of Alcohol, Tobacco and Firearms when it allowed labels on wine bottles to suggest that a glass or two might be healthful. Using his seniority and reputation for bottling things up in the Senate, Thurmond unleashed the full force of his powers on the regulators at Treasury—all the way up to the secretary's office.

ATF Bows to Thurmond in Wine War

The Washington Post, October 29, 1999—Call it Strom Thurmond's revenge on the wine industry.

The Bureau of Alcohol, Tobacco and Firearms this week threw open the controversial question of whether the government should prohibit labels on wine and other alcoholic beverages that make health claims without detailed qualifications about the risks of drinking. It also wants to make sure that consumers are not confused or deceived by labels that make such claims.

It also asked for comment on whether the "negative consequences of alcohol consumption" should be reason enough to prohibit the industry from making any health claims, including directing consumers to the government's dietary guidelines or their doctors, as winemakers are now allowed to do.

The rule-making essentially is directed at the wine industry, which in February was granted authority by ATF to put "directional" labels on its products, in essence telling consumers that wine is good for them. The labels do not explicitly say wine drinking is healthful, but they suggest that consumers check with their doctors or the federal government's dietary guidelines, which mention that "moderate drinking is associated with a lower risk for coronary heart disease in some individuals."

This change infuriated Sen. Thurmond (R-S.C.), who opposes any labeling on wine bottles that might contradict the message of the government warning already found on bottles that tells pregnant women not to drink and warns of health problems. (He lost a daughter to a drunken driver in 1993.)

Before the first directional label was pasted on a bottle, he blasted the decision as "irresponsible, subjective and . . . poor public policy." That afternoon, he called Robert Rubin, then secretary of the Treasury, ATF's parent department.

He uncorked a carafe of bills that would have stripped ATF of its authority to approve wine labels, increased taxes on the wine industry and blocked the two directional labels.

Plus, he attached a provision to the Department of Agriculture's appropriations bill that would have cut millions of dollars the domestic wine industry receives from an Agriculture Department program to boost exports. He asked for investigations by the inspectors general at the departments of Agriculture and Health and Human Services into whether the wine industry influenced the dietary guidelines.

And, to really focus the Clinton administration on his feelings about health claims and wine labeling, he held up the nominations of four top Treasury nominees in the Senate.

On April 21, a chastened Rubin wrote Thurmond a letter saying he supported banning health claims on labels and that ATF would start a rule-making. "I regret that we did not consult with you more closely prior to the approval of two wine labels containing health-related statements," he said.

After Rubin left Treasury, Thurmond also made it clear in several published reports that Treasury Secretary Lawrence H. Summers's confirmation might go more smoothly if he supported the rule-making.

A senior Treasury official, who asked not to be named, said the rule-making was an attempt to set formal policy on these issues. For the past 60 years, ATF has been giving the industry informal guidance on what is permissible on alcoholic-beverage labels. It always has taken a dim view of suggesting that alcohol has any curative or therapeutic value, holding that "distilled spirits, wines and malt beverages are, in reality, alcoholic beverages and not medicines of any sort."

"Senator Thurmond suggested we put existing policy out there and have a full debate on that," he said.

The wine industry says it welcomes that debate, even though it accused Thurmond of coercing Treasury into examining the issue with "unrelenting year-long pressure." The wineries also have the support of the California congressional delegation, and they have used free-speech arguments to bolster their position that the labels should be allowed.

"If anything, the science is more compelling than ever on the health effects of moderate drinking," said John DeLuca, president of the Wine Institute in San Francisco.

But the proposal also could be a setback if the ATF decides directional labels are out of bounds after all. "Maybe the best thing might be no directional labels or health claims—only the warning label," said John DeCrosta, spokesman for Thurmond. "This will be a good forum for people to talk about how foolish this campaign by the wine industry is."

Such a decision would reverse the work of the Wine Institute, which for the past several years has worked tirelessly to put a health claim on wine bottles to tout its belief—and the belief of some doctors and scientists—that a glass or two of wine a day with a meal is not only civilized but also good for your health. In its newsletters and public relations material, the industry widely disseminates the view that drinking in moderation—particularly red wine—lowers the risk of heart disease.

"This would put a lid on health claims by making the requirement for balance so onerous," said George Hacker, director of the Alcohol Policies Project for the Center for Science in the Public Interest.

As for Thurmond, he was positively giddy Monday when the proposal was published. He called it "refreshingly responsible action" and added he couldn't imagine why anyone would oppose the proposal.

———————————

Congress has another special interest in regulation: reforming the process that goes along with it. In chapter 4, I will explore congressional unhappiness with how the regulatory system works and numerous legislative efforts to change how rules are evaluated and made. The debate that took place in the 1990s over the proper role of regulation in American life and government was one that was as heated and important as the arguments that arose about the role of regulation after the New Deal and in the 1970s when another large expansion of the regulatory state took place. No period since the middle of the twentieth century was so vital to the debate over the role of government in the personal and business lives of the nation. The attempt to change the process deserves close attention by students of regulation who seek to understand how business executives try to negotiate the shoals of regulation, how regulation affects employees adjusting to the realities of the new workplace, and how average Americans unwittingly live by the rules made in Washington.

 ## Summary

Chapter 3 zeros in on the effect that special interests have on the rulemaking process in Washington. It gives an overview of the diverse groups and individuals who lobby Congress and the regulators, as well as their goals, which can be very specific to one industry or individual, or very broad, covering a whole swath of American business or individuals' interests. To understand how the process works, the chapter looks at the years-long campaign on the part of business interests to defeat the ergonomics rule—its strategy and the outcome. The outcome of an intense, expensive lobbying campaign by the General Electric Co. to defeat an Environmental Protection Agency decision to remove pollutants from the Hudson River is also examined closely. The role of Congress as a special interest is considered. And, finally, to make the point that there isn't a regulatory issue immune from special interest lobbying, a full account of attempts to change the dog treat rule and toilet flushing rule is included.

To Learn More

To get the idea of the magnitude of the ergonomics standard proposed on November 14, 2000, by the Clinton administration, you can go directly to the page of the *Federal Register* and view it in its entirety. This is a good exercise to see the language of a rule, its complexity, and how the agency intended to apply it. Go to www.access.gpo.gov/su_docs/fedreg/a001114c.html. This will take you to the table of contents of the *Federal Register* for that day; scroll down to the Occupational Safety and Health Administration and look for "Occupational Safety and Health Standards: Ergonomics Program." This will take you to the text of the rule, which is broken up into numerous sections because it is so lengthy.

Where there are special interests, there is lobbying. Where there is lobbying, there is money. Business interests and individuals cannot contribute directly to agency regulators, but they do spend money on presidential and congressional campaigns. The outcomes of elections, in turn, influence regulatory policy. The two best sources of information on the money flow in Washington are sites maintained by the Center for Responsive Politics—www.opensecrets.org—and PoliticalMoneyLine, which can be found at www.tray.com. Opensecrets, for example, has down to the penny the contributions from Enron Corp. and Arthur Andersen LLP, as well as who received money from the companies. This would be the place to start the compilation of a case study to trace contributors and the issues that were important to them before the scandal broke. As they say, follow the money.

Notes

1. Cornelius M. Kerwin, *Rulemaking: How Government Agencies Write Law and Make Policy* (Washington, D.C.: CQ Press, 1994), 162.

2. James Deakin, *The Lobbyists* (Washington, D.C.: Public Affairs Press, 1966), 1.

3. Thomas K. McCraw, *Prophets of Regulation: Charles Francis Adams, Louis D. Brandeis, James M. Landis, Alfred Kahn* (Cambridge, Mass.: Belknap Press, Harvard University Press, 1984), 300.

The End-of-the-Century
Crucible of Reform:
The Critical Testing
Ground for Regulation

Roadblocks to Reform: A Bipartisan Bill
Runs into a Lott of Opposition

The Washington Post, March 20, 1998—It's never been easy to get broad-based regulatory reform legislation passed in the House or the Senate. For the past 20 years, legislative proposals to change the way federal agencies propose and make rules have cratered with resounding thuds whether they were proposed by the highest-ranking member of the Senate or a firebrand newcomer in the House.

Sens. Fred D. Thompson (R-Tenn.) and Carl M. Levin (D-Mich.) thought their compromise bill to "reform" many aspects of the federal system just might sidestep such a fate. That was until Senate Majority Leader Trent Lott (R-Miss.) lobbed a small asteroid last week, once again endangering a bill that Thompson and Levin have been working on for almost a year.

Before this unexpected event, the Thompson–Levin bill looked like it could survive both the carping of conservatives who thought it did not restrain regulators and the attacks of liberal groups who branded it as just another attempt to cripple federal agency rulemaking capabilities.

The bill has the support of the Business Roundtable, whose members are Fortune 500 companies, the National Governors' Association, and other business groups. Experts in the economics of regulation applauded Thompson and Levin for attempting to bring some rational analysis to rulemaking. And Thompson and Levin promoted the bill widely as the best attempt yet at introducing concepts such as cost-benefit analysis of rules, better defining the role of the judiciary in challenges to federal rules, and requiring agencies to explain how they arrive at a rule.

To try and keep competing constituencies happy, the bill was modified numerous times. It took note of concerns the Clinton administration raised—though environmentalists and public interest groups never wavered in their opposition. On the other side of the issue, several changes proposed by Sen. Don Nickles (R-Okla.) were made, reflecting things that business wanted to see in the bill, including giving companies flexibility to meet standards several different ways. It was progress.

But the walk down the yellow brick road came to a quick halt when Levin and Thompson learned just before the committee vote that Majority Leader Lott had a bill of his own. The Thompson–Levin bill passed the Senate Governmental Affairs Committee, but without warning, Lott threw the fate of the compromise bill into serious question and signaled his belief that it's better to try to change the system incrementally.

The Lott bill, the Risk Assessment Improvement Act, speaks only to "risk assessment"—requiring agencies to decide what are the real risks to the environment, human health and workplace safety. It does not pursue a broader regulatory "reform" agenda that addresses nettlesome issues including peer review of rules, challenges to rules, and what measures should be used to assess costs and benefits of rules.

"I believe that a targeted bill like this one would address the most important part of regulatory reform," Lott explained when he introduced the bill on March 6. Lott commended Thompson and Levin for their efforts, but said, "A comprehensive approach offers many complexities, both substantively and procedurally." He called it an "incremental and doable step toward real regulatory reform."

A spokeswoman for Lott said, "We hoped this would be a bill that would be more likely to move through. We would have liked to have Thompson and Levin on board."

Lobbyists on both sides of the issue had their own interpretations. Some figured that Lott's move was payback, reflecting the differences he has had with Thompson over other issues such as campaign finance reform. Others calculated that Lott never liked the compromise bill, and would not bring it to the floor, especially since the business community was not enthusiastic in all quarters, sources said.

One source familiar with the struggle to pass regulatory reform legislation—and the trouncing Republicans took the last time they tried to pass sweeping legislation—said conservatives believe the best strategy may be to move incrementally, and wait for big change until a Republican is back in the White House.

Even business lobbyists interpreted the Lott maneuver as an "in your face" gesture to Thompson and Levin. "It gives some angst," said one of the lobbyists.

To make matters worse, the Clinton White House came down like a ton of bricks just before the bill was to be voted on in committee on March 10. Its negative reaction surprised the bill's drafters who thought they had won some support from the administration after changing the original legislation.

Instead, the Office of Management and Budget said in a letter that the bill does not meet the "simple test" of truly improving the regulatory system and making sure that the legislation "does not impair—by creating more litigation, more red tape, and more delay—the agencies' ability to do their jobs."

On the same day, Sens. John H. Chafee (R-R.I.) and Max Baucus (D-Mont.), the chairman and ranking minority member of the Senate Environment and Public Works Committee, poured more cold water on the bill.

They said they believed the best approach was to revisit existing laws and change them on a case-by-case basis—as they did in the reauthorization of the Safe Water Drinking Act and the Endangered Species Act.

"We are concerned that an omnibus approach, which makes changes across a wide range of statutes, may have serious unintended consequences," said Chafee and Baucus.

That leaves proponents of the Thompson–Levin approach needing more Republican, Democratic and business support to somehow get the bill to the floor of the Senate. But before that ever happens, Lott would have to be satisfied that the bill was worth fighting for—a decision he seems to have made already.

But that can't stop the oddsmakers.

"I don't think it gets adopted this year, though I wish it would," said C. Boyden Gray, chairman of Citizens for a Sound Economy, a conservative think tank that has an interest in changing the current regulatory system. "I don't think either of them will go anywhere."

———————————

The Levin–Thompson bill never passed, and neither did others like it. But the attempts were symptomatic of two constants in the world of federal regulation: There is broad dissatisfaction with the system, and someone is always trying to fix it. Both the executive and the legislative branches of government have had their share of ideas on how to make regulation work better—in some cases, to make it work better by working less—and have nameless regulators be more accountable for their decisions. Over the past half century, there have been numerous attempts to "reform" the regulatory system—and bring in more capable regulators—through independent commissions, legislation, and executive orders issued by presidents. Each of these attempts had a political tinge to it, reflecting the philosophy of the administration in the White House or the party in control in Congress. All of the sweeping attempts to affect broad reform on the regulatory system have failed, even when the efforts have been bipartisan and ranking members of Congress have led those efforts.

The column you have just read illustrates the difficulties that proponents of procedural reform had in advancing their legislation. Even though several years of work in the 1990s went into Republican-led efforts to "reform" regulation, and even though the atmosphere was ripe politically for some kind of change, the result was disappointing for those who wanted to see permanent alterations to the system. Political divisions, lobbying by opposing special interests, and a lack of Democratic support doomed this major effort. In the words of one regulatory expert, attempts by Congress to change the regulatory status quo were hollow efforts that resulted in a few peripheral procedural changes but no substantial, noteworthy change.

Throwing Bombs

Reform can mean different things when it is applied to federal regulation. There have been periods in history, most recently the early 1990s, when conservatives in Congress, aligned with business interests, have viewed reform as an opportunity to restrain severely the ability of agencies to regulate. Regulatory opponents were not so much interested in fine-tuning regulation and adjusting the process as they were in curtailing regulation altogether—it wasn't so much reform as relief. They agitated for fewer rules, worked to repeal rules, tried imposing moratoria on rulemaking, and proposed the elimination of some federal agencies. They wanted drastic measures to restrain regulators and to erect procedural hurdles that would make it almost impossible to regulate. They supported the primacy of individual rights and the states' role in regulating over the prerogatives of Washington—if there was going to be any regulating at all. They pushed for more oversight of the regulators. They backed more deregulation of major industries.

Outspoken opponents of regulation like former Rep. David McIntosh (R-Ind.) wanted to seize the moment that came with a Republican-controlled Congress to curtail rulemaking. It became a hot-button issue in the House and Senate that engendered stormy floor debate, a slew of amendments, filibusters, competing legislative drafts, and accusations over the motives of parties on either side of the debate.

The other approach is the one highlighted in the opening column of this chapter—procedural, or process, reform. It is a more measured—and equally controversial—approach to changing regulation. It involves passing legislation that would require agencies to use various economic, scientific, and legal tests to determine whether a rule should be issued at all. It often provides

Deregulation vs process reform

opportunities for judicial review of rules. It makes it much more difficult for an agency to issue a rule without justifying its cost or coming up with alternatives. This is the approach lawmakers such as Sens. Fred Thompson, the Tennessee Republican, and Carl Levin, the Michigan Democrat, advocated in the late 1990s, as did others before them such as former Sens. William Roth, a Democrat from Delaware, and Robert Dole, the Republican from Kansas. Those who have supported this technique believe that using analytical tools such as cost-benefit analysis, risk assessment, and aggressive peer review are improvements in the regulatory system that result in more rational, cost-effective rulemaking that is easier for Americans to understand.

Process reform could have had a far-reaching effect on whether the federal government has a heavy or a light touch in regulating. Proposed regulations that are held to stringent scientific and economic standards are likely to take longer to issue and attract more criticism. Regulators who are forced to come up with regulatory alternatives that may be better than the plan under consideration might have to abandon the initial course they set out on. Peer review of proposed rules may disprove the initial reason for regulating. "It is a disincentive to promulgate onerous regulations. Our intent is to really make it pinch," said Rep. Lamar Smith, a Republican from Texas, referring to legislation that was under consideration in 1995 that included some of these regulatory review provisions.[1]

For this reason, consumer and environmental groups were vigilant about beating back efforts for significant process reform. Their opposition to broad regulatory reform legislation, which was expressed through painting the Republican Congress as antienvironment and antisafety, largely derailed any far-reaching attempts to change the system. Watchdogs of the federal regulatory process, like OMB Watch and a coalition of groups it created called Citizens for Sensible Safeguards, thought the changes being contemplated in Congress would result in the agencies being unable to do their jobs because they would be immersed in complying with requirements for extensive analysis. They would drown is a sea of paperwork.

In 1995, Citizens for Sensible Safeguards, and the 230 organizations that were its members, was successful in stopping a broad regulatory reform bill sponsored by Sen. Robert Dole (R-Kan.) from being voted on in the Senate after eleven days of debate and three unsuccessful attempts to end debate. With lightening-fast speed, however, the House, led by House Speaker Newt Gingrich, passed a series of regulatory bills that addressed the risk assessment of rules, cost-benefit analysis of proposals, paperwork reduction for businesses, and compensating property owners when federal action affected the value of a property. The idea was stopped in the Senate after opponents managed to put what they called a "human face" on the drive to reduce regulations.

Gary Bass, executive director of OMB Watch, said opponents stressed that the bill would weaken food safety laws and other protections. The country had experienced several outbreaks of food-borne illness, some resulting in deaths, and was sensitive to how the federal government was handling the problem. Several years later, when another bipartisan regulatory bill was advanced, opponents pounced again. They brought to Washington the mother of a boy who succumbed to a food-borne illness. "It made the Republicans look evil, nasty, and hardened. It had enormous impact. This was the regulatory battle royale," said Bass in an interview.[2]

A Contract on Regulation

Extreme process reform—or regulatory reform on steroids, as one former congressional staffer put it—was part of the Republican agenda outlined in the "Contract with America," the insurgent GOP manifesto that was the vehicle that former House Speaker Newt Gingrich and his Republican allies used to catapult themselves to power in the House in 1994 for the first time in four decades. It called for votes on ten budget, regulatory, and congressional procedural items. Those who supported the regulatory tenet in the Contract preferred to think of the change ahead—which never materialized to the extent some hoped—as a regulatory revolution.

The following story captures some of that early fervor in the time before the more cautious Senate addressed the legislation.

Hill Republicans Promise a Regulatory Revolution; Lawmakers Target Rules and Rulemakers

The Washington Post, January 4, 1995—After years of debate over the way the federal government regulates American businesses and individuals, the Republican capture of Congress has created the moment when everything from how rules are made to how they are enforced could be changed.

"The notion of a regulatory reform revolution is not overstated at all," said Jerry Jasinowski, president of the National Association of Manufacturers. "The center of gravity has moved to the right and ideas that were dismissed before are now more acceptable. We've never had anything of this magnitude and muscle."

If the Republican lawmakers championing deregulation succeed, government regulators, for the first time, would have to justify every new rule with exhaustive scientific and economic analyses that critics say would overwhelm and render useless every federal agency. The cost of new federal regulations would be capped, limiting the number of rules any one agency could issue annually.

Another major change would be to put more power in the hands of the regulated. Landowners who cannot develop their land because of environmental restrictions would have to be compensated. Citizens would be able to initiate legal challenges against regulators.

And even if they do not achieve all their goals, the Republicans have triggered a rethinking of how to regulate—or not regulate—the nation's workplaces, banks, drug industry, financial markets and educational system. No rule, federal program, government agency or bureaucrat is exempt from scrutiny—everything from turtles protected by the Endangered Species Act to procedures for disposing of industrial waste.

The current system, critics complain, costs the country about $500 billion annually, stifles innovation and acts as a hidden tax on businesses and consumers.

Some public interest groups fear Republican initiatives will rip apart an intricately woven safety net of protections that they say Americans have come to expect: Safe workplaces, clean water and clean air.

"To the extent you can reduce burdensome red tape and still protect the public, we believe in that," said Gary Bass, president of OMB Watch, a public interest group that is organizing opposition to business- and Republican-led deregulation efforts. "That's real regulatory reform. Their agenda is to dismantle federal programs."

As part of their "Contract With America," House Republicans have pledged to bring legislation intended to curb new federal rules and regulations to a vote within the next 100 days. They also plan to move quickly on an immediate moratorium on new federal regulations, which, by their count, would freeze 4,300 pending rules in their tracks. And the Nov. 8 elections have breathed new life into the Clinton administration's efforts to prune unnecessary regulations.

The strongest push for deregulation is coming from the politically powerful small-business community. Big corporations, which often find it easier than small businesses to pay for the cost of regulations, are less strident about regulatory rollback, but most agree they are wrapped too tightly in red tape spun by such agencies as the Environmental Protection Agency and the Occupational Safety and Health Administration.

Led by Whip Tom DeLay (Tex.), House Republicans are pressing a measure that would make it more difficult for new rules to be developed. Agencies would have to provide more justification for their rules and businesses would have a bigger say in what rules were put on the books. States would gain because they would be freed from paying for programs that the federal government now "mandates" they fund.

Proponents of the legislation said it is an effort to restore balance to the regulatory systems. Public interest groups call it "dangerous legislation cloaked in agreeable rhetoric."

If the legislation passes, the most vulnerable targets would be the Clean Air Act, the Superfund Act and the Safe Drinking Water Act, all of which are up for renewal. Yet-to-be proposed rules designed to reduce repetitive-motion injuries and smoking in the workplace also are in danger, critics of the measure said.

"Americans believe Washington has gone too far in regulating and they want to turn the clock and the paperwork back," said Frank Luntz, the Republican pollster who helped House Speaker-to-be Newt Gingrich (R-Ga.) draft the "Contract With America."

"Americans need to see a Republican Congress fighting against the regulators," said William Kristol, a Republican strategist who heads the Project for the Republican Future. "It's important for Republicans to find [regulatory] excesses right away, hold hearings and move on them—turn back five, 10, 20 examples of regulatory excess."

Along with encouragement from Kristol, congressional proponents of changes in the regulatory order are getting intellectual ammunition from conservative think tanks that are assembling hit lists to help lawmakers select their targets.

The Competitive Enterprise Institute, a lobbying group that wants environmental rules linked to free-market principles, is circulating a report called "Dirty Dozen: Soft Targets for Elimination at Energy, Interior and EPA." Kristol's group recently sponsored a panel discussion called "What to Kill First: Agencies to Dismantle, Programs to Eliminate, and Regulations to Stop." Among its targets: the Americans with Disabilities Act, automobile fuel economy standards and federally mandated paid leave for workers with family or medical emergencies.

"Rein in what I call the 'Nanny State,'" said William A. Niskanen, chairman of the Cato Institute, a libertarian think tank. "Stop telling states where to set speed limits. . . . Stop telling businesses about whether and when employees and customers may smoke."

Fearing the political momentum is against them, groups such as the Wilderness Society, Public Citizen, Save the Children and close to 200 others are scrambling to mobilize their constituencies to save programs that protect the environment, public lands, the disabled and the disadvantaged.

"Our strategy is to make sure the public knows what they are up to," said David Hawkins, senior attorney with the Natural Resources Defense Council. "They trot out small-business representatives but behind them are large, irresponsible business interests that know what the rules require and how to comply."

Regulatory advocates are looking to the administration to put a brake on the wholesale change that Republicans are pushing—but the election results have forced the administration to do cutting of its own.

The EPA already is being accused of backing away from provisions of the Clean Air Act that would have required more stringent auto emissions testing, the sale of reformulated gasoline in more areas and broader use of electric cars to cut pollution.

And other regulators may not be as bold now that Republicans have oversight authority over their agencies and will cast key votes on Clinton nominees for important jobs.

That would be a reversal for agencies such as the Consumer Product Safety Commission, which under Ann Brown, its new chairman, has gone after manufacturers over everything from bunk beds that can collapse to toy necklaces with beads that children might choke on.

Similarly, Mary L. Schapiro, the newly arrived head of the Commodity Futures Trading Commission, has vowed to aggressively regulate risky financial instruments such as derivatives. Arthur Levitt Jr., chairman of the Securities and Exchange Commission, has made investor protection a priority. Anne K. Bingaman, assistant attorney general in the antitrust division at the Justice Department, revived a moribund antitrust legal staff and hired dozens more lawyers to police corporate mergers.

But these are just the preliminaries in what promises to be a polarized debate over how much regulation is too much regulation.

"Translating this [anti-government] animus into a workable political consensus for specific reforms is going to take more than 100 or 200 days," said

Christopher DeMuth, president of the American Enterprise Institute for Public Policy Research, another conservative think tank. "It is going to take imagination. It is going to take research. It is going to take persuasion."

Or, as James Gattuso, vice president of policy development of Citizens for a Sound Economy, a lobbying group that promotes free enterprise, put it: "We're not uncorking our champagne yet."

Organizing against Regulation

This was a heady, exciting time for those who thought federal regulators were too heavy-handed under both Democratic- and Republican-controlled White Houses—that is, Bill Clinton and George H. W. Bush. They viewed the Republican takeover of Congress an as opportunity to undo the regulatory excesses of the past and put in place policies that would make it more difficult to regulate in the future. The legislation that was introduced shortly after the Republicans took control of Congress was intended as a rebuke directed at anonymous bureaucrats, a Democratic president, and Democrats in Congress who supported regulation. "For years, business and industry have been forced to jump through hoops to satisfy regulators in the bureaucracy," said House Rules Committee Chairman Gerald B. H. Solomon, a Republican from New York. "Well, if this legislation becomes law, we are going to turn that around."[3]

For conservatives, this was an unparalleled opportunity to change the system and unmask the anonymous regulators. Opponents of regulation who had been agitating as a minority in the background now could exert their influence with the House leadership, which was in accord with their views. In this column, we hear from some of the conservative firebrands who became a kind of kitchen cabinet for regulatory "reformers" in the Congress, especially the House.

Advice as a Growth Industry: In Regulatory Assault, GOP Has a Lot to Be Thankful For

The Washington Post, December 2, 1994—The next few years could be a golden age for critics of federal regulation.

Now that the Republicans are in ascendancy on Capitol Hill, conservative think tanks, business-oriented trade associations and other anti-regulatory activists are plotting how to topple the established regulatory order.

Scholars and policy makers at places such as the Heritage Foundation, Cato Institute, Hudson Institute and other conservative centers have spent years preparing for the coming counterrevolution. In fact, some of their ideas—such as freeing the states from paying for regulatory "mandates" imposed by the federal government and cost-benefit analyses for new regulations—have become conventional wisdom for both Republicans and even some Democrats.

But the legitimacy of their ideas really was confirmed when the GOP included an anti-regulations plank in its "Contract With America" and introduced an ambitious bill called the Job Creation and Wage Enhancement Act, which embodies many of the initiatives considered mainstream in conservative circles.

Now, demand for their work is high. As a result, conservative think tanks and business organizations are working overtime to provide intellectual ammunition for lawmakers intent on overthrowing more than 30 years of regulatory history.

"We try not to proceed without bouncing our ideas off of them," said Monica Vegas, legislative director for Rep. Tom DeLay (R-Tex.), who heads the regulatory reform coalition in the House.

Groups such as Cato now will assume more prominence, especially since Edward Hudgins, Cato's director of regulatory studies, has years of experience working the anti-regulation issue on Capitol Hill (he has worked closely with Rep. Richard K. Armey (R-Tex.), soon to be House majority leader).

Hudgins is developing a list of regulations and laws ripe for review. He's calling this hit list "The Dirty Dozen—Beyond the Contract."

He wants Congress to consider ditching the existing Superfund legislation. He said the current law is a "horror story," because it spends more for lawyers and bureaucracy than for actually cleaning up the environment. Where there isn't a serious problem, he suggests, why not put a fence around the site rather than haul dirt away from it—a more expensive option? He suggests that when businesses pollute and there is identifiable harm done, the problem should be handled in court and the company should pay fines proportionate to the damage done to the victims, not the state. Similarly, he thinks responsibility for clean air and water should be turned over to states and localities.

Other items on Hudgins's endangered legislation list include the Community Reinvestment Act, which calls for banks to better serve minorities, the Civil Rights Act and the Americans With Disabilities Act.

Susan Eckerly, deputy director of economic policy at the Heritage Foundation, said Hudgins's ideas "aren't considered far out at all in this environment. . . . This is an excellent opportunity to change the focus of the debate." Other observers, however, doubt Congress will take such extreme measures.

Heritage, which for years has been stressing the harsh economic impact of regulations, said it will try to help new members of Congress understand regulatory issues. Early next year, Heritage will publish what Eckerly calls "a compilation of [regulatory] horror stories from the various agencies."

Many of the individuals who are prominent in the regulatory debate are Council on Competitiveness alumni who went to work for Citizens for a Sound Economy, a group that promotes market-based policies. The group's chairman is C. Boyden Gray, White House counsel in the Bush administration, and a senior adviser is James C. Miller III, director of the Office of Management and Budget from 1985 to 1988 and a big proponent of deregulation. Other members include James Gattuso and Nancy Mitchell, both of whom were associate directors on former vice president Dan Quayle's Competitiveness Council.

Another likely leader in next year's anti-regulatory push is David M. McIntosh, a newly elected House Republican from Indiana. He was executive director of the Council on Competitiveness and was later a senior fellow at Citizens for a Sound Economy and at the Hudson Institute.

Not to be left out are huge lobbying forces such as the National Association of Manufacturers and the U.S. Chamber of Commerce.

The Chamber has started a regulatory affairs committee whose members will work on regulatory reform legislation, public education and research. The NAM has started a group called Alliance for Responsible Regulation, which says it will push for more emphasis on science, risk assessment and economics in the regulatory process. The group already has about 1,000 members.

The new enthusiasm for regulatory rollback and reform has many public interest groups worrying that conservatives are "using good-sounding rhetoric to dismantle the government," said Gary Bass, executive director of OMB Watch, a public-interest group that monitors the regulatory process. "We're losing sight of valuable regulations that Americans depend on."

———————————

Picking on the Rulemakers

In the view of opponents of regulation, there was plenty of blame to go around and much to fix. Conservative voices such as the Heritage Foundation chastised former President George Herbert Walker Bush for allowing too many new rules such as expanding wetlands protection and protecting disabled Americans. Heritage commentators said, "Though George Bush projects himself as an avid foe of regulation, his Presidency has seen an enormous resurgence of regulation."[4] They pointed to the burgeoning of pages in the *Federal Register,* increased staffing at federal agencies, more money spent on administering federal regulatory programs, and appointees who were eager to regulate. Even though the Bush administration was viewed as accommodating to business interests in easing some regulations, it also had the reputation of being a regulator.

As for the Clinton years, the scorecard for opponents of regulation was worse. Conservatives blamed the Clinton administration for saying that it would cut tape and reduce regulation when, in fact, they perceived an increase in regulatory initiatives and power given to the federal agencies. The Heritage Foundation claimed that fewer major rules were being reviewed by the Office of Management and Budget than during the Reagan and Bush years. A Heritage Foundation report issued in 2000 said,

> Today, OMB reviews about 10 percent of rules issued annually by agencies. Under Presidents Reagan and Bush, it acted as a powerful check on overeager agencies, reviewing as much as 50 percent of the rules issued by agencies each year. Removing this check on agencies has given new life to the pro-regulatory urgings of the [Clinton] Administration. It also has allowed agencies to be increasingly slow, sloppy and secretive about providing justification for their rules.[5]

The takeover of Congress by antiregulation forces presented a moment at which "reformers" felt much could be done. Even if legislation were controversial, extreme, and likely to be vetoed by Clinton, Republicans felt they had the momentum to move ahead. Business interests felt that, for the first time in a long time, they not only had a place at the table but also sat at the head of it during deliberations in Congress about regulatory policy. The following column is a sample of the sentiment in the business community and the exhilaration it felt having a Republican Congress in its corner.

Dome Alone II: How Small Business Won Congress's Heart

The Washington Post, January 6, 1995—The National Federation of Independent Business surged to prominence last year when it helped trounce health care reform. But that was just the beginning. With the new Republican Congress, the 60,000-member small-business group is in the big leagues.

"They are the most plugged-in general membership organization in town," said one Republican lobbyist. "They have tremendous grass-roots capability and the [congressional] leadership likes them."

What this means is that the business agenda being advanced by Republicans—with its heavy emphasis on rolling back federal regulation—tracks many of the same themes the NFIB has sounded in recent years. Indeed, the group put out its own legislative agenda this week, a first in its 52-year history.

No surprises there. In fact, save for a few additions here and there, it looks a lot like the Republicans' "Contract With America." And, although the NFIB is concerned about taxes, deficit reduction and health care reform, its top priority is "relief from federal regulation, red tape and paperwork."

"Our members want the federal government off their backs, out of their pockets and off their land," said Jack Faris, the NFIB's fast-talking chief executive officer from Tennessee, formerly head of the Republican National Finance Committee.

With the Republican majority on its side, the NFIB, like other business groups, may get the regulatory relief they are seeking.

"This is very much a role reversal for us," Faris said. "We're being called on by committee chairmen asking, 'What do you want?' Can you imagine [former House member Dan] Rostenkowski asking us what we wanted?"

To enhance its political clout, the NFIB hired R. Marc Nuttle, a Republican campaign strategist whose specialty is grass-roots organizing. Nuttle, who ran Pat Robertson's presidential campaign and was executive director of the National Republican Congressional Committee, comes to the job with a mission in mind.

Nuttle sees small business as a group like the Christian Right—an independent column of voters that can swing elections and play a big role in influencing the nation's agenda.

"Christians did not realize how big they were," Nuttle said. "Pat Robertson put a face on them and I intend to do that for small business."

After its victory in derailing the Clinton administration's health care plan, the NFIB threw its members into 220 congressional races; its candidates won in 180 of them.

As a result, the newly elected Congress is full of members sympathetic to small business interests. For example, in the last Congress, House Majority Leader Richard K. Armey (R-Tex.) and House Ways and Means Committee Chairman Bill Archer (R-Tex.) voted 100 percent of the time with the NFIB.

The net effect for the NFIB is that instead of having to wrestle with every federal regulator that stands in its way—including the Darth Vaders from the Internal Revenue Service, the Environmental Protection Agency, and the Occupational Safety and Health Administration—the group can appeal to Capitol Hill to fight its regulatory battles.

Faris predicts that small-business owners will be popular hearing witnesses on Capitol Hill. If there is a problem with a workplace regulation, the group will be able to ask for an amendment rather than wait for an appointment at the Labor Department.

Or, as a new NFIB's poster says: "Suddenly, the voice of small business isn't so small."

The Agencies and Reform

The dramatic change in Congress put the Clinton administration on the defensive. The administration may have been populating the agencies with its appointees, but Congress now had the power to cut the purse strings of agencies, hold oversight hearings to pick apart rules it did not like, and generally try to embarrass the administration about individual rules. Some agencies found that they were spending all their time on damage control, fending off nasty, personal attacks about their regulating. The Clinton administration's "reinvent the federal government" strategy, which emphasized efficient, customer-friendly government, suddenly did not have all the answers that highly critical Republicans were looking for about regulatory programs that they wanted to eliminate or at least curtail. This column highlights how one federal agency, the Occupational Safety and Health Administration, mustered a defense when conservative think tanks and members of

Congress targeted it, trying to paint it as an abusive regulator that laid down nonsensical rules.

OSHA Marches Out Its "Truth" Team to Take on Detractors. Are They Lies, Damned Lies?

The Washington Post, March 3, 1995—After weeks of being pilloried by its detractors on Capitol Hill, the Occupational Safety and Health Administration is trying to set the record straight. As the debate on regulatory "reform" has unfolded, the agency has become a favorite target for the "unregulators"—those who argue that federal regulations need to be rolled back or removed.

To rescue its reputation, the agency has created a "rapid response team" that looks and listens for assertions about OSHA it believes are not true, or only partially true. The team's job is to catalogue and correct the examples of "abuse" that OSHA opponents use with abandon in congressional debates and hearings and news conferences.

Four employees from OSHA field offices have been brought to Washington to do the truth-squadding.

"We had to hit back," said Joseph A. Dear, OSHA administrator. "People repeat these things whether they are true or not. The stories achieve the status of urban legends."

But it's an uphill battle. No company can say the word "OSHA" now without thinking about whether Joy dish detergent is a hazardous substance. (You only have to fill out the forms if it's used in quantities that exceed normal usage or if it's mixed with other chemicals.) Or the accusation that OSHA killed the tooth fairy when it stopped allowing dentists to give extracted teeth back to kids. (Teeth are indeed covered under OSHA's blood-borne pathogens rule but it's up to the dentist whether to return teeth to their owners.) And then there's the belief that OSHA has 140 standards for ladders. (OSHA says it's four, soon to be two.)

The agency, which is charged with protecting workers from health and safety hazards, is trying to get its story out with missives called "Fact or Fable?" that state the "headline grabber" next to the "up-to-date reality."

OSHA's critics don't buy the agency's explanations. "It's a bucket brigade," said Craig Brightup, director of government relations for the National Roofing Contractors Association, which has been fighting an asbestos standard. "They say, 'There. We've taken care of that.' Their answers are incomplete at best."

Meanwhile, OSHA has another fire to put out.

A recently published best-selling book, *The Death of Common Sense*, chastises OSHA for the volume of its regulations, its determination that sand is poisonous and its tedious inspections of a brickmaking company in Pennsylvania.

OSHA has responded with a point-by-point rebuttal. For example, it said the brickmaking company has had fatalities and serious accidents that go unmentioned in the book. Sand, they said, isn't dangerous on the beach, but it can be in industrial situations when it's finely ground.

OSHA isn't the only federal agency coming up with fighting words.

The Consumer Product Safety Commission defended itself last week when Rep. David Martin McIntosh (R-Ind.) maligned the agency for considering a regulation that would have put holes in five-gallon buckets to eliminate a drowning hazard for children. (In the last decade, 500 babies have toppled into buckets and drowned. The most recent fatality happened yesterday when a 1-year-old in Chicago drowned.)

"The commission never issued such a recommendation or requirement, nor did it ever even consider doing so," said Ann Brown, chairman of the CPSC. Instead, she said, the CPSC and the industry have agreed to a voluntary labeling standard.

And Carol Browner, administrator of the Environmental Protection Agency, fired off a letter to Rep. John D. Dingell (D-Mich.) Tuesday fuming that the EPA was being erroneously assailed by its critics, who cited an arsenic standard and the regulation of "white-out" correction fluid as examples of inept regulation.

Browner said the critics got the wrong arsenic and the wrong level, and the correction fluid rule was California's. "The rhetoric against us is very powerful," she said in an interview. "The reality takes a few more minutes to explain."

Another way Congress put agencies on the hot seat was to tinker with their budgets and attach "riders" to legislation that would hamper them from funding an enforcement program or proceeding with a rulemaking. It was an effective way to hamstring the agencies and was used liberally after

Republicans took control of Congress in 1995. It was a punitive sort of reform that in some cases made Clinton administration regulators more ginger about regulating—unless congressional supporters of regulation managed to insert protective "riders" of their own.

Industry's Court of First Resort: Rulemakers Discover Hill's Power Over the Purse Strings

The Washington Post, September 15, 1995—When the insurance industry decided to challenge the Department of Housing and Urban Development's efforts to enforce anti-discrimination regulations, it didn't waste time trying to get the agency to change its mind.

Instead, a group of influential Republican members of the House and Senate agreed with the industry that HUD's enforcement proposals for property insurers would preempt state regulations. Appropriations bills in the House and Senate order that no HUD funds are to be spent on issuing, implementing or enforcing anti-redlining insurance regulations in fiscal 1996.

HUD isn't the only agency having its regulatory authority tweaked by the congressional appropriations process. While broader efforts at overhauling how federal regulations are issued and enforced are stalled in Congress, appropriations subcommittees and committees have become the venue of choice to air regulatory gripes, cut funds for specific regulatory programs or throw up roadblocks to enforcement of rules.

Sneak attacks against regulators in appropriations bills are nothing new. But this year's crop—in their volume, their unpredictability and their aim at specific regulatory initiatives—has put every federal agency on alert. Usually when they find out they have been hit, the vote already has been taken.

Aida Alvarez, director of the Office of Federal Housing Enterprise Oversight, a two-year-old agency that regulates Fannie Mae and Freddie Mac, didn't know until the day before a Senate appropriations subcommittee voted that her operation may be transferred to the Treasury Department.

"This came as a total surprise," Alvarez said, complaining that the quick vote was "a rude way to deliver the message."

The Agriculture Department may have to drop its work on a rule that mandates labels distinguishing fresh chicken from frozen chicken. A

Senate appropriations subcommittee indicated the department would be prohibited from spending money to issue or enforce the rule—which consumer groups have been urging for more than a year.

But it isn't all bad news for the regulators. Several appropriations bills in the Senate actually struck special provisions that the House had inserted in its own legislation.

Sen. Christopher S. "Kit" Bond (R-Mo.), chairman of a Senate appropriations subcommittee, eliminated 16 of 17 "riders" added by the House constraining the Environmental Protection Agency from enforcing a variety of laws and regulations. Only the House provision prohibiting EPA from requiring employee car pooling remains.

Similarly, Sen. Arlen Specter (R-Pa.), chairman of the Labor appropriations subcommittee, restored much of the funding for the Labor Department's Occupational Safety and Health Administration and dropped controversial House riders such as liberalization of OSHA's current fall protection standard.

Some of the Senate's reluctance to embrace the House's agenda may be the result of a coordinated lobbying campaign by labor, environmental and public interest groups, arguing that the riders would undo years of public health and safety regulations.

Last week, Citizens for Sensible Safeguards, a coalition of 230 groups, issued a report called "Back Door Extremism: Misusing the Appropriations Process to Gut Public Protections," an exhaustive review of 165 "backdoor provisions" that the group called a "grotesque misuse of the budget process."

Senators may have read the report, but it doesn't mean they have dropped all of their plans to include special intentions in appropriations legislation.

Bond added six "legislative provisions" of his own—such as stopping EPA from adding new sites to the Superfund cleanup list until the Superfund law is reauthorized. It's expected that a House push to prohibit OSHA from issuing a workplace ergonomics rule will reappear as an amendment on the Senate floor.

As anyone who has watched the process knows: They've only just begun.

Other Approaches to Eliminating Rules

Republicans who favored extreme "reform" measures had several weapons in their arsenal besides comprehensive changes in the regulatory system or stealth insertions in appropriations bills. The new Republican speaker of the house, Newt Gingrich, came up with a plan called "Corrections Day" to take aim at individual rules. The idea was to institute a shortcut legislative procedure that would enable lawmakers to eliminate rules that were, as Rep. David McIntosh put it, "dumb and expensive." The plan was emblematic of Republicans' distaste for regulation and the authority that had been vested in unelected bureaucrats. Democrats were fearful that if Corrections Day got going, it would be a way to eliminate rules with little fanfare. At the time he announced the Corrections Day procedure, Gingrich said he hoped bureaucrats would be cowed into regulating less so they would not be held responsible for corrections bills.[6] In the end, Corrections Day never lived up to its potential, much to the chagrin of conservatives who hoped Congress would play a major role in eliminating rules and thwarting new ones.

There also was the idea of a regulatory moratorium, a pause that House Republicans, in particular, favored. The House bill, which passed, provided a moratorium through the end of 1995 and covered rules issued after November 20, 1994. Though the moratorium legislation was the opening salvo in the war on regulation in the House, the Senate did not see it quite that way. The GOP-dominated upper house expected opposition from Democrats and the Clinton administration—which it got—stalling the legislation. The White House fought back by tallying a long list of regulations that potentially would be affected by a moratorium and including the damage that would be done to them—and the public. It publicized these widely, predicting that the health and safety of Americans would be harmed. The following column looks at how the Clinton administration, which called the moratorium a "blunt instrument," devised a political strategy that helped kill it.

Clinton's Answer to a Juggernaut: Show Who Gets Hurt

The Washington Post, February 24, 1995—President Clinton tried to keep it light Tuesday when he unveiled a four-point plan to reform the federal government's regulatory process. He joked that Vice President Gore had been assigned to read the entire Federal Code of Regulations. He said when he was Arkansas governor he shut a state agency down every couple years just to see if anyone noticed.

But it was hard to make jokes about what congressional Republicans have accomplished since November in throwing fear and uncertainty into the heart of every federal regulator. It's also hard to dispute that Republican-sponsored legislative time bombs—one of which is moving to the floor of the House today—have forced the Clinton administration to focus on coming up with a reform program of its own.

The administration announced a highly deliberative plan that tells regulators to inventory their rulemakings and come up with some to cut or change by June. The other three directives sound good on any campaign stop: Reward results, not red tape; get out of Washington and create partnerships; negotiate, don't dictate.

The president said he couldn't support a regulatory moratorium and preferred to "change the culture of regulation."

The timing of Clinton's plan was obvious. This week the congressional calendar was jammed with "regulatory reform" hearings, news conferences and floor debate—more evidence that the Republicans continue to move at warp speed to produce a grand plan to turn the federal regulatory system inside out, if not disable it.

Earlier in the week, the Senate put its own brand of regulatory "reform" on the fast track. The Senate Governmental Affairs Committee held a hearing on moratorium legislation and scheduled a meeting next Tuesday to put final touches on it. Senate Majority Leader Robert J. Dole's (R-Kan.) jumbo regulatory reform package was aired in two days of hearings in the Senate Judiciary subcommittee on administrative oversight and the courts.

To guard its flank rather than advance the battle, the administration concentrated on highlighting the hurt and injury that it says a moratorium would cause. Clinton ticked off a series of regulations he said would be affected by a moratorium: commuter airline safety standards, burials at Arlington National Cemetery, standards for safe bottled water and the hunting season for certain migratory birds.

The strategy—especially the bird hunting threat—tied Republicans in knots as hunting groups screamed foul. The administration offensive infuriated regulatory rollback firebrands in the House and Sen. Don Nickles (R-Okla.), author of the Senate's moratorium legislation.

"Most of his comments were completely inaccurate," Nickles said. "Our legislation does not tie his hands."

That may be true, but no one seems to be too concerned about accuracy as the debate ensues.

Pro-moratorium lawmakers chided the Consumer Product Safety Commission yesterday for considering a rule that would have had manufacturers of five-gallon buckets redesign their products to eliminate drowning hazards for children. The agency decided Feb. 15 to allow manufacturers to voluntarily label the buckets instead.

Republicans had more success with the Unfunded Mandates Act, which eliminated some of the regulatory requirements that are imposed on states and local government by federal law without federal funding, such as pollution control. It was among the first pieces of legislation to pass in 1995 under the umbrella of the "Contract with America," garnering support from Republicans and conservative Democrats who thought that regulatory burdens had been increasing on state and local governments. The Clinton administration, in two executive orders, tried to curb unfunded mandates, but not with the specificity that the legislation provided.

The legislation that passed was milder than what the Contract had originally envisioned—not allowing federal agencies to enforce any program that was not federally funded. Instead, the version that passed, after Democrats tried to offer dozens of amendments to slow the debate, called for the Congressional Budget Office to measure the nonfederal cost of a mandate costing more than $50 million. Congress, knowing the cost of the mandate, then would have to vote explicitly to proceed with legislation. The bill exempted many mandates and limited judicial review of them, but it did force Congress to reckon with such expenditures before a bill was passed. It told federal agencies to conduct cost-benefit analyses of rules and consult with state and local governments before issuing a new mandate. Business also was interested in this legislation and pushed for recognition that unfunded federal mandates were a burden for the private sector, too. The following column shows how business interests got involved in the debate months before the bill passed and walked away with a provision that said mandates costing the private sector more than $100 million annually also had to be subject to the same congressional treatment.

The Unfunded Mandates Debate: Business
Finds Hill Help in Getting a Load Off Its Mind

The Washington Post, January 13, 1995—And you thought unfunded mandates involved a battle between the states and the federal government over who picks up the tab for regulations created in Washington.

They do. But, for the U.S. Chamber of Commerce, the National Association of Home Builders and other powerful business groups, this isn't strictly a federalist tiff. For them, the debate in Congress that intensified this week presented an opportunity to speak up about business's mandate burden.

To hear them tell it, there is a federal mandate for businesses lurking behind almost every regulation—from the Clean Air Act to paying the minimum wage to workers—and no one in Washington really knows the costs of these programs. Worse yet, what states and localities can't afford gets turned over to businesses in the form of increased taxes, fees and building assessments.

"We call them hidden housing taxes," said Robert Bannister, senior vice president of the National Association of Home Builders. "If the feds pass a mandate for clean water and the locals can't pay, it ends up on the doorstep of home buyers. It can be thousands of dollars." But it looks like business lobbyists are headed for success in fixing at least part of the problem. Proposed legislation in the Senate and House to limit unfunded mandates would require the Congressional Budget Office (CBO) to figure out the financial impact on the private sector from a particular federal program if it exceeds $200 million (in the Senate version) or $100 million (in the House bill). There also is the possibility that federal agencies will have to produce similar analysis before Congress can dish out new mandates.

"We now have a terrific opportunity to send a loud and clear message . . . that the shift of good intentions is about to end," said Bruce Josten, senior vice president at the Chamber of Commerce.

Business hopes that the CBO requirement would give it real numbers to wave in the faces of lawmakers before votes on business-sensitive legislation that would result in voluminous regulations.

At a news conference on Capitol Hill yesterday where business groups urged passage of the Senate bill, Sen. Dirk Kempthorne (R-Idaho), who introduced the bill, said, "How many organizations . . . can make decisions that may be multimillion or multibillion [dollars] in size without any idea of the cost before they make the decision? I can't think of any except Congress."

Critics of current legislative efforts say the approach is all wrong.

"Find a solution to funding the mandates, not gutting the mandates," said Gary Bass, head of OMB Watch, a public interest group. "All this does is put up roadblocks to enacting protections."

The Congressional Review Act: The Big Kahuna

Without much fanfare, Congress voted itself a potent regulatory review provision as part of the Small Business Regulatory Enforcement Fairness Act of 1996. The section in the new law was called the Congressional Review Act, and it was crafted to give Congress overarching authority to review final rules and eliminate them under very streamlined procedures that limit debate and negotiations between the House and Senate and require only a simple majority vote. Under the new law, agencies had to verify that they performed cost-benefit analyses and other assessments on new rules. Most important, if Congress voted to revoke a rule, an agency could not issue another one that is substantially similar without approval from Congress.

This arrangement was attractive to conservatives who wanted to see Congress take responsibility for the laws it passed and the ensuing regulations written to implement the laws. They also thought that the new law would prevent agencies from issuing rules that were not well thought out, especially because the scope of the legislation was extremely broad and included for review guidance, policy statements, and other pronouncements from agencies.

> It is not the primary purpose of the CRA, nor is it necessary for its success, for Congress to overturn a great number of the rules that are submitted by the agencies. Because the rejection of only a few rules can send a powerful message to the regulatory agencies, the CRA's success will be measured in part by how few rules Congress must overturn before the regulatory culture is changed,

said Todd Gaziano, who was involved in drafting the legislation, in an article written for the conservative Federalist Society.[7]

Conservatives at think tanks in Washington hoped the law would be used aggressively. Instead, frustration grew as Congress did not use the law at all. Groups such as the Heritage Foundation chastised Congress for being weak and cowardly in not standing up to the agencies. It predicted that federal agencies, confident that Congress did not want to be criticized for rolling back rules, would not change their behavior because Congress would not use its oversight authority effectively. This column reports on the state of inactivity surrounding the Congressional Review Act, a situation that changed dramatically when George W. Bush became president, allowing the Republican Congress to use its one-strike authority to revoke the Labor Department's controversial ergonomics rule—an event described in chapter 3.

Inaction with the Review Act: Will Congress Wake Up to Its Rule-Blocking Weapon?

*The Washington Post, February 13, 1998—*The Congressional Review Act was supposed to be a single-shot assault weapon for members of Congress who want to block, or at least delay, federal regulations.

Instead, the law has been about as effective as a popgun in removing even a single one of the 7,408 regulations that flowed out of dozens of agencies last year.

What the Review Act is supposed to do is make Congress more accountable for regulations—some policy analysts view the authority as a kind of regulatory veto power for the legislative branch.

Under the act, Congress has 60 legislative days to review a rule; during that time, it can pass a joint resolution of disapproval, which would stop the rule from taking effect. The president can veto Congress's action, but the law provides the Hill the opportunity to override the veto.

Meanwhile, the General Accounting Office is now supposed to keep a running tally of agencies that are analyzing rules for their costs and benefits, effect on states and small businesses, and the paperwork the rules created. GAO is required to submit reports to Congress on all the major rules it reviews.

Members' lack of interest in the law has left some conservatives chagrined.

One group figures too many in Congress prefer business as usual and don't want to risk political capital on attacking regulations that the public seems to support. For instance, when the Clinton administration proposed highly controversial, costly rules designed to protect the ozone layer and limit particulate matter in the air, no one made a peep about subjecting the rules to congressional scrutiny.

"Republicans were traumatized by the government shutdown and the reelection of Clinton. They don't want to be perceived as being nasty," said Edward Hudgins, director of regulatory studies for the Cato Institute, a libertarian think tank.

Others believe the disinterest is due to the strong economy.

"Businesses can pass along the costs," said Merrick Carey, president of the Alexis de Tocqueville Institution, a conservative think tank. Fighting regulation, he added, "doesn't have a lot of traction because the economy is so strong." Carey predicts, however, any slowdown in the economy will, once again, bring the cost of regulation and taxes to the fore.

Other regulatory analysts have upbraided Congress for not using the weapon it voted itself to sidetrack rules or at least spark debate over them.

"The clear message to the watching agencies is that they need not be concerned about Congress asserting accountability. So what if there is congressional review?" said Robert Coakley, a former House Small Business Committee staffer and an expert in regulation.

Some members, who originally supported passage of the provision and expected it to be used, hear their critics. In the past month or so, the subcommittee staffs of Reps. George W. Gekas (R-Pa.), David M. McIntosh (R-Ind.) and Sue W. Kelly (R-N.Y.) have been hosting briefings for members' staffs to remind them the law is there and how to use it.

"To date, Congress has not fully implemented this powerful new oversight tool. Since CRA became effective, only a handful of resolutions to disapprove a rule have been introduced, and not a single one has been passed," said a letter to Republican members from Gekas, Kelly and McIntosh.

To back them up, House Republican Majority Leader Richard K. Armey (R-Tex.) urged his colleagues to attend the briefings "and learn how to use this important and underutilized congressional tool."

"Along with the means, the CRA gives Congress the responsibility to reject inappropriate rules and regulations. If Congress fails to do so, agencies may say that Congress has tacitly approved their actions," Armey wrote.

Congressional staff members and some policy analysts believe there is a learning curve that has to be climbed before members and their staffs feel comfortable using the law.

Attendees of the briefings are given a rundown on what the Review Act is, and what might be a good candidate for a resolution. One of the background papers instructed staff on what rules might be appropriate for review: "Any rule you feel you can oppose politically; any rule that is ill-conceived, ill-considered, needlessly burdensome, or just plain stupid."

While the act may not be working as some intended, some regulatory analysts see great value in having the agencies report on every rule to the GAO and Congress—especially since GAO has established an Internet database for the Review Act.

"This breaks the monopoly on information that has traditionally been held by the agencies," said Angela Antonelli, deputy director for economic policy at the Heritage Foundation, a conservative think tank. She believes Congress now will be able to finally grasp what agencies do every day.

When Antonelli picked through the database she came up with what she calls the worst final rules of 1997: the almost-one-a-day rule at the Internal Revenue Service—255 IRS rules for the year; the 231 Federal Communications Commission rules to deregulate the communications industry; and everything from the Agriculture Department's marketing order for Irish potatoes from Colorado to the "Importation of Ratites and Hatching Eggs of Ratites."

So far, agencies have been dutifully shipping their rules over to GAO for analysis. But a few have slipped through the cracks.

At the Environmental Protection Agency, for example, Assistant Administrator Fred Hansen told his troops in a recent memo that he would tolerate nothing less than "proper and timely notification to Congress and the GAO" because final rules do not go into effect until the 60-day clock has run out. He told offices with regulatory responsibility to establish a "fail-safe mechanism" to make sure no rule missed review.

An EPA official said that out of some 900 rules sent to GAO, there were 40 "minor actions" that were not sent to GAO and Congress. All have since been sent, and the agency announced new dates for the rules to become effective.

What was that about paperwork reduction and regulatory burden?

The More Things Change,
the More They Stay the Same

By 1996, it was clear that the regulatory revolution—if there ever was one—was over. Republicans, who had been criticized for shutting down the government twice in 1995 and for being antienvironment and antisafety, pulled in their horns. The energetic drive to pass broad, process reform legislation was dead until Sens. Thompson and Levin tried again with a more moderate approach in 1998. And then that effort failed, too. Several other less ambitious pieces of legislation to tweak regulatory performance and oversight did not move forward over the next several years.

Outside of passing unfunded mandates legislation and the Congressional Review Act, Republicans were stymied in efforts to bring sweeping change to the regulatory system. There was some transformation: Small business got some concessions, and the Office of Management and Budget was required to do an annual report on the costs and benefits of regulation. A bipartisan effort to revise the Safe Water Drinking Act included a first-time provision that the Environmental Protection Agency had to consider costs and benefits of the rules it would issue under the law.

But not that much had changed on the regulatory front. The federal regulatory establishment was intact. The spending bill that Congress approved in 1996 virtually turned the funding back on at the agencies it had been trying to strangle. The Interstate Commerce Commission, which was created in 1887 and was the oldest federal regulatory agency, was gone, but there was a successor in its place: the Surface Transportation Board. The Departments of Commerce and Education stood untouched. The much maligned Environmental Protection Agency got a budget increase. Business lobbyists abandoned plans for sweeping change to the regulatory system and said that they would settle for incremental change. Even David McIntosh, the Republican from Indiana who had been part of the effort in the House to push regulatory relief, said that he would have to settle for half a loaf. Regulatory opponents agreed that they had misjudged and underestimated the passion of their opponents in defending environmental, health, and safety regulatory programs. Among themselves, Republicans agreed that maybe the idea was not to topple the regime but, rather, just tip it to the right. The following column recaps the results of the regulatory "reform" revolution, a battle that was over in little more than a year.

Small Victories: Why the GOP Isn't Serving a Volley of Anti-Rule Rhetoric

The Washington Post, August 23, 1996—Remember the House Republicans' post-election "Contract With America" and its manifesto on regulatory reform? It was replete with pledges that the federal regulatory system would be revolutionized to give relief to businesses and the states. Endangered small businesses, not endangered species, would be running the regulatory show.

It was a valentine to businesses and their lobbyists who long had been toiling to get federal regulators off their backs, cut the amount of paperwork that had to be done, and eliminate rules considered too costly to implement. It was a promise to topple the fortress of federal rules that took 30 years to build.

Fast forward to the just-completed Republican convention, where mention of regulatory reform was relegated to the text of the Republican Party's platform, a document that the party's candidate and chairman openly admitted they have not read.

There, many of the old themes got a reprise: Get rid of federal departments and agencies such as Commerce and Energy; make the Occupational Safety and Health Administration a partner instead of an adversary; use peer-review to vet new regulations; and keep a "regulatory budget" to get a true accounting of regulatory costs. Pretty stale stuff.

During the choreographed segments of the Republican convention there was not much mention of the taxing effect that regulations have on the economy or a parade of horror stories of regulatory excess that dominated in the new Republican Congress.

Even the party's most visible anti-regulatory warrior, House Speaker Newt Gingrich, avoided the "R" word. Instead, Gingrich touted the virtues of beach volleyball—now an Olympic sport—and the fact that its ascension in the sports hierarchy had nothing to do with a bureaucrat inventing it.

Regulatory analysts assume the low profile accorded to regulatory issues is consistent with the retreat Republicans started taking after efforts to dismantle departments, strip agencies of their funds and shut down the government resulted in negative poll ratings—especially concerning perceptions of the party's environmental stewardship.

"The Republicans got burned in 1995 when they tried to push through their regulatory package," said Thomas Hopkins, an economist at Rochester Institute of Technology, who analyzes the cost of federal regulation. "I think they created an obstacle to their success by being too severe and micromanaging."

William Niskanen, chairman of the libertarian Cato Institute, said Republicans made the mistake of trying to find a silver bullet to put an end to all the programs and rules they didn't like. "That was a mistake," Niskanen said, and no substitute for the hard work that would have to go into changing the regulatory system statute by statute.

What the platform's views about regulation do not reflect is that some changes they support in the regulatory process actually have been made. Republicans, for example, were happy to have cost-benefit analysis incorporated in the reauthorization of the Safe Water Drinking Act. Changes to regulations governing the use of pesticides loosen a controversial zero-tolerance policy for any residue of cancer-causing chemicals on food, now allowing their use as long as there is "reasonable certainty of no harm."

Angela Antonelli, deputy director for economic policy studies at the conservative Heritage Foundation, credits Congress for "progress toward a more flexible and less burdensome regulatory system." She cites passage of legislation ending unfunded mandates to states; provisions that make it easier for small business to comply with regulations, and congressional review of regulations.

Antonelli does not credit the Clinton administration for its efforts to "reinvent" the government and discounts them as "repackaging the same old regulatory system and passing it off as something new."

But the Clinton administration's inertia on major regulatory issues has resulted in slower growth of the regulatory state than under Republican president George Bush, according to several regulatory analysts.

"There wasn't much of a regulatory agenda [from Clinton] and not much was offered to Congress," said Niskanen. In an upcoming article in Cato's *Regulation* magazine, Niskanen notes, "The legislative record of the Clinton administration is consistent with its own rhetoric—it is neither pro-regulation nor anti-regulation."

The rhetoric the Democrats will use at their own convention next week will promise to end the era of big government, and expand "opportunity, not bureaucracy," according to their platform.

The platform also gives them a pat on the back for shrinking the federal payroll, taking thousands of pages out of the *Federal Register,* and resisting Republican attempts to eviscerate environmental laws.

All that may sound nice, and some of it is true, but Americans still don't really know how much federal regulations cost and if the "smartest" rules are always put on the books.

And that would be useful information no matter who is running the regulatory state.

The Clinton Brand of Reform

While Congress was throwing brickbats at the regulators, the Clinton administration pursued its brand of reinvention and reform. On September 30, 1993, President Clinton issued an executive order that set the tone and the direction that his administration would take in regard to regulatory policy. The order said,

> The American people deserve a regulatory system that works for them, not against them: a regulatory system that protects and improves their health, safety, environment and well-being and improves the performance of the economy without imposing unacceptable or unreasonable costs on society; regulatory policies that recognize that the private sector and private markets are the best engine for economic growth; regulatory approaches that respect the role of State, local and tribal governments, and regulations that are effective, consistent, sensible, and understandable. We do not have such a regulatory system today.[8]

The Clinton administration wanted to return the upper hand in regulatory decision making to the agencies, institute a more open form of rulemaking, and give back to the Office of Management and Budget its traditional role of executive review of proposed rules. The order laid out twelve principles of regulation. It set up timetables for reviewing "significant" rules, and it told agencies that they had to analyze the costs and benefits of most rules. Both business and public interest groups found it hard to disagree with the sentiment but reserved judgment on the result.

Out with the Old, In with the New

The first thing to go, just days after Clinton took office, was the Bush administration's Council on Competitiveness, which was established on March 31, 1989, and headed by Vice President Dan Quayle. Made up of top-ranking members of the Bush administration and its own staff, the council was a powerful regulatory group that critics viewed as secretive and dominated by business interests. Usurping the traditional role of the Office of Management and Budget, which had line authority to review the work of agencies, the Bush administration instead relied on the Council to handle rules that were problematic. It addressed major regulatory issues, such as proposing changes in the Clean Water Act, and offered its own interpretations of provisions of the Clean Air Act. The Democratic Congress and consumer groups were outraged at the power of the group and agitated throughout the Bush administration to have it abolished or at least force it to be more accountable and open in its decision making. The council did not keep records of discussions with lobbyists or of its own internal proceedings. "The council is operating, perhaps for special interests, to undo the government's regulatory clout without leaving tell-tale fingerprints. The central issue is the council's secrecy in thwarting congressionally mandated policies to protect the public's health and safety," complained Senator John Glenn, a Democrat from Ohio who was in 1991 chairman of the Senate Government Affairs Committee.[9]

The Clinton administration decided to restore authority to the Office of Management and Budget's Office of Information and Regulatory Affairs. OIRA was created on April 1, 1981, to centralize the executive review of rules and administer the Paperwork Reduction Act of 1980. OIRA, which has a modest-sized staff of low-profile career professionals in economics and law, was allowed to play almost no roll during the George H. Bush administration. The office, which can be a very powerful one, did not even have a political appointee as its head. Clinton appointed a legal expert in administrative law, Sally Katzen, to open and preside over a new era in regulatory reform, one that would restore to the agencies authority to make rules, with oversight from OIRA.

Thawing Out a Watchdog Agency: OMB's Sally Katzen Lets Rules In—and Out—the Door

The Washington Post, May 20, 1994—In the days before the Clinton administration, it wasn't unusual that a proposed regulation going to the

Office of Management and Budget for review fell into a deep black hole. Unless you had an inside track with Vice President Dan Quayle's Competitiveness Council, your chances of finding out what really happened in a top-level review were slim to none.

Now, the Office of Information and Regulatory Affairs at OMB, run by superlawyer Sally Katzen, is the place to check—and you can actually find some things out. Like how long it took to review a certain rule. What "outsiders" talked to OMB during deliberations. And what rules got eyeballed at the highest levels.

"OIRA is a completely different kind of shop in terms of openness and accountability," said Gary Bass, director of OMB Watch, a group that monitors the OMB.

The agency thinks so too. In a six-month self-evaluation ordered by the White House, OIRA gave itself high marks for quick turnarounds on proposals—or taking a pass on reviewing them at all. Katzen said OMB looked at 578 rules from October 1993 through the end of March, about half the number in similar prior periods. It also has speeded up reviews of "significant" regulations to meet a 90-day deadline.

Katzen has thawed relations with agencies. "I had an uphill battle with my own staff," said one official at another agency. "They were conditioned to an extremely defensive approach in dealing with OMB."

Not that Katzen, a former partner at Wilmer, Cutler & Pickering, is Sherrie Lewis.

She is regarded as outspoken and tough-minded. Regulators and the regulated largely consider her fair and a good listener with a mastery of one of government's most demanding subjects. Bass said it's no problem for her to keep the details of 1,000 or so regulations in her head.

But even when she's slightly incapacitated (she's hobbling around because of a household accident) she can appear forceful. It's better to have Katzen on your side, than not, those who know her suggested.

But despite the new open-door policy, it still remains unclear at times how decisions are made.

The business community worries that OMB, which is supposed to be the overlord of the federal regulatory morass, may be giving too much discretion to agencies to decide what rules should be second-guessed. The business community also wants a rewriting of rules already on the books that don't make social or economic sense to it.

Public interest groups also are trying to read the tea leaves. David Vladeck, director of Public Citizen's Litigation Group, was disappointed when OMB held up a proposed regulation of smoked fish and sent it back to the Food and Drug Administration for more work. But there was surprise, and delight, in Vladeck's camp when an Occupational Safety and Health Administration proposal on indoor air quality got OMB's blessing.

Said Katzen, not showing her hand: "I just want to get better rules. There is still a lot of work to be done."

Let's Reinvent It

The other part of the Clinton regulatory reform equation was its government "reinvention" effort, which began in 1993 and had at least two phases. Headed by Vice President Al Gore, "Reinventing Government," or REGO, as it was known in White House circles, had a more powerful impact on the shape of the federal government than did some congressional initiatives. "The government is broken and we intend to fix it," said President Clinton, posing on the South Lawn of the White House in front of a forklift loaded with thousands of regulations in its maw.[10] The blueprint for this reform was a report called "From Red Tape to Results: Creating a Government that Works Better & Costs Less." One of its themes was "Improving Regulatory Systems," a perennial for reformers.

Under the reinvention rubric, thousands of federal jobs were cut, the federal procurement process was streamlined, and federal employees got "Hammer Awards" for efforts to improve government programs or eliminate waste. Agencies laid out management plans to "reinvent" themselves. Others were under orders from the White House to make themselves more customer friendly. Critics viewed the program as window dressing and predicted that it would stall. To some extent it did until 1995 when Republican rule in Congress revitalized the effort.

The political appointee in charge of the reinvention program was Elaine Kamarck. In the following column she explains why the administration pinned its hopes on reinvention as the best bet to reform the system.

Taming the Beast, Act II: Reinventing Regulation

The Washington Post, December 30, 1994—When Elaine C. Kamarck took the job of heading Vice President Al Gore's National Performance Review, the work of whipping the federal government into shape seemed daunting.

She had to turn the procurement process inside out, reduce the number of government employees, make federal agencies more customer-oriented, forge partnerships between federal workers and management, and reorganize departments.

In other words, Kamarck became the engine behind reinventing government. With the help of a couple hundred employees, Kamarck says she accomplished 93 percent of what the National Performance Review suggested needed to be done to streamline the federal government.

"The first six months were just brutal," Kamarck, 44, remembers. "The last month has been pretty intense, too."

Maybe if the Republicans had not swept Congress, her job would be mostly done. She had cut her staff to 40 people, but now is hiring again for "Phase II," reinventing the regulators.

Since the Nov. 8 election, the Republicans' loud insistence that government is still too fat and that regulators are still overbearing and intrusive has taken Kamarck into new territory: Figure out how the federal regulatory agencies are run and try to do it better.

The regulators should not underestimate her.

As one of the Democratic Party's foremost experts on presidential nomination rules, her appetite for the arcane is endless, and she knows firsthand what a real rules fight is. She has known disappointment—she worked in losing Democratic presidential campaigns (Walter Mondale's and Bruce Babbitt's) and briefly in the Carter White House. Trained as a political scientist, she is regarded as a tireless worker who has a tough, outspoken approach to running things.

The question that Kamarck says she and other administration officials will ask every federal regulatory agency is, "Why are you here?"

Her job, in part, will be to figure out ways to provide "better government." This may mean reorganizing, eliminating or combining various pieces of the dozens of federal agencies.

Some may view this as too kind and gentle an approach.

Jack Faris, president of the National Federation of Independent Business, said the Clinton administration should not be afraid to cut too much too quickly. He assessed what has been done so far as "throwing a bucket of water at the Chicago fire."

But Kamarck calls the Republican proposal to choke off funding for some programs and simply eliminate the rest "a really simple-minded view of government. Their slash-and-burn techniques will not stand up to reality. People do expect to be protected [by the government]."

But some complaints of the anti-regulators already have been heard. The administration has been running hard to come up with initiatives such as the reorganization of the Department of Housing and Urban Development, the possibility of closing the Department of Energy and "corporatization" of the air traffic control system.

But Kamarck doesn't underestimate that much needs to be done, especially with recalcitrant regulators who buck change.

She got some perspective on the problem when her shop published a 160-page guide of customer service standards for just about every organization in the federal government. She said the feedback she got from many agencies was, "'We are regulators. We don't have to be nice and figure out a better way to do this.'"

What was that about better government?

Appointees like Kamarck, now a Harvard professor, were on the front line in 1995 when the Republicans swept Congress and set their sights on regulatory "reform." When Republicans started shouting for radical changes in how the agencies and administration operated on the regulatory front, the Clinton administration was forced to not only reinvent but show resolve that it could rein in the regulators. The administration responded by unveiling a new reinvention initiative to reduce regulatory burden but continue to protect health and safety—a distinction the administration hoped voters would make with the Republican agenda.

"I am determined to see reform of our regulatory system, so that it costs less, meddles less, and puts more responsibility in the hands of the people themselves. But while we reform regulation, we cannot strip away safeguards for our children, our workers, our families," said President Clinton at a White House press conference with the heads of all the federal agencies in attendance.[11] The administration made it clear that it was willing to sharpen the budget knife on its own. The administration promised a new Occupational Safety and Health Administration and Environmental Protection Agency that would embark on experimental programs that rewarded voluntary effort to comply with rules.

Did Reinvention Work?

Rule watchers saw changes taking place, in both the agencies' approach to regulation and the culture of regulation. Though the Clinton administration saved its firepower for the big issues such as tobacco regulation, tightening an important air pollution law, and pushing ahead on ergonomics, there were subtle responses from the White House to Republican oversight of the agencies and the political realities of the day that are captured in this story.

Slowing the Flow of Federal Rules; New Conservative Climate Chills Agencies' Activism

The Washington Post, February 18, 1996—Under pressure from congressional Republicans, budget cuts and the Clinton administration's efforts to cut red tape, the federal agencies charged with protecting Americans from unhealthy workplaces, pollution and unsafe products have begun to fundamentally change the way they do their job.

Bureaucrats who for a generation dictated enormous volumes of rules are more readily compromising with the industries they regulate. Others are finding that they don't have enough money to enforce rules or conduct inspections. And still others find themselves ordered practically overnight to reverse longstanding policy.

The result is a de facto deregulation of American business that marks a significant departure from decades of government policy.

"Some agencies now are hesitant to push regulations that will encounter stiff political resistance," said Edward Hudgins, director of regulatory studies for the libertarian Cato Institute, which supports reducing the power of regulatory agencies. "Some businesses see an opportunity to challenge certain rules and establish more lenient, implicit rules that are followed by an agency but not necessarily stated in writing."

The Environmental Protection Agency was forced to scrap proposed rules requiring employers to set up car pools for employees in severely polluted areas.

The Occupational Safety and Health Administration has been forced to limit its inspections of workplaces for lack of funds.

The Food and Drug Administration has cut approval times for new products after criticism that it had been painfully slow.

The Interior Department is making it easier for developers to build on land that may have been off-limits because of rules protecting endangered species.

To be sure, agencies are adhering to their regulatory agendas where they can, and business groups note that some major rule-makings are going forward. But, according to many observers and some of the agencies themselves, the new change in tone and substance of many initiatives has resulted in some of the very reforms that the Republican Congress failed to effect with legislation.

Donald Kettl, professor of public affairs at the University of Wisconsin, said the nation's regulatory superstructure is having to conform to a new operating environment—there is neither the money nor the congressional will to authorize or enforce a host of controversial rules. "Agencies have had to get a whole lot smarter, faster, because the job hasn't gone away, but there are greater expectations and lower budgets," he said. "Congress clearly has turned up the heat, forcing agency managers to move further than they ever would have. . . . There hasn't been much strategic about it."

Critics of the changes say the agencies are being intimidated by Congress and thwarted by corporate lobbyists. The ad hoc changes taking place, they say, can have significant impact on weakening the resolve and reach of regulators.

"They are just wearing these agencies down," consumer activist Ralph Nader said.

But deregulation proponents say the changes are coming none too soon. Rep. David McIntosh (R-Ind.), a freshman who had advocated radical changes in the regulatory system, said he believes the steps the agencies are taking are in the right direction. "I do think we have changed the culture," he said. "The agencies are being much more reasonable with the public."

Hanging by Purse Strings

Early in his administration, President Clinton hoped to use an orderly "reinvention" strategy to teach agencies how to better manage themselves and operate more efficiently. The emphasis was on partnerships with business, simplifying regulations and focusing on results rather than process and punishment.

The focus—and the pace—changed when the Republicans took over Congress and the House made regulatory reform one of its "Contract With America" proposals.

Congress specifically barred OSHA, for example, from spending any money to issue a workplace ergonomic rule, which would have set new standards for offices and factory floors to protect workers from repetitive strain injuries, one of the country's fastest-growing categories of occupational illnesses.

"Even though OSHA reform legislation has not moved forward yet, some of the pressure points in the legislation are happening de facto," said John Tysse, vice president at the Labor Policy Association, which represents companies on employee-related issues.

At the EPA, a major regulatory effort has stalled because of delays caused by the government shutdown and scarcity of funds. The agency each year puts out a report based on information filed by manufacturers releasing certain chemicals into the air, water and land. The EPA report is the only source for local communities that want to find out what pollutants are being discharged by area manufacturing plants.

This year's report will be delayed several months because of budget cuts and the shutdowns. The EPA also will not have the resources to check the quality of the data filed by companies or be able to offer guidance to new industries expected to report, according to an analysis by Friends of the Earth, an environmental group.

The Consumer Product Safety Commission has not been a visible target in Congress, but it has been hit hard by the shutdowns, forcing it to be less vigilant in some cases, officials there said.

"It has increased our anxiety as to what has come in during that time and it may increase our workload in the future," said Kathleen Begala, a spokeswoman for the agency.

Rhetoric to Reality

Budget shortages aren't the only reasons agencies are changing. The Federal Trade Commission turned the reinvention rhetoric into reality. Its goal is to maintain its ability to enforce rules while also partnering with industry. Rather than just going after businesses that may not be complying with its rules, the FTC now is trying to get them to cooperate and through that dialogue avoid further run-ins with the agency, officials there said. That can save the FTC a lot of money and allow it to concentrate its enforcement muscle on more serious offenders.

For example, the FTC recently fined several funeral homes for not disclosing to consumers the prices of their services, as required under its Funeral Home Rule. At the same time, the agency entered into a regulatory partnership with the National Funeral Directors Association, which has agreed to run a program to discipline offenders.

High-profile battles over changing the Endangered Species Act—which has been blamed for throwing loggers out of work, preventing farmers from planting crops and holding up real estate development—also have caused the Interior Department to rethink its approach to enforcement.

Interior has begun negotiating dozens of voluntary agreements with timber companies and real estate developers that allow the "incidental" killing of endangered species in return for the protection of certain blocks of habitat.

Murray Pacific Corp., a timber company in Tacoma, Wash., negotiated such a deal. Under the agreement, the company will establish reserves where it won't cut trees on 10 percent of a 55,000-acre tree farm and take other measures such as providing stream buffers to protect spotted owls, marbled murrelets, salmon, steelhead trout and other species. In return, the company will not be penalized if some animals die on other parts of the farm, known as "incidental take" of imperiled species. Moreover, Murray Pacific will be immune from new endangered species restrictions for 100 years.

Agreements such as the one with Murray Pacific are key to the administration's drive to change the Endangered Species Act "from a regulatory program to more of a cooperative program with state and local governments and private landowners," said George T. Frampton Jr., assistant interior secretary for fish and wildlife and parks.

Mixed Reviews of FDA

The Food and Drug Administration, one of the most heavily criticized agencies, gets mixed reviews for its deregulatory efforts. For example, it kicked off the year by enraging conservatives with its proposal to regulate nicotine as a drug.

But it has changed its mind on certain product approvals that had been languishing for years and Ken Reid, editor of the *Enforcement Letter*, has recorded slight dips in some areas of enforcement.

"They're not stopping regulating altogether," Reid said. "But there certainly are things they probably would not have done if not for the Republican takeover."

Sidney M. Wolfe, executive director of Public Citizen's Health Research Group, said that since the 1994 election, the FDA has all but ignored the petitions he has sent in requesting that the agency require drug manufacturers to warn patients about adverse health effects related to certain drugs. "These fall into the category of . . . hunkering down and not wanting to seem too regulatory in the current climate," Wolfe said.

Pushing for More Reform

Though de facto deregulation has delivered some of the results that conservatives have sought for years, it's expected that business groups will push again for significant regulatory reform legislation that would hold agencies as well as Congress more accountable for rules.

Business lobbyists, several of whom said they felt burned by the stalled legislation of last year and negative perception that they were trying to gut environmental and safety rules, said they are likely to use a more temperate deregulatory message and downplay controversial proposals such as judicial review or preempting rules already on the books.

But they are set to chisel in legislative stone some of the ad-hoc regulatory changes to guard against losing ground. "The moment the fear is gone, agencies will go to excesses again," said David Ridenour, vice president of the National Center for Public Policy Research, a conservative research group.

Throughout the remainder of the Clinton administration there was continuing tension between the Republican Congress and the administration. Regulating continued apace, though some programs were delayed because of congressional moves to halt funding or call for more studies. By the end of the administration, many important rules such as ergonomics, which had been in the works for years, were issued. They became known as "midnight regulations" because of the lateness of their issuance, and many of them were "frozen" for additional review when the new Bush administration came to Washington. Largely, the push for radical reform had been averted.

As for reinvention, the General Accounting Office found in 1997 that the elimination of thousands of pages of published regulations did not necessarily reduce the burden of compliance. Even more eye-opening was GAO's observation that some of the agencies' totals did not include the pages they added during the review exercise. As one regulatory analyst put it: It was a hollow exercise.

Silent Reform: Executive Review

"There is no doubt that the President needs to coordinate regulatory policy. Each one since Richard Nixon has tried. The issue is how it can best be done," said William D. Ruckelshaus, who was Environmental Protection Agency administrator in the Nixon and Reagan administrations.[12] One of the most powerful ways to influence change and effect reform in the regulatory system is the least noticed: the executive order. For the past thirty years, presidents have used it to shape, restrain, and reform the process of regulation. Executive orders are issued by the president and then are printed in the *Federal Register*. Often orders are issued by presidents to revoke previous orders on the same topic. In the case of the Clinton Executive Order on Regulatory Planning and Review, it annulled a similar order issued by President Reagan.

Issuing an executive order is an arbitrary way to intervene in the regulatory process; it can result in the regulatory spigot being turned on, or off, with no public comment. Over the years, executive orders concerning regulation have instituted executive-level reviews of rules, moratoria, or extensive analysis of rules. In fact, some of the most far-reaching process reform legislation that Republicans were promoting in the mid-1990s was an attempt to codify what recent presidents had set out to achieve in various executive orders.

Though presidents Nixon, Ford, and Carter had requirements they wished to impose on the regulatory process, it was President Reagan who had the most significant imprint on the process of regulating. Agencies were ordered to prepare regulatory impact analyses that would determine the "potential net benefits" of new rules. "Regulatory action shall not be undertaken unless the potential benefits to society for the regulation outweigh the potential costs to society," the order, issued on February 17, 1981, stipulated.[13] Agencies were instructed in a separate order to submit annually to the Office of Management and Budget a "draft regulatory program" that would allow OMB reviewers to see in advance what agencies were planning and if the programs were in accord with the administration's broader goals for reform. This meant that regulators had to justify, or at least attempt to rationalize, the monetary as well as intrinsic value of regulation—an order that federal agencies complied with haphazardly over the years. President Bush lived under the Reagan orders, with the added twist of the Competitiveness Council and a moratorium that he imposed to slow down the rulemaking process. It was not until President Clinton took office that the notion of regulatory reform was again reinterpreted: The Clinton executive order gave a deep bow to cost-benefit analysis of rules, but it removed the stipulation that a rule's benefits must outweigh its cost—a central tenet of the Reagan reform program. Instead, the Clinton executive order stipulated that "each agency . . . propose or adopt a regulation only upon a reasoned determination that the benefits of the intended regulation justify its costs."[14]

The difference is more than a nuance. As we see in chapter 5, the question of what the real cost of regulation is—and its net benefit—has been a source of deep disagreement among regulatory experts, economists, scholars, and regulators, each group coming to different conclusions. The question has become a prominent one in the George W. Bush administration, with its emphasis on the agencies' use of a controversial analytical tool called cost-benefit analysis, which is a way of evaluating the worth and necessity of federal regulation.

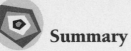 ## Summary

Chapter 4 is a survey of the numerous attempts by Congress and various administrations to "reform" the regulatory process by bringing more consistency, rigor, and analytic discipline to it. This movement is examined in light of the political realities of the time—the Republican takeover of Congress in

1995, a Democratic White House, and the increasing power of the business lobby. The chapter looks at the legislation that was introduced to effect change and what succeeded and what did not succeed. It examines how federal agencies reacted to conservatives in Congress who wanted to impose a moratorium on rulemaking, cut agency budgets, and make it more difficult for regulators to regulate. It discusses the role of the Office of Management and Budget in reviewing rules and setting standards for cost-benefit analysis. It looks at the Clinton administration's "Reinventing Government" initiative and the effect it had politically and substantively on regulation.

To Learn More

To understand the political ferment of the 1990s, a firsthand look at the Republican "Contract with America" will give you an understanding of what the newly elected Congress wanted to accomplish on the regulatory front and in other areas of domestic policy. It can be found at www.house.gov/house/Contract/CONTRACT.html (May 8, 2002). The Job Creation and Wage Enhancement Act, which passed the House, contains the legislative language calling for unfunded mandates reform, cost-benefit analysis and risk assessment of rules, and other changes to the regulatory process.

Two reports from the General Accounting Office examine the results of the Clinton administration's regulatory reform initiative and the effect that the Unfunded Mandates Act had on agency rulemaking. Both are worth reading to see the practical effect of an administrative decision and a new law; each was supposed to improve the regulatory process. Go to GAO's website, www.gao.gov, to find "Regulatory Reform: Agencies' Efforts to Eliminate and Revise Rules Yield Mixed Results" (GAO/GGD-98-3, October 1997). The other report is "Unfunded Mandates: Reform Act Has Had Little Effect on Agencies' Rulemaking Actions" (GAO/GGD-98-30, February 1998).

There are at least two executive orders that give key insights into attempts to reform the regulatory process; one is from a Republican president, and the other, a Democrat. The regulatory master plan of the Clinton administration is Executive Order 12866, which the new president issued on September 30, 1993. This plan revoked an earlier executive order issued by President Reagan. Sections 1, 2, and 4 of the Clinton order are a good summary of the reform effort undertaken by that administration. It can be found in the *Federal Register,* vol. 58 (October 4, 1993): 51735. Reagan's Executive Order 12291 should be read for its treatment of what thresholds must be met by agencies before rules are issued. It can be found in the *Federal Register,* vol. 46 (February 17, 1981): 13193.

Notes

1. "Senate Filibuster Derails Efforts to Limit Federal Regulations," *Congressional Quarterly Almanac,* 104th Congress, vol. 51 (Washington, D.C.: Congressional Quarterly Inc., 1995), 3-6.

2. Interview with Gary Bass, director, OMB Watch, January 31, 2002.

3. "Senate Filibuster Derails Efforts to Limit Federal Regulations," 3-7–3-8.

4. William G. Laffer III and Nancy A. Bord, "George Bush's Hidden Tax: The Explosion in Regulation," *The Heritage Foundation,* Backgrounder no. 905 (July 10, 1992): 4–5.

5. Angela Antonelli, "Regulation: Demanding Accountability and Common Sense," in *Issues 2000: The Candidate's Briefing Book* (Washington, D.C.: Heritage Foundation, 2000), 141.

6. Kevin Merida, "Corrections Day to Hit Twice Monthly; Some House Democrats See Red as GOP Sets Tuesdays to Cut Unnecessary Tape," *Washington Post,* June 21, 1995: A19.

7. Todd Gaziano, "SBREFA and Other Landmark Regulatory Reform Laws of the 104th Congress," *Administrative Law and Regulation News* 1, no. 2 (spring 1997): 10.

8. President, "'Regulatory Planning and Review,' Executive Order 12866, Revokes Executive Order 12291, 12498," *Federal Register* 58 (October 4, 1993): 51735.

9. Philip J. Hilts, "At Heart of Debate on Quayle Council: Who Controls Federal Regulations?" *New York Times,* December 16, 1991: B11.

10. Ann Devroy and Stephen Barr, "Clinton Offers Plan to Fix a 'Broken' Government," *Washington Post,* September 8, 1993: A1.

11. White House Office of the Press Secretary, "President Orders Governmentwide Reform of Regulatory System: Reinvention Initiative to Reduce Burdensome Regulations, Protect Public Health and Safety" (February 21, 1995), 1.

12. William D. Ruckelshaus, "Who Will Regulate the Regulators," *New York Times,* February 2, 1993: A23.

13. President, "'Federal Regulation,' Executive Order 12291, Revokes Executive Order 12044," *Federal Register* 46 (February 17, 1981): 13193.

14. President, "'Regulatory Planning and Review,'" 51735–36.

The Price Tag of Regulation: The Cost-Benefit Equation

Tire Sensors Gain among Automakers

The Washington Post, September 15, 2000—Timing is everything. Taking advantage of the attention on tire pressure that the Firestone recall has generated, General Motors Corp. is expected to extend to sport-utility vehicles and trucks the computerized "tire inflation monitoring system" it already offers in cars.

Ford Motor Co. President Jacques Nasser told a recent congressional hearing on the tires, which are used mainly on Ford Explorer SUVs, that he supports the idea of such technology. He said the device "would be a very popular option, but it needs to be friendly to the customer. It can't be a scientific device that is so difficult that you need a German professor of engineering to figure it out."

Ford hasn't announced any plans to offer the devices.

GM, which already offers it on 1.6 million vehicles, ranging from its high-end Corvette sports car to the Chevrolet Impala, a family sedan, is considering introducing the tire monitoring system on its sport-utility vehicles and light trucks by 2003.

"We're being very responsive to the marketplace. The rollout plan is being formulated," said Brook Lindbert, GM's director of tire and wheel systems.

In the 2002 model year, DaimlerChrysler Corp. will offer monitoring systems in Dodge and Chrysler minivans, Jeep Cherokees and four of its full-size passenger cars.

Two Mercedes-Benz cars have a tire monitoring system as a $600 option for the 2001 model year.

The idea that drivers should not have to keep track of their tire pressure, much as they do the status of their gas tanks, has until now been confined to race cars, heavy trucks and mining equipment.

Consumers have been expected to use tire gauges to check their tire inflation regularly, a chore that often has been neglected as more dependable radial tires replaced bias-ply tires and full-service gas stations disappeared.

In January 1981, as President Jimmy Carter was leaving office, the National Highway Traffic Safety Administration proposed requiring manufacturers to put a warning light on the dashboard or a device on the tire that would signal a leak.

The Reagan administration killed the idea seven months later, dismissing it as too expensive, unreliable, or better addressed through consumer education. The agency estimated at that time that the on-tire devices would cost $5.

Joan Claybrook, NHTSA administrator during the Carter administration, said manufacturers should have adopted the proposal anyway, adding that it could have been a lifesaver for owners of Firestone tires that have experienced tread separation. Tread separation can result from riding on underinflated tires.

GM offers the tire monitoring system on many of its models as standard equipment. Some of them have wireless sensing systems connected to the wheel, while others incorporate wheel-speed sensors connected to the anti-lock braking system.

"It's not rocket science," said Dick Humphrey, GM's liaison for safety affairs in Washington. "It's a good idea. It gives you a forewarning that something bad is about to happen. You'd sure like to know that when you're driving down I-95 so you can get it off and get it fixed."

The system includes a wireless sensor on each wheel. The sensors monitor either air pressure or the speed of the tire, which is affected by how much air it contains. The sensor sends the information to a receiver, which relays it to the driver.

On some devices, a deviation of between five and 10 pounds per square inch sets off a signal, which may be a light on the instrument panel and an audible chime. A computerized voice reminds the driver to check tire pressure or, on other systems, a display on the instrument panel shows the pressure of each tire.

In GM's 2001 Cadillac DeVille, for instance, a driver can press an "info" button and get a reading for each tire, such as "34 PSI LF Tire OK." Deviations show up as "tire low" or "tire high." The 2000 Oldsmobile Alero sounds an alert if the pressure in one tire deviates by 12 psi from the other three.

Another part of the latest generation of tire technology is the run-flat tire, which can run at speeds up to 50 mph for 50 miles or more even when it is not inflated.

Consumers can buy off-the-shelf tire monitoring systems. SmartTire Systems Inc., a Canadian company, has been researching and designing tire-monitoring systems since 1987, primarily for use with heavy equipment.

The company adapted its system to be used with run-flat tires, and then with conventional tires. The system uses wireless technology to monitor air pressure and temperature through sensors mounted on the inside of each wheel.

The receiver is similar in size to a radar detector and can be placed on the dashboard or anywhere else in the car. It gives readouts only when the car is rolling.

The system retails for about $400 and is sold by tire retailers—including Bridgestone/Firestone stores.

In the aftermath of the government investigation of what went wrong with Bridgestone/Firestone tires and the 271 fatalities that many suspected were linked to underinflation in the tires, Congress ordered the National Highway Traffic Safety Administration to come up with a fix that would keep passengers safer: a tire-monitoring system like the ones mentioned in the above column that would automatically send an alert to the driver. The question of whether some of the Firestone tire accidents could have been avoided centered around whether Ford Motor Co. had recommended a tire pressure for its Explorer sport utility vehicles, which were involved in most of the accidents, that was too low, causing tread separations and tire blowouts. There also was the question of whether vehicle owners neglected to keep the proper air pressure in the tires and if an automatic sensing system might be the way to alert them to keep their tires inflated properly. At any rate, Congress decided to prod the agency to make sensors mandatory, instead of leaving it up to car manufacturers to offer them as they saw fit.

Fast-forward a bit more than two years after this column was written. In the interim, NHTSA got to work on a proposal to require automakers to use by 2007 a direct warning system that would tell drivers when up to four tires are 25 percent or more underinflated. Sensors would be placed in each wheel to measure directly the amount of air in each tire and send an electronic warning to the dashboard for the driver. The system would be capable of pinpointing which tire has low pressure. In the interim, automakers could use a less expensive approach, communicating to drivers that tire pressure is low through computers integrated in the antilock braking system. The brakes are used to measure the rotation speed of the tires; those with low pressure rotate faster, causing a signal to be sent to the driver that pressure is low. But unlike the case with the direct system, the driver would not know which tire is underinflated. In addition, the vehicle must be moving to get a reading. "Any system for monitoring tire pressure should provide the most accurate information possible about *all four tires,* and potentially the spare tire as well," said Consumers Union in comments on the proposed rule.[1]

Comments on the rule were also made by the tire industry, companies that make the sensor systems, and the auto industry. Jeffrey Runge, who was Bush's pick to head the auto safety agency, sent NHTSA's proposed final rule to the Office of Management and Budget for review on December 17, 2001. As with any major rule, OMB's Office of Information and Regulatory Affairs reviewed the rule, checking to see if it made sense from a scientific and financial point of view. In other words, would the proposed system work, and would the cost of it yield sufficient benefits in terms of safety?

John D. Graham: Return to Sender

In those two years, there was another important development. President George W. Bush made a controversial appointment to OMB's Office of Information and Regulatory Affairs, the office that reviews and approves most major rules written by the agencies. OIRA is the federal government's nerve center for passing judgment on the rules produced by the agencies; its sway over the agencies' work has been different with every administration since the office was created in 1981. Its response to agency rulemakings over the years has ranged from intensely negative to extremely supportive.

John D. Graham, the Bush administration's appointee, was a professor at Harvard University and director of its Center for Risk Analysis. When Graham arrived at OIRA he decided to strengthen the executive review of major rules and subject them to strict cost-benefit and risk assessment tests, his area of professional expertise. Graham signaled immediately that OIRA would play a major role in conceptualizing as well as approving rules. This approach was troubling to Graham's critics, who believed that Congress and the agencies should have primary authority over rulemaking. While Graham was awaiting confirmation by the Senate, public interest groups unleashed an outpouring of opposition to his appointment because they believed that he would be biased toward corporate interests that oppose regulation. Some of the same companies that would be affected by new regulation, they argued, were corporate donors to Graham's Harvard Center for Risk Analysis. The following column was written to set the stage for the tight vote (sixty-one to thirty-seven) in the Senate that approved Graham's nomination.

Nominee Gets Mixed Reception; Graham, Tapped for Post at OMB, Says He'll Soften Rhetoric

The Washington Post, May 18, 2001—The Harvard University risk-assessment expert nominated to be the Bush administration's chief reviewer of agency regulations said yesterday that he will tone down provocative statements he has made about agency decisions if he is confirmed.

"It was the kind of thing I could do as a college professor, but . . . I would assume agency risk assessors are public-spirited without regard to impact on their agency, unless I had reason to believe otherwise," John D. Graham told the Senate Government Affairs Committee, referring to a statement he once made that agencies have more incentive to regulate than not regulate.

Graham, head of Harvard's Center for Risk Analysis and a leading proponent of assessing the economic effects of rulemakings, faced 2 1/2 hours of questioning, the most pointed coming from Sen. Richard J. Durbin (D-Ill.). Durbin said he will oppose Graham when the committee votes next Wednesday on his nomination to head the regulatory branch at the Office of Management and Budget.

Several senators quizzed Graham, who has been under fire from public interest groups that fear he will be pro-business, about corporate contributions to the center, whether he would be impartial in his decision-making, and how he would use analytical tools such as cost-benefit analysis and risk assessment to make regulatory decisions.

Graham said he would uphold the statutes underlying the regulations he reviews. He assured members that the use of cost-benefit analysis will not result in fewer or more rules but a "smarter regulatory system."

"These analytical tools can be a force for more protection at less cost than we are seeing today," Graham said. He also said he would concentrate on making rules more cost-effective by working with agencies and Congress in planning rules and agency budgets.

Republicans on the panel defended his record, intellectual ability and integrity. Sen. George V. Voinovich (R-Ohio) said Graham is "hands down, one of the most qualified people for this position." Sen. Robert F. Bennett (R-Utah) said the nominee has been subject to a "character assassination attempt" by his opponents.

Sen. Fred D. Thompson (R-Tenn.), the committee chairman, said Graham had adhered to conflict-of-interest and disclosure requirements that are tougher than those required by the university.

The GOP members pointed out that Graham had received hundreds of letters of support, including one from five past administrators of both parties at OMB's Office of Information and Regulatory Affairs. The committee combed Graham's reports and public statements for examples of his support of regulatory initiatives—a move designed to answer charges by Graham's critics that he is an opponent of regulation.

Nine high-level regulators from Democratic administrations, including former Labor secretary Robert B. Reich and former Occupational Safety and Health Administration chief Charles Jeffress, told the committee in a letter that it should "conduct a thorough investigation into Dr. Graham's suitability for the position."

Sen. Carl M. Levin (D-Mich.), the senior Democrat on the committee, said he found Graham to be "moderate and thoughtful" in prior dealings. Sen. Joseph I. Lieberman (D-Conn.) said it was "a provocative nomination" that has caused some anxiety because the new administration has already made decisions such as suspending an arsenic drinking water standard.

Durbin accused the nominee of "trivializing environmental concerns." He questioned Graham about a statement he made about dioxin being a "likely anti-carcinogen" and not being harmful at certain levels of exposure.

Graham said yesterday that at high doses dioxin causes cancer in animals, but in low doses there is some evidence it acts to prevent cancers. He said the "protective effect, if it exists, is in the female mammary tumors in rodents."

Graham added that in humans the evidence is more mixed. He said he has stressed other negative effects of dioxin "which provide the rationale to continue reducing exposure to dioxin."

Durbin also questioned the contributions Graham's center accepted from the Philip Morris Cos. In 1991, the center solicited a donation from the tobacco company and received a $25,000 check. The money was returned when the School of Public Health, which houses the Center, decided it could not take money from a tobacco company.

Graham told Durbin he argued against returning the money and said, "I still have some serious reservations about that decision."

Subsequently, Graham asked Kraft General Foods, a Philip Morris subsidiary, for a $20,000 donation, which he received in 1992. From 1994 to 1997, Kraft donated another $60,000.

Durbin asked Graham if he saw any ethical problem in "getting out of the pocket of Philip Morris" and then asking Kraft for money. Graham replied that the school determined that Kraft's money was acceptable.

Asked about a computer that a Philip Morris official sent the Center in 1993, Graham said it was a "personal donation" from the scientist, not a company contribution.

The verdict from Graham on the tire sensor rule was that NHTSA flunked the cost-benefit test. On February 12, 2002, OIRA sent a "return" letter to the regulators at NHTSA telling them to consider a different approach—the cheaper one tied to the braking system that automakers wanted included in the proposal. The rationale was that promoting the system that worked through the brakes would encourage automakers to install more antilock brake systems, for only about two-thirds of the fleet now offers the safety feature. It would also make installation of a sensing system cheaper. OIRA said that it would save more lives and avoid more injuries than did the NHTSA proposal. "Before NHTSA finalizes a rule that disallows indirect systems, OMB believes that the potential safety benefits from more vehicles with anti-lock brakes need to be considered," said the letter that Graham sent to the agency.[2]

Besides sending shock waves through the agency, the letter was notable because it signaled a different philosophy toward regulation. It focused debate on the role of cost-benefit analysis in rulemaking and, ultimately, how the government's corps of regulators should use this powerful tool. It was a very public stand on the influential and controversial role that cost-benefit analysis would play in the White House's expectations about what rules would go forward.

The bottom line was that the agency had to go back to the drawing board. On May 30, 2002, NHTSA announced that automakers could use either system for three years beginning in November 2003. The agency said that it would evaluate their effectiveness and make a final decision for vehicles built after 2006.

Until Graham took over, the role of cost-benefit analysis was acknowledged as important, and even essential, by OMB, but it was not often the determining factor in whether a rule would become final. In fact, during the eight years of the Clinton administration, OIRA returned fewer rules to the agencies than Graham did in his first seven months on the job.

Looking at the Fine Print

The letter that was sent to NHTSA from Graham is worth examining in detail to understand the shape of the debate and the increasing power of cost-benefit analysis. In this case, the economic analysis done by OIRA trumped the agency even though NHTSA believed that its analysis showed that its choice of sensing system might have saved more lives. By doing the calculation differently and giving additional weight to another regulatory alternative—the indirect system tied to the brakes—the White House exerted executive review authority over the agency. This result was favorable to auto companies, which felt both options were equally safe, but drew the ire of consumer groups such as Public Citizen. "The administration is playing a game here," said Joan Claybrook, president of Public Citizen and a former administrator of the NHTSA.[3] "Essentially what this allows is for those vehicles that have antilock brakes to jury-rig a tire inflation system, but it doesn't work very well."[4] Public Citizen eventually sued the Department of Transportation over the rule issued in May 2002. Tire manufacturers did not like the final rule either and asked the agency for a rewrite of it. They feared that the warning light would not go on in some cases until tires were already in an unsafe condition. Their objections were backed up by congressional sponsors of the safety legislation, including the Republican chairman of the House Energy and Commerce Committee, Rep. W. J. Billy Tauzin (R-La.).

The OMB rejection of the tire sensor rule provides a concise case study of how rules are reviewed by OIRA and the effect special interests can have on the outcome of a rule. In this case, the automakers had a meeting with top officials at OIRA, including Graham, to advance their argument that both systems have merit and should be allowed.

In its written comments to NHTSA, the Alliance of Automobile Manufacturers, which includes most of the major automakers, said that one of its concerns was that the new rule "provide for reasonable cost-benefit."[5] In an interview, Robert Strassburger, vice president, safety and harmonization at the Alliance, said that the group found many of NHTSA's assumptions—such as how many people would respond to direct or indirect systems—unsubstantiated. "When we corrected for things [in the proposal] that were not well documented, we found both systems can provide equal safety benefits," said Strassburger. As for the difference in cost, Strassburger characterized it as "huge," estimating that the direct systems would cost perhaps $100 per car. Using the antilock brake system to supply the information, he estimated, would be "around $15 per car."

Whose Numbers Add Up?

When an agency proposes a major rule that costs the economy more than $100 million annually, it is required to perform a cost-benefit analysis of the rule that then must be reviewed by OMB's Office of Information and

Regulatory Affairs. OIRA has ninety days to complete its review and to decide whether to clear the rule for publication in the *Federal Register* or to send it back to the agency for more work. During this time, the agency can also withdraw the rule itself and continue to work on it. OIRA reviews about six hundred major rules a year.

Under this process, NHTSA had to compile what is called a preliminary economic assessment that compared the costs and benefits of both direct and indirect tire-sensing systems. The agency found that the direct system would be more expensive—$66.33 per car. But adding in the benefit of fuel savings and reduced tire wear, the net cost would be reduced to $23.08 per vehicle, the agency said. The cost to outfit the 16 million vehicles produced annually would be about $1 billion.

The indirect sensing system tied to the brakes would add $30.54 to the cost of a new vehicle, a total of $489 million or about half the cost of a direct system; adding increased fuel economy and reduced tire wear would reduce the final cost to $8.63, the agency estimated. This is a big difference in cost when multiplied by the 16 million vehicles produced annually.

The other important factor in assessing the two systems is the benefits they provide: How many injuries and fatalities would be averted? In this calculation, NHTSA estimated that direct sensing systems would prevent 10,635 injuries and seventy-nine deaths. Indirect systems were found to be less effective in this calculation. They would prevent 6,585 injuries and forty-nine deaths.

The agency looked at some of the disadvantages of indirect systems, such as their inability to detect air loss in all four tires, the lack of antilock brake systems in some cars, and their inability to detect small losses of air. The benefits of using the existing antilock brake systems on vehicles are lower cost and minor changes to the vehicle.

On the benefit side for direct systems, the agency found that they have better sensitivity to small losses of pressure and can measure pressure at any time in any tire, including the spare. The disadvantages of the direct sensors, which are installed on the rims of tires, include possible maintenance problems and higher cost.

After analyzing all of this information, the agency formulated its proposal and sent it to OIRA for review. It suggested that automakers should be allowed to use indirect systems for several years but that in 2007 they had to begin using direct systems that would transmit readings from all four tires.[6]

Then the trouble began. OIRA, using updated figures from the agency and other assumptions, came up with different estimates. It told the agency that there would be substantially greater safety benefits at lower cost if indirect systems could be used indefinitely, an option that the agency did not explore. OIRA said that it liked this approach because it would encourage automakers to install antilock brakes and avoid the extra cost of providing a direct sensing system.

According to OIRA's calculation, it would cost $66.50 per vehicle to install a direct system. If the vehicle already had antilock brakes, it would cost $13.29 to add indirect sensing, reducing the cost of compliance by $53.00 per vehicle. For cars and trucks without the brakes, the cost of a direct system would be avoided altogether.

OIRA then went on to extrapolate how many lives would be saved and injuries averted from having more antilock brakes than there otherwise would have been on the road. It estimated that at least forty-seven more lives could be saved annually (and maybe up to 195) compared with the option preferred by NHTSA—the direct system. And unlike the billion-dollar price tag on the direct systems, allowing indirect systems indefinitely would reduce the cost to $726 million.

OIRA told NHTSA to go back to the drawing board and evaluate this option on its own. The OMB letter said,

> OMB believes that a rule permitting indirect systems may provide more overall safety than a rule that permits only direct or hybrid systems. This additional safety may be available at a lower total cost to the public. Although direct systems are capable of detecting low pressure under a greater variety of circumstances than indirect systems, the indirect system captures a substantial portion of the benefit provided by direct systems. Moreover, allowing indirect systems will reduce the incremental cost of equipping vehicles with antilock brakes [ABS], thereby accelerating the rate of adoption of ABS technology.[7]

Finally, OIRA chastised NHTSA for the quality of its analysis, telling the agency that it needed to better explain how it arrived at its cost-benefit estimates. It told the regulators at NHTSA that they missed the regulatory objective—enhanced highway safety—by overlooking the indirect option.

Congressional Oversight

It did not take long for Congress to get wind of the controversy and to intervene. On February 28, 2002, the House Commerce, Trade and Consumer
Protection Subcommittee of the Energy and Commerce Committee
wanted a briefing on the rule because it was part of a larger hearing on the
progress the NHTSA was making in implementing other auto safety rules
that were supposed to be implemented as a result of the Firestone tire
tragedy. Graham was asked to explain his rebuke of the agency, and the
agency was asked when it would have a rule ready. By the end of the hearing, it became apparent that some sort of "compromise" was in the mix that
would avoid a stalemate. It appeared that the agency had agreed to give
automakers the choice of either system through the 2006 model year. Then
a study would be done to determine what should be required for the future.
In Washington-speak, this kind of decision usually appeases the complaining party (in this case, the automakers that want a choice of systems), and it
often puts off indefinitely any decision that might be contrary to what that
party wants.

Rep. Edward Markey (D-Mass.), who sponsored the legislative provision
calling for tire sensors, pointed out to Graham at the hearing the shortcomings of the indirect system that OIRA prefers. Primary among them is the
system's inability to sense underinflation in two or four of the tires. In other
words, if all the tires were underinflated, no warning would be sent to the
driver. Markey said in his hearing statement:

> Now it's hard to see how a system where two tires on a vehicle could
> be significantly underinflated, or where every tire is underinflated, and
> where the driver has a tire pressure warning system yet remains unin-
> formed of the safety risk could conceivably meet the mandate from
> Congress that drivers be informed with a warning system when a tire
> is significantly underinflated. Such systems may be fine during a tran-
> sition and ABS systems may be wonderful technology and may also
> save lives. Yet ABS systems were not required by the TREAD Act. If
> OMB feels so strongly that ABS systems are a compelling safety feature
> we look forward to the administration's proposal to require ABS as a
> standard feature in all vehicles. Until we receive that proposal, however,
> the TREAD Act requirement for tire pressure safety warnings for
> motorists should not be undermined or unduly delayed.

And to show his disagreement with OIRA's cost-benefit res
added: "As the author of the provision, I think NHTSA got it right the first
time and we should move toward implementation as soon as possible."

Markey said that he would like a specific date for the end of the transition period when automakers are supposed to meet the standard with either
system. And to show his skepticism about the effectiveness of antilock
brakes and their role in the whole debate, he asked if they would be necessary so that, "when the tires blow, you'll be able to brake faster."

The Role of Cost-Benefit Analysis

Over the past two decades, economists, regulatory scholars, and legal experts
have given increasing weight to cost-benefit analysis as a way to determine
how effective a rule will be compared with what is spent to implement it. The
executive branch, Congress, and the judiciary all consider to some extent the
cost of regulating and what inherent benefits a rule offers in protecting
Americans. In many, though not all, cases, calculating cost has become a factor in issuing rules and in tallying up the total cost of regulation. Increasingly,
it also is at the center of politically charged debates over the proper role of
regulation in government, the growth of federal regulation, and how much
society is willing to spend on government regulation. "Gradually, and in fits
and starts, American government is becoming a cost-benefit state. By this I
mean that government regulation is increasingly assessed by asking whether
the benefits of regulation justify the costs of regulation," writes Cass R.
Sunstein, a professor at the University of Chicago Law School.[8]

Questions like these are posed: How much does society want to spend to
save a worker from benzene exposure? How much pollution control will abate
rising incidences of asthma among children? What do the numbers show as
far as how much arsenic is acceptable in water supplies? Is it worth requiring
child safety seats in airplanes, or will the cost drive passengers into their cars,
a less safe alternative to flying? How much is society willing to pay to diminish
certain risks, and how does one calculate what that avoidance is worth? Who
pays for all this? Business? Taxes on individuals? Increased prices that get passed
on to consumers? This is where the theoretical arguments about the necessity
of regulation in society become practical questions of economic cost.

On an emotional level, most people support regulation to lessen risk,
preserve the value of an intangible such as a mountain vista, or alleviate pain
and suffering. They expect the federal government to play a prominent role

in affording certain protections, especially when tragedy strikes, such as fatal food poisonings or mining accidents. But sometimes, supporters of cost-benefit analysis say, numbers must drive the decision because the average person is unreliable at assessing and valuing the nature of the risk.

The following column discusses how the Federal Aviation Administration decided in 1995 that it is safer not to require safety seats on airplanes for babies. To most people it seemed like an odd decision because they assumed that the safety risk of an infant being unbelted in an airplane was high. But what the FAA calculated was that more lives would be saved by keeping kids flying unbelted than having them ride in cars if their parents decided that it was too expensive to buy them airplane seats. In other words, more children would be put at risk if a rule were instituted than if it were not because it is less safe to drive than to fly.

The agency revisited the issue in 1998 after the White House Commission on Aviation Safety and Security recommended that infants and small children be restrained in child safety seats on aircraft. The FAA issued an advanced notice of proposed rulemaking, which is similar to a request for information, but no rule has been put in place. Instead, the FAA "strongly recommends" that parents use child safety seats on airplanes.

Cost-Benefits & Babies: FAA Ruling on Child Safety Seats Running into Turbulence

The Washington Post, June 16, 1995—At the cool, calculated heart of regulatory cost-benefit analysis is this question: How much is a baby's life worth?

Any parent would say priceless. But when it comes to strapping them into child safety seats on airplanes, things such as fares, the availability of proper restraints and the remote chance of an accident affect their judgment. The majority choose to hold infants on their laps—a precarious position in case of an accident or turbulence—to avoid paying for a seat.

The Federal Aviation Administration considered these very factors in its cost-benefit analysis of whether to mandate that children younger than 2 be secured in child safety seats on airplanes instead of riding in an adult's lap.

This is the kind of analysis—numbers-based and objective—that regulatory "reformers" want all agencies to do in proposing new rules.

After studies by economists, technicians and statisticians, the FAA recently decided that families who fly are so "price sensitive" that they would choose to drive if forced to buy an airplane seat for an infant. And so, the FAA concluded, more children would die, since air travel is statistically safer than driving.

"If the choice is to drive rather than fly, then it's preferable to hold the child," said John Rogers, director of the FAA's office of aviation policy and plans.

The agency weighed the cost to travelers against the benefit that would be gained—fewer injuries and fatalities. The FAA said requiring infants to fly in their own seats would cost families an additional $1 billion over 10 years—$200 a trip for the average traveling family.

For that money, the agency said, five infant fatalities would be avoided over the next 10 years. Conversely, if families were driven into their cars, there would be a net increase of 82 infant and adult fatalities over that time.

Since 1978, nine infants have died in what aviation experts consider survivable crashes. In some cases, their mothers, who survived, were holding them.

"It's bad policy based on bad analysis," said Christopher Witkowski, the Association of Flight Attendants' air safety director. "They are not providing the highest degree of safety. Sure, it's okay if it's someone else's baby" who dies in a crash.

The flight attendants group's own analysis is that parents would not be driven off planes because of the availability of low-cost carriers.

The National Transportation Safety Board also challenges the FAA's reasoning, concluding: "Small children traveling on aircraft should be provided crash-worthiness protection that is at least equivalent to other passengers."

The FAA agrees. It would like to see all kids strapped in. The difference is in the approach.

"Regulation is not the only way to get to this objective," said FAA Deputy Administrator Linda Daschle, who had supported a mandate until she saw the studies. Instead, she said, the agency will push a public awareness campaign and encourage airlines to offer "incentives" for families to fly. She noted that Southwest Airlines charges infants 58 percent of regular fares.

The airlines supported a mandate until they realized that there continued to be questions about the safety of some child restraints used on aircraft. "We didn't want to mandate things that weren't safe," said Chris Chiames, an Air Transport Association spokesman.

The flight attendants group said it will press on until it's "the law of the land—or the skies."

Or, as Rep. Jim Lightfoot (R-Iowa), author of a bill to force use of the seats, said: "It is incredible that a flying passenger's luggage is afforded a higher level of protection than an infant child."

The Critics Weigh In

Decisions such as these strike fear into the hearts of proponents of health, safety, and environmental regulation. They worry that number crunching will overrule ethical judgment and discourage important rulemakings—particularly rules that are intended to save lives. They dispute the conviction of a growing number of economists and conservatives that expenditures on regulation need to be quantified according to standardized accounting rules, even if that means assigning a value to each life saved or lost. They object to the idea that an elite of technocrats and other experts should be given deference in assessing risk and recommending solutions. "On this view, what matters, for law and policy is what people actually fear, not what scientists, with their own, inevitably fallible judgments, urge society to do. Populists insist that the very characterization of risks involves no simple 'fact,' but a host of normative judgments," writes Sunstein in his book *Risk and Reason: Safety, Law and the Environment,* characterizing the views of those who are deeply skeptical of cost-benefit analysis.[9]

Joan Claybrook, president of Public Citizen, has made that argument, and her remarks are reflective of what other groups in the consumer, environmental, and labor communities have expressed about the perils of "regulatory accounting."

"Calculating the impacts of a rule in preventing human suffering and death in monetary terms is a practice that is utterly out of touch with public notions of the value of life, and this deep discontinuity should matter to democratic decision makers. In fact, these regulatory decisions must be a matter of human judgment, relying on shared notions of value, as well as data and other quantitative calculations," Claybrook said.[10]

Lisa Heinzerling, a law professor at Georgetown University, has been an outspoken opponent of the misuse of cost-benefit analysis, saying that it leads to flawed results by reducing everything to monetary terms. Heinzerling, who opposed Graham's nomination, has testified and written widely about the federal government's growing dependence on cost-benefit analysis to determine the outcome of rules: "Cost-benefit analysis is a deeply flawed method that repeatedly leads to biased and misleading results. Far from providing a panacea, cost-benefit analysis offers no clear advantages in making regulatory policy decisions and often produces inferior results, in terms of both environmental protection and overall social welfare, compared to other approaches."[11] She called placing a price tag on human life the single most controversial idea in regulation, one that is thick with moral meaning.[12]

The issue of cost-benefit analysis came up repeatedly in the weeks leading up to Graham's confirmation at OIRA. Though Graham had the support of Republican senators, Democrats such as Sen. Richard Durbin (D-Ill.) campaigned against him on the basis of Graham's use of risk assessment to determine the need for regulation. Durbin viewed Graham's research at Harvard as antiregulation, and he expected that philosophy would permeate OIRA under Graham. "Graham is an academic in the field of risk analysis. His philosophy, which involves 'discounting' lives, is that we should get the biggest bang for the buck when reducing risks. Why spend society's scarce resources on programs that would save, say, only 100 lives when, for the same amount, we could save 1,000?" Durbin wrote.[13]

The Politics of Cost-Benefit Analysis

Although cost-benefit analysis is a highly technical, economic exercise, the results of such analyses—and how they can be used to determine the outcome of a rulemaking—have practical and political applications. For opponents of regulation, in particular, a cost-benefit analysis can tip the scales toward less costly regulation, another regulatory alternative (as in the tire sensor rule), or no rule at all. Sunstein points out that cost-benefit analysis gets plenty of criticism from opponents, but it also can be responsible for spurring regulation, as it has with some environmental rules. Basically, the calculation involves, as law professor Eric A. Posner put it, "a loose balancing of the advantages and disadvantages of a project." Into that calculation go survey data about market behavior and consumer preferences. Various costs have to be taken into account and whether lives or life years are saved. How much people are willing to avoid the risk of death counts. The numbers must be discounted to reflect the passage of time, and the possibility of alternative regulations and their costs must be considered, Posner writes.[14]

Some economists and regulatory analysts have argued that knee-jerk reactions to perceptions of risk—particularly environmental risks identified in the 1970s—created the current regulatory state that had grown exponentially; they have encouraged Congress to think about injecting cost-benefit analysis in any broad reform regulatory legislation that it might pass and to consider it an essential part of the reauthorization of any environmental statutes that now disallow risk assessment and cost-benefit analysis. Scholars like Robert Hahn, director of the AEI–Brookings Joint Center for Regulatory Studies, have urged that more discipline be imposed on the regulatory process. Hahn writes:

> Society could spend its regulatory dollars more wisely, and a system to allocate regulatory dollars efficiently does not exist. To improve the regulatory process, Congress and the White House must enforce the economic analysis requirements they publicly support. They must take advantage of existing reform proposals—designed on the basis of decades of work by regulatory scholars—to improve agency decision-making. The success of such efforts requires high-level political support, adherence to established principles of benefit-cost analysis, and rigorous review of agency analyses of regulations by an independent entity.[15]

The business community views cost-benefit analysis as part of any template for sensible and acceptable regulation. It has supported an exercise that would emphasize evaluating the magnitude of the risks involved and analyzing whether a regulation designed to solve one problem would create another (such as whether regulating increased fuel economy in cars would make them less safe, always a contentious debate) and whether scientific and economic analysis was factored into the regulatory equation. Various valuations would be placed on life.

The attempt to quantify the cost of rules intensified in tandem with criticism from the business community and other opponents of federal regulation who insisted that federal agencies do not pay enough attention to the cost of rules—even though some major statutes such as the Clean Air Act do not allow the consideration of cost to enter into the setting of some standards. They urged that regulators should be required to bring more rigor and consistency to their cost-benefit analyses of regulations, bringing them in line with the analyses done on other expenditures such as those within the federal budget.

Hahn and others have examined closely the track records of agencies in preparing cost-benefit analyses of their rules and have found them lacking. Hahn reports in his research that agencies used different discount rates from regulation to regulation, did partial analyses, or did not project the costs and benefits for future years. Some agencies, such as the Occupational Safety and Health Administration, are statutorily restricted from using costs and benefits as a way to set health standards. Independent agencies such as the Federal Communications Commission are not required to do such analyses. "My analysis of regulatory impact statements shows that they lack analytical consistency and that agencies only superficially comply with the requirements in the Reagan and Clinton executive orders," Hahn writes.[16] The General Accounting Office has concurred, saying in a report that agencies' estimates of costs vary according to their assumptions about what constitutes regulatory cost. It has concluded, not surprisingly, that estimates could vary widely.[17]

Conservatives who pushed for better regulatory accounting also wanted more disclosure, or "transparency," about how agencies go about their calculations and choose regulatory alternatives. "Regulations really are a hidden tax. They really are very easy to pass. What you don't measure, you don't pay attention to. Treat regulations like a budget item. Like a tax. Attach a regulatory authorization to every bill—the cost couldn't exceed X," said Wendy Gramm, former administrator of OIRA in the Reagan administration and now director of the Regulatory Studies Program of the Mercatus Center at George Mason University, in comments she gave at a conference in December 2001.

The analyses that agencies do on individual rules are also used to calculate the aggregate cost of regulation, a number that has political usefulness for those on both sides of the regulatory wars in Washington. And no matter how inconclusive or unreliable the number, many regulatory analysts applaud the exercise as a step toward rationalizing federal regulation and making regulators more accountable. "Prior to 1980, if you mentioned the cost of regulation before a congressional committee, you'd be excoriated. We've come a long way," said Murray Weidenbaum, chairman of the Weidenbaum Center at Washington University in St. Louis and former chairman of the Council of Economic Advisers.[18]

Supporters of regulatory accounting looked to Congress to reform the system and codify provisions for how agencies would have to do their rulemakings. As discussed in chapter 4, there were serious attempts to reform the regulatory process, and increasing the role of cost-benefit analysis in rulemaking was a large part of that debate, with Democrats and Republicans largely dividing into opposing camps on the issue. There were Democrats like Sen. Carl Levin (D-Mich.) who supported more analysis of rules as a way to produce better regulation, not necessarily less of it. Levin unsuccessfully sponsored legislation with Sen. Fred Thompson (R-Tenn.) to push agencies to come up with better estimates on what rules will cost, disclose the options that were considered, and justify why a particular alternative was chosen. The legislation provided for judicial review to ensure that agencies actually did the analyses.

But instead of broad changes to the process, there were incremental changes. Major statutes like the Safe Water Drinking Act were rewritten with provisions that would allow the Environmental Protection Agency to analyze costs and benefits and consider the element of risk reduction when it regulates a contaminant. For new drinking water standards, EPA now has to conduct cost-benefit analysis and determine whether the cost of a standard is justified by the benefits. Before the amendments, EPA was expected to order the removal of contaminants and not consider cost.

Another step was taken in 1995 when the Office and Management and Budget under the Clinton administration made an attempt to systematize how agencies do their cost-benefit sums. It discussed challenging issues such as how to evaluate risk, how to value a life, and how to quantify future gains and losses from a rulemaking. The guidance was finalized on January 11, 1996—after two years of work—and OMB stressed that the document "is not in the form of a mechanistic blueprint, for a good EA [economic analysis] cannot be written according to a formula."[19] At the behest of Congress, the Clinton administration in 2000 gave the agencies further guidance on preparing economic analyses. Despite assurances that hard numbers alone would not drive decision making, there was controversy over the guidelines and the motives behind issuing them, as the following column shows.

Putting a Value on Life: Agencies Question OMB's Cost-Benefit Balancing Act

The Washington Post, November 3, 1995—One of the fundamental beliefs of regulatory reformers is that federal agencies should be sure that the costs of the rules they write are in line with the potential benefits yielded to society.

In regulatory shorthand, it's called cost-benefit analysis and it is the underpinning of much of the legislation that Congress is pushing to make regulators more accountable.

Though it may sound like a simple, logical way to think about the cost of regulation, an attempt by the Office of Management and Budget to write guidelines on how agencies should approach such tricky valuations shows it is uncertain work.

To start with, there are imponderables, such as how to measure risk, who will be affected by the rules, and how much people are willing to pay to be safer in the workplace and have clean water. And there are the political implications of writing and enforcing the guidelines.

Draft OMB guidelines are raising hackles in some agencies because they would require more uniform calculations of how many lives would be lost or saved on the benefit side of the equation.

But actually doing the analysis sometimes can be impossible, complain some agency officials.

Clinton administration officials familiar with the Environmental Protection Agency's rulemaking procedures said putting values on the benefits of many rules involves "tremendous uncertainty and complexity."

The agency now sometimes uses the numbers it comes up with to "inform but not dictate decisions."

The Occupational Safety and Health Administration does estimates on risks to workers and costs to employers, but it is not as specific as the draft OMB guidance.

From the administration's point of view, issuing "guidance" to the agencies may mollify Republicans who insist that rigorous cost-benefit analysis would rein in overzealous rule writers.

Critics of the proposal claim OMB is pushing agencies to accept that "it's as important to save money as to save lives."

"Economists go through contortions to try to put valuations on everything," said an environmentalist who has been monitoring development of the guidelines. "We're at the stage of alchemy here. It's not feasible to do it in any rigorous fashion."

The EPA recently wrote a letter to Sally Katzen, administrator of OMB's Office of Information and Regulatory Affairs, saying agencies should have the option not to put a dollar figure in valuing fatal risks.

"Valuing life raises issues that make the proposed guidelines difficult for the agency to implement," said David Gardiner, EPA assistant administrator.

He also said the risk assessment portion of the guidelines remained "unacceptable."

EPA declined comment on the letter.

An administration official familiar with EPA's concerns said many of the agency's suggestions have been incorporated into the latest draft of the guidelines.

OMB does not want to talk about the guidelines until they are issued.

Agencies are expected to do economic analyses on major rules. But there are differences in approaches among agencies and even within agencies. Also, there are instances in which rules emerge without full consideration of cost.

In the case of the Clean Air Act, standards are set on the basis of health effects. Because of the way the statute is written, the agency has to do cost-benefit analysis, but it cannot consider cost in setting the rules.

Some experts in federal regulation believe it's a worthwhile exercise for OMB to expect more uniform cost justification of rules. But they are also wary that things may not be as black and white as the green-eye-shade folks at OMB think.

"I'm especially surprised that at a time when Congress is pushing so hard for the agencies to make more use of cost-benefit analysis, EPA has chosen to resurrect rhetoric from the early 1970s to the effect that 'There's no price tag that can be put on a human life,'" said Paul Portney, president of Resources for the Future, a think tank specializing in environmental issues.

The question, he said, is whether people are willing to pay for less risk and if the trade-offs they make say something about the value of a program.

The OMB Reports

Around the same time, Congress took another stab at trying to put in place a system that would give an annual reading on the total costs and benefits of regulation. Championed by Sens. Ted Stevens (R-Ark.) and Fred Thompson (R-Tenn.), the Regulatory Right-to-Know Act passed, requiring OMB to do an annual report on how much regulation costs. The report is an estimation of costs and benefits based on data supplied by the agencies for individual rules. This approach was expected to bring discipline to agencies that did not routinely put their rulemakings through the cost-benefit paces. Conservatives applauded the legislation as a way for the American people to become informed about how much they are spending on regulation; they pushed OMB to calculate regulatory expenditures at the same time it released the federal budget every year. Susan Dudley, a senior research fellow at the Mercatus Center at George Mason University, in testimony before the House Committee on Government Reform Subcommittee on Energy Policy, Natural Resources and Regulatory Affairs, said,

> A better understanding of regulatory impacts, or results, can help [con-gressional] appropriators allocate budgets toward regulatory agencies and programs that produce the greatest net benefits. Congress and the Executive branch must always consider, implicitly, if not explicitly, the costs and benefits of different programs as part of the budget process. If they are to allocate our nation's resources more efficiently and effec-tively to achieve greater benefits from our regulatory programs, infor-mation in OMB's Regulatory Accounting Report must be available during the fiscal budget process.[20]

The accounting has been shaky, and the bottom line numbers have been broad ranges. Under the Clinton administration, the OMB went through the exercise but cautioned that knowing the exact amount of costs and benefits in the aggregate is of little use to making sound regulatory policy. The adminis-tration somberly pointed out the shortcomings of the methodologies it was forced to use; the report issued in 1999, reflecting the cost-benefit scorecard for the previous year, was an example of how unsatisfactory such an estimation could be. The following column captured how the exercise was not of much practical use to anyone because the range of numbers it offered was so broad. The problem was that the bottom line included calculations about the costs and benefits of the Clean Air Act, ranges that were breathtakingly unreliable.

A Cost-Benefit Analysis:
OMB Tries to Add Up the Bill for Federal Rules

The Washington Post, February 12, 1999—There's the apples-and-oranges problem. There are the gaping data gaps. There are deep differences over methodology. There is the baseline problem. There are the politics of writ-ing about a touchy subject.

From an accountant's point of view, it's not an auspicious beginning for compiling "Report to Congress on the Costs and Benefits of Federal

Regulation, 1998," the Office of Management and Budget's second attempt at estimating how much federal regulation benefits society and the corresponding costs.

Despite the limitations, which OMB discusses at length in the report, the administration came up with an estimate on the aggregate benefits and costs of all kinds of social and economic regulation, such as ozone control and automobile safety. And what an estimate it is.

Factoring in a recent study that the Environmental Protection Agency did to assess the benefits of the Clean Air Act, OMB estimated the net benefits from health, safety and environmental regulation at between $30 billion and $3.3 trillion annually. Costs fall somewhere between $170 billion and $230 billion.

Jacob Lew, director of the OMB, explained that there might be a bit too much breathing room in the range of numbers offered. In a letter to Congress accompanying the report, he warned that " . . . the state of knowledge regarding costs and benefits of regulatory programs is still relatively rudimentary" and "significant methodological problems remain to be resolved."

Paul Portney, president of Resources for the Future, a public policy group that specializes in environmental issues, called the effort "the mother of all benefit-cost assessments—a somewhat dubious assignment, at best."

Portney saw little usefulness in the big numbers, but thought OMB did "a pretty straight-up and respectable job." He added, "One of the things the report does give lie to is saying that we don't get anything out of environmental regulation—even if the estimates are stratospheric."

Gary Bass, executive director of OMB Watch, a public interest group, said the report demonstrates for the second year "how difficult it is to do this and why these numbers should not be used for public policy purposes."

OMB cautions repeatedly not to read too much into the numbers. "We must underline the uncertainty of these estimates. As discussed above, the baseline, apples and oranges and other methodological problems significantly reduce the likelihood that these findings are robust," it said.

Figuring out the contributions and costs of economic regulation is even more problematic, the report said. Tax compliance, which was pegged at $140 billion annually in OMB's draft report, wasn't mentioned in the final product.

Last year, OMB did not have the benefit of the EPA study and relied mostly on estimates done by economists outside the government. The result was a far more modest estimate of $300 billion in benefits and $279 billion in costs.

Republicans have been pushing the Clinton administration to quantify the cost of regulation and the public's return on it.

"I believe the public has a right to know credible estimates of the costs and benefits of regulatory programs. We need to improve regulatory accounting so we can make our government more accountable, efficient and fair. We can do better—and should," said Sen. Fred D. Thompson (R-Tenn.), chairman of the Senate Governmental Affairs Committee, and author of the legislation requiring OMB to do the report.

Republicans want OMB to do more than offer broad, sweeping estimates and rely on agency data to come up with estimates on the price tag of individual rules. They insist that OMB should make its own assessments and offer recommendations on what programs are worthwhile and which should be eliminated. They want OMB to "drill down" and get into the details of various regulatory programs so their monetary worth can be estimated more precisely.

OMB supporters said progress has been made in this year's report. They say that OMB economists brought consistency to some of the agencies' cost-and-benefit estimates. It analyzed how two agencies calculated a variety of rules and how they overestimated and underestimated the effects and costs of the rules. OMB also addressed concerns that economists and others raised about the report.

But regulatory experts insist that OMB should rely less on information from the agencies and more on its own judgment.

"They have better information than what's here," said Richard Belzer, a former economist at OMB who now is regulatory program manager for the Center for Study of American Business.

Robert Hahn, director of the AEI–Brookings Joint Center for Regulatory Studies, agreed. "I would like to see a bold report where they have the courage of their convictions—and this isn't it." But he said this year's effort "is a point of departure for discussion" and he's glad to have it.

And there's always next year's crop of oranges and apples.

Despite the unreliability of the reports, the results could be used to different political ends. High costs allowed business groups to reiterate that regulation was a drain on productivity and profits. Generous numbers on the benefit side of the ledger supported the arguments of those who saw great intangible value in regulations that protected or saved lives. These reports also were a way to peer over the shoulder of OMB, which, until 1997, did not have to disclose its numbers and kept its correspondence with agencies under wraps.

Since then, OMB has published four annual cost-benefit reports, with economists at OIRA crunching the numbers. Under John Graham, the Bush administration got its first chance to pin down some numbers in the 2002 annual regulatory report. Graham reported that the number is not totally reliable because the underlying data were not produced solely by the agencies or reviewed by OMB, but he estimated that the cost of all rules that are in effect ranges from $520 billion to $620 billion per year; the benefits could be anywhere from one-half to three times the total costs.[21] Other estimates, such as the one mentioned in chapter 1 produced by W. Mark Crain and Thomas D. Hopkins, arrive at higher numbers: $800 billion annually in costs.

The OMB numbers may not be as solid as economists would like, but the sophistication of the reports has increased. A Republican OMB might view the reports not as an assigned chore from Congress but as an opportunity to expand its influence over a contentious policy area. The opening remarks in the 2002 OMB report reflect movement in this direction: "The Bush administration is committed to developing a smarter regulatory system based on sound science and economics. A smarter system adopts cost-effective rules when market and state and local efforts fail, revises existing rules to make them less costly and/or more effective, and rescinds outmoded rules whose benefits do not justify their costs."[22]

The Bush OMB

Those sentiments were conveyed by OMB Director Mitch Daniels to Congress even before the 2001 OMB accounting report was issued. Daniels made it clear in the following column that OIRA would play a preeminent role in shaping regulatory policy and that agencies that did not do their accounting properly would have rules sent back to them—a threat that materialized with the tire sensor rule.

OMB Chief Vows Scrutiny of Agencies; Daniels Wants Consultation with States on Major Rules

The Washington Post, May 25, 2001—Mitchell E. Daniels Jr., director of the Office of Management and Budget, said yesterday that his office will expect federal agencies to consult with states and carefully weigh costs and benefits before they issue major regulations—or his office will send their proposals back for more work.

"It will be our hope that this will happen rarely," Daniels said of rejecting rules. He also made it clear during a House subcommittee hearing that he plans to lean on Harvard professor John D. Graham, nominated to be the OMB's regulatory czar, to police agency compliance.

"We will insist," Daniels said, on making cost-benefit analyses "as sound and credible as they can be."

Daniels made his comments at an oversight hearing on agencies' performance since the Republican-controlled Congress passed an "unfunded mandates" law in 1995. It established procedures for the legislative and executive branches to consider the cost of proposed rules on state and local governments and the private sector.

The new OMB director, who was a pharmaceutical company executive before joining the Bush administration, criticized agencies' track record on the "unfunded mandates" front during the Clinton years. Agencies issuing rules that call for expenditures of $100 million or more by states or the private sector are expected to prepare "mandates impact statements," which include assessments of what rules will cost, their benefit and whether cheaper alternatives are available.

"It appears that agencies have attempted to limit their consultative processes, and ignored potential alternative remedies, by aggressively utilizing the exemptions" in the law, he said.

Daniels said he would direct Graham's office "to return a rule that is not in compliance with the [unfunded mandates law] to the agency from which it came. If an agency is unsure whether a rule contains a significant mandate, it should err on the side of caution," he said.

Regulatory experts and representatives of the business community considered Daniels's warning indicative of how the balance of power is changing between the agencies and the OMB in the Bush administration.

They expect that the OMB will be involved in the early stages of rule-making and will expect uniform compliance with administration directives on how costs and benefits should be used in rulemakings. The Clinton administration deferred to the agencies' expertise in most cases.

Asked by Rep. Doug Ose (R-Calif.) whether the OMB will develop standards for agencies to follow, Daniels said he would rely on Graham, a leading proponent of risk analysis in regulations, to handle that job.

"We have everything to gain with better-informed rules. That will be my guidance to Dr. Graham and he'll have to fill in the blanks," he said.

Daniels based his criticism of agency regulations on a 1998 General Accounting Office report that said many rules the agencies issued in the first two years after the "unfunded mandates" law was passed were economically significant, but underwent no economic analyses.

Rep. John F. Tierney (D-Mass.), ranking minority member of the subcommittee, noted that in all but two of 80 cases the GAO studied, the agencies were in compliance with the law because of exemptions that absolve them doing a special look at costs.

The Power of OIRA

The authority given to OMB to review and reject rulemakings has been a source of controversy since OIRA was created in 1981. OIRA is not as obvious and accessible as most federal agencies. Its work is highly technical and inscrutable to most who are not expert in regulatory subject areas; and as one regulatory expert put it: "OMB historically runs one of the worst spin machines in Washington."[23] The work done by OIRA "desk officers," who have expertise in the regulatory affairs of various agencies, was kept among the agencies, OMB, and the White House despite interest on the part of lobbyists, professionals in regulatory analysis, public interest groups, congressional overseers, and a few reporters. The office is sparsely staffed (compared with the size of the regulatory bureaucracy that it oversees), and the fifty-four OIRA professionals—some who have worked there almost their entire government careers—do not give interviews or remove their cloak of anonymity eagerly.

Each succeeding presidency since Richard Nixon's has had an interest in executive review of rules and what that should entail, but there were differences in the interpretation and extent of the authority that OIRA wielded. In the Clinton administration, OIRA deferred to the agencies and their expertise on most rules. Republican administrations conferred more authority on OIRA or on regulatory offshoots at the executive level, such as the Council on Competitiveness, to pass judgment on rules from the agencies. The judgments passed on rules can be fraught with political meaning or can pass completely unnoticed except by insiders at the agencies who might feel that OIRA's "mere existence stops some very, very stupid proposals."[24]

Graham's arrival at OIRA opened another chapter in regulatory that his critics and supporters have said will have broad implications for how federal bureaucrats—unelected and largely anonymous—manage the regulatory state, determining the level of regulatory protections offered to Americans. The Bush administration brought with it the resolve to use an aggressive approach to get agencies to heel and comply with strict cost-benefit analysis guidelines—or suffer returns of their rules.

In its 2002 draft report to Congress, OMB waded into territory that the Clinton administration never approached. It made it clear that it would do more than review significant rulemakings; it would suggest priorities for agencies with what it called "prompt" letters. It promised to demystify the regulatory process with more openness. It announced the development of a government-wide website so that average Americans can find and comment on proposed rules via the Internet, instead of using the individual websites of various agencies. It said that it was serious about the quality of new rulemakings and would "return" them to agencies when they suffered from "inadequate analysis." OMB expected that agencies would do cost-benefit analyses even if they were not called for under statute and would have their findings peer reviewed. OMB began the process of standardizing the elements of a cost-benefit analysis, suggesting what discount rate agencies should use and how they should evaluate the risk of premature death. It promised that it would be crisp and efficient in reviewing—and returning—rules to agencies.

"The regulatory reforms now being implemented and described below, while modest, incremental and generally procedural in nature, promise to have a powerful positive long run effect on the quality of federal regulation," the 2002 OMB draft report predicted. "With regard to federal regulation, the Bush Administration's objective is quality, not quantity. Those rules that are adopted promise to be more effective, less intrusive, and more cost-effective in achieving national objectives while demonstrating greater durability in the face of political and legal attack."[25]

With those marching orders, the Bush administration set the tone for how regulatory policy would be set. But much of the process "reform" that the Bush administration had in mind when it came to office was overtaken by two other significant events—the terrorist attacks of September 11, 2001, and the collapse of a major energy company called the Enron Corp. As noted in the final chapter, the trajectory of regulatory policy was changed dramatically. In the space of six months, there was more regulatory activity than at any time since the Great Depression, though, philosophically, the inclination of the administration was to minimize the need for federal regulation.

Summary

Chapter 5 gives you an intensive look at how cost-benefit analysis and risk assessment, two analytical tools, work in rulemaking and why they have become increasingly important. A rule proposed by the National Highway Traffic Safety Administration is used to examine how the agency analyzed the rule, how the agency's work was reviewed by the Office of Management and Budget, and why OMB rejected it. This is an up-close look at how the analysis itself was done and why it is a key step in the regulatory process that can determine the fate of a rulemaking. The chapter exposes you to the controversies surrounding trying to put a price tag on rulemaking and airs the arguments on both sides. It looks at the growing use of economic and scientific analyses in rulemaking, the power of executive review at OMB, and attempts to legislate cost-benefit analysis.

To Learn More

It is essential to become familiar with the website of the Office of Management and Budget, www.whitehouse.gov/omb. Clicking on "Regulatory Matters" and then "Regulatory Review" will give you a bull's-eye view of much of what the current administration is doing on the policy front as well as an archive of memos and executive orders. The site also includes the full accounting of the "return letter" to the NHTSA regarding the tire sensor rulemaking, as well as other return letters and "prompt letters" that encourage agencies to look at an issue with a potential regulation in mind. It also has copies of all the regulatory accounting reports prepared by OMB since 1997.

For a discussion of how to assess the cost-effectiveness of rules through the use of "league tables," or rankings, go to the fiscal year 2003 U.S. budget documents, "Analytical Perspectives," Section 24, and the "Technical Appendix" (February 4, 2002). This assessment tool is a good starting point for a discussion on using controversial measures such as "life years saved" to determine the cost-effectiveness of a rulemaking.

To see how the National Highway Traffic Safety Administration did its calculations for the tire pressure sensor rule, the entire document can be viewed online in the NHTSA electronic docket. Go to www.NHTSA.gov and click on "Docket Management System." Follow the search prompts and use the docket number of the rulemaking, 8572, to find the report. Then scroll down to NHTSA-2000-8572-57, "Preliminary Economic Assessment," published on July 1, 2001. For purposes of discussion, compare this analysis with the one done by OMB's Office of Information and Regulatory Affairs. That can be found on OMB's website under OIRA's "return letters": "Letter to the Department of Transportation National Highway Traffic Safety Administration on Tire Pressure Monitoring Systems" (February 12, 2002).

Notes

1. Consumers Union, "Federal Motor Vehicle Safety Standards: Tire Pressure Monitoring Systems; Controls and Displays," Docket No. NHTSA 2000-8572-89 (August 27, 2001).

2. Office of Management and Budget, Office of Information and Regulatory Affairs, "Letter to National Highway Traffic Safety Administration," February 12, 2002.

3. Caroline E. Mayer and Frank Swoboda, "Top Regulator Delays Tire-Monitor Rule," *Washington Post,* February 14, 2002: E1.

4. Danny Hakim, "Regulation on Tire Safety Rejected by Budget Chief," *New York Times,* February 14, 2002: C16.

5. Alliance of Automobile Manufacturers, "Federal Motor Vehicle Safety Standards: Tire Pressure Monitoring Systems; Controls and Displays," Docket No. NHTSA 2000-8572-16 (March 26, 2001).

6. Stephen Power, "White House to Seek Changes in Proposed Tire-Safety Rule," *Wall Street Journal,* February 13, 2002: B4.

7. Office of Management and Budget, Office of Information and Regulatory Affairs, "Letter to National Highway Traffic Safety Administration," February 12, 2002.

8. Cass R. Sunstein, *The Cost-Benefit State: The Future of Regulatory Protection* (Chicago: American Bar Association, 2002), ix.

9. Cass R. Sunstein, *Risk and Reason: Safety, Law and the Environment* (New York: Cambridge University Press, 2002), 46.

10. Joan Claybrook, *Regulatory Accounting: Costs and Benefits of Federal Regulations,* prepared for the Subcommittee on Energy Policy, Natural Resources and Regulatory Affairs, House Government Reform Committee (105th Cong., 2d sess., March 12, 2002).

11. Lisa Heinzerling and Frank Ackerman, "Pricing the Priceless: Cost-Benefit Analysis of Environmental Protection" (Washington, D.C.: Georgetown Environmental Law and Policy Institute, Georgetown University Law Center, 2002).

12. Lisa Heinzerling, "Don't Put the Fox in Charge of the Hens," *Los Angeles Times,* July 19, 2001: 15 (Metro Desk).

13. Dick Durbin, "Graham Flunks the Cost-Benefit Test," *Washington Post,* July 16, 2001: A15.

14. Eric A. Posner, "Controlling Agencies with Cost-Benefit Analysis: A Positive Political Theory Perspective," *University of Chicago Law Review* (fall 2001): 5.

15. Robert W. Hahn, *Reviving Regulatory Reform: A Global Perspective* (Washington, D.C.: AEI–Brookings Joint Center for Regulatory Studies, 2000), 63.

16. Robert W. Hahn, *Regulatory Reform: Assessing the Government's Numbers,* Working Paper 99-6 (Washington, D.C.: AEI–Brookings Joint Center for Regulatory Studies, July 1999), 5.

17. General Accounting Office, *Regulatory Reform: Information on Costs, Cost-Effectiveness, and Mandated Deadlines for Regulations,* GAO / PEMD-95-18BR (March 1995), 2.

18. Murray Weidenbaum, "Executive Regulatory Review: Surveying the Record, Making It Work," Weidenbaum Center Forum, National Press Club, Washington, D.C., December 17, 2001.

19. Office of Management and Budget, "Memorandum for Members of the Regulatory Working Group: Economic Analysis of Federal Regulations under Executive Order No. 12866" (January 11, 1996).

20. Susan E. Dudley, *Regulatory Accounting: Costs and Benefits of Federal Regulations,* prepared for the Subcommittee on Energy Policy, Natural Resources and Regulatory Affairs, House Government Reform Committee (105th Cong., 2d sess., March 12, 2002).

21. John D. Graham, *Regulatory Accounting: Costs and Benefits of Federal Regulations,* prepared for the Subcommittee on Energy Policy, Natural Resources and Regulatory Affairs, House Government Reform Committee (105th Cong., 2d sess., March 12, 2002).

22. Office of Management and Budget, Office of Information and Regulatory Affairs, *Making Sense of Regulation: 2001 Report to Congress on the Costs and Benefits of Federal Regulations and Unfunded Mandates on State, Local, and Tribal Entities* (December 2001).

23. Richard B. Belzer, "Executive Regulatory Review: Surveying the Record, Making It Work," Weidenbaum Center Forum, National Press Club, Washington, D.C., December 17, 2001.

24. Neil Eisner, "Executive Regulatory Review: Surveying the Record, Making It Work," Weidenbaum Center Forum, National Press Club, Washington, D.C., December 17, 2001.

25. Office of Management and Budget, Office of Information and Regulatory Affairs, "Draft Report to Congress on the Costs and Benefits of Federal Regulations," *Federal Register* 67 (March 28, 2002): 15013.

The Future of Regulation: From Enron and Homeland Security to Globalization

---

EPA to Kill New Arsenic Standards;
Whitman Cites Debate on Drinking Water Risk

The Washington Post, March 21, 2001—The Environmental Protection Agency announced yesterday it will revoke a Clinton administration rule that would have reduced the acceptable level of arsenic in drinking water, arguing the evidence was not conclusive enough to justify the high cost to states, municipalities and industry of complying with the proposal.

The measure was one of dozens of environmental regulations and rules issued in the final months of Bill Clinton's presidency that were put on hold after President Bush took office Jan. 20 and subjected to further review.

In ordering the withdrawal of the standard, which was to have taken effect Friday, EPA Administrator Christine Todd Whitman said there is "no consensus on a particular safe level" of arsenic in drinking water. She rejected the arguments of environmentalists that studies show the limits are essential to protecting millions of Americans from cancer and other health threats, and suggested that a lower standard might be more appropriate.

"I am committed to safe and affordable drinking water for all Americans," Whitman said. "When the federal government imposes costs on communities—especially small communities—we should be sure the facts support imposing the federal standard."

Meanwhile, the Interior Department's Bureau of Land Management will announce today a proposal to suspend new hard-rock mining regulations for public lands that would have toughened environmental standards and made it more difficult for mining companies to escape financial liability for violations of anti-pollution laws, an Interior Department official said. The new rules—adopted Jan. 20—have prompted four lawsuits from mining groups, and bureau officials say it makes more sense to shelve the regulation while the disputes are settled.

These and other decisions in recent weeks provide a strong signal that Bush has embarked on a radically different course on the environment, energy production and federal land use than was taken by Clinton— a course that was not fully outlined during last year's presidential campaign.

A week ago, Bush announced that he would not seek reductions in carbon dioxide emissions at power plants, breaking a campaign pledge. Then administration officials signaled that they might consider a court settlement that would significantly scale back a Clinton rule placing a third of the national forests off-limits to logging and road construction.

"They are mounting a bigger assault on the environment and public health than any other administration or the Gingrich Congress did," said Philip Clapp, president of the National Environmental Trust, referring to former representative Newt Gingrich (R-Ga.), House speaker from 1995 to 1998.

At least 34 million people in the United States are exposed to drinking water supplies with elevated levels of arsenic that occur naturally or as a result of industrial pollution and mining operations, according to studies by environmental groups. A National Academy of Sciences study concluded that arsenic in drinking water can cause cancer of the lungs, bladder and skin.

Experts say the biggest problems are found in the Southwest, Midwest and Northeast, while the Washington area has a relatively minor problem. The proposed rule, issued Jan. 22 after years of study, would have reduced the acceptable level of arsenic in water for the first time since the 1940s—from 50 parts per billion to 10 parts per billion.

Congress mandated a toughening of the standard, and the measure promulgated by the Clinton administration would have brought the United States into compliance with a standard adopted by the World Health Organization and the European Union within five years. Opponents and proponents differ sharply over the cost of implementing the rule, but state and local communities and industries would have had to spend billions of dollars collectively to replace filtration systems, switch to alternative water supplies and launch programs to educate the public on the dangers of arsenic.

Senate Budget Committee Chairman Pete V. Domenici (R-N.M.) praised the administration's decision to shelve the arsenic regulation, saying that it would spare states onerous costs.

"Communities faced with the daunting task of finding the money to adhere to the stricter standards can breath a sigh of relief," Domenici said. "I believe the rules rushed to print in January are excessive and based on insufficient science."

However, Erik Olson, a senior attorney with the Natural Resources Defense Council, which sued the EPA in February 2000 to issue the revised standard, said the administration's decision "will force millions of Americans to continue to drink arsenic-laced water."

"This outrageous act is just another example of how the polluters have taken over the government," Olson said.

To undo the regulation, the EPA must launch an administrative procedure that includes a public comment period. "This is in line with what Congress intended," said John Grasser, spokesman for the National Mining

Association. "Congress gave the agency more time to examine the science and costs and the last administration chose, instead, to rush it out."

The George W. Bush administration's vision of making the regulatory system more effective and less intrusive almost immediately ran into a buzz saw of disapproval from environmental and public interest groups that viewed decisions like the one it made on arsenic as misguided and dangerous. The controversy that erupted over the arsenic rule is only a glimpse of what the future is likely to bring on the regulatory front: deepening divides between business interests and public interest groups and labor over environmental issues, use of public lands, health and safety, corporate governance, and the role of the United States in deciding regulatory issues that have international ramifications.

The National Resources Defense Council, a major environmental group, sued the administration for suspending the arsenic rule without scientific or legal justification. Newspapers editorialized against the decision. An angry Congress was ready to force the Environmental Protection Agency to tighten the standard. And the agency received 57,000 comments asking that it remove even more arsenic from the water than the Clinton administration rule recommended. So much ruckus was raised over the suspension of the rule—which the Bush administration said was necessary to review the science behind the decision—that the new cadre of regulators finally let the Clinton administration rule stand.

The response the Bush administration got to this decision prompted it to moderate its tone, if not approach, toward regulation. Moreover, events that it could not control—like the terrorist attacks of September 11, 2001, and the financial fallout from the collapse of the Enron Corp.—dramatically changed the regulatory agenda. A collapsing stock market, disillusioned investors, the bankruptcy of several major companies, and political pressure from Democrats and environmentalists to address economic problems with regulation forced the administration to take a more activist posture. By summer 2002, President Bush called for increasing the budget of the Securities and Exchange Commission and a crackdown on corporate fraud. Federal Reserve Board Chairman Alan Greenspan admitted that the accounting industry needed more regulatory supervision. And, most significantly, President Bush found himself signing legislation in July 2002 to beef up corporate governance and police the accounting profession even though he preferred a less aggressive approach. Suddenly, the corporate world was facing more economic regulation than it had seen since the 1970s.

There were other rules with lower profiles that were given the go-ahead: They include ones to protect ironworkers from hazards on the job, salmonella testing of ground beef in school lunches, two Clinton-era energy-efficiency rules for washing machines and hot water heaters, and the reporting of toxic lead pollution by industrial facilities. The Bush administration rejected pleas from the Republican House and truck engine manufacturers to postpone a rule to cut emissions from diesel truck engines.

The Future of Regulation and Business

The arsenic decision—before it was reversed—was viewed by critics of the Bush administration as predictive of the future. These critics expected that regulation under the Bush administration would be dominated by business, both because many top members of the new administration, including Vice President Richard Cheney and President Bush, had business backgrounds and because business interests had contributed heavily to the Bush campaign. By 2002, there were some thirty former energy industry executives, lobbyists, and lawyers appointed to influential jobs within the Bush administration—a reversal from the previous eight years when the energy industry complained that environmentalists had the ear of the Clinton administration.[1]

Fueling critics' suspicions were eager pronouncements by influential business lobbies that offered guidance to the new administration on what rules to kill or to review for potential change or elimination. The following column, written early in the new Bush administration, gives vent to the aspirations of business interests in regard to federal regulation.

Bush versus Clinton White House:
Lining Up to Lobby for Rule Recision

The Washington Post, February 6, 2001—Take a number. Industry groups are lining up to make their case to the new Bush administration that rules they don't like should be killed.

Some already have had some success.

Federal contractors won a reprieve late last week from a controversial new rule to have government officials consider past violations of labor, environmental and consumer laws and regulations in awarding new contracts.

It became known in business circles as the "blacklisting" rule and business groups already were challenging it in court.

Last Friday, the General Services Administration and other civilian agencies quietly issued what's called a "class deviation" to the rule—effectively suspending it for at least six months.

Randy Johnson, vice president of labor and employee benefits for the U.S. Chamber of Commerce, said the action "points out how agencies themselves are unable to comply with the rule." It should be repealed government-wide, he added.

"There are folks in the halls of the Pentagon right now urging DOD Secretary Donald Rumsfeld to do the same thing," said Elaine Guth, an attorney with the Manufacturers Alliance/MAPI, a policy research organization representing manufacturers. The group has written two letters urging the Bush administration to repeal the rule.

David Drabkin, GSA's deputy associate administrator for acquisition policy, said the delay was needed because GSA did not have enough time to comply with the new rule. He added that a broader rollback is being considered.

"We are working as fast as we know how to undo this," Drabkin said, noting that federal contracting officers weren't eager to have to make judgments about prospective contractors' regulatory track record. "It's the first time we've been sued over a procurement rule. We have been working to get a new rule that will deal with the old rule and that has not been easy."

The AFL-CIO, which supported the Clinton rule, said the Bush administration had "launched a secret and outrageous assault on regulations designed to make sure that taxpayer-funded projects are rewarded to responsible companies—not chronic lawbreakers."

Business groups also are expecting President Bush to sign draft executive orders soon overturning other Clinton administration decisions favorable to labor.

The draft orders would include revoking labor-management teams, ordering federal contractors once again to inform workers about their right not to join a union, and eliminating a provision that required contractors to keep existing unionized workforces.

On the energy front, the National Petrochemical & Refiners Association has brought two major issues to the attention of the new administration: repealing the Environmental Protection Agency's recent rule mandating a reduction in sulfur content for diesel fuel for trucks and buses, and pushing for streamlining environmental air and water rules to make it easier to get permits to build new refineries.

"We're going to continue to discuss this [diesel] rule with people in Congress and in the administration every chance we get so it can be reviewed," said Robert Slaughter, general counsel of the refiners association. "We do support significant reductions in diesel fuel though this goes too far, too fast."

The Chamber, meanwhile, is reviewing other executive orders issued by President Clinton, many of which set regulatory policy. It came up with a list of 15 that it thinks need to be rescinded.

The Chamber has even written a draft executive order of its own that it hopes the new administration will use as a template for rewriting its policy on regulation—how rules should be reviewed, the role of the Office of Management and Budget, and the economic and scientific criteria that agencies should apply to rule-making.

"If you fix that one, you rein in all the agencies," said Bruce Josten, the Chamber's executive vice president for government affairs, reflecting the sentiment of the business community that the agencies have been over-aggressive regulators over the past eight years.

The Business Roundtable, a group of top executives of large companies, plans to issue an environmental agenda for the administration's new regulators on Thursday. It suggests, among other things, more regulatory flexibility for companies that achieve "superior" environmental performance.

On at least one major front—stopping what's in the regulatory pipeline—the administration hasn't waited for advice.

On Jan. 20, White House Chief of Staff Andrew Card issued a memo that extends the effective date of rules by 60 days. Six days later, OMB director Mitchell E. Daniels Jr. gave the agencies more detailed instructions on how to proceed, including withdrawing any rules that are awaiting review at OMB.

This rush to review has caught the eye of Democrats, who worry the memos are just the first steps in eliminating a host of Clinton-era rules.

"We intend to closely monitor the implementation of the Card memorandum, particularly where it applies to measures to protect health and safety, consumers and the environment," Sen. Joseph I. Lieberman (D-Conn.) and Rep. Henry A. Waxman (D-Calif.) wrote yesterday in a letter to Daniels.

Lieberman and Waxman asked OMB to supply the paperwork on all the rules affected by the Card memo—and to supply it routinely to the public.

The lobbying was effective. The contracting rule was withdrawn, and the administration made other rule changes and appointments that were favorable to the business community. A bevy of regulatory decisions came down in the first year of the Bush administration, reversing decisions made by the Clinton administration or striking out in new directions altogether. Business interests felt that they had a place at the executive-level policy-making table, much as they did with influential House Republicans.

The General Accounting Office examined the number of rules that the Bush administration froze under the moratorium it imposed on Inauguration Day in 2001—the so-called Card memo discussed in the introduction. The agency found that ninety of the 371 rules that were subject to the freeze had their effective dates delayed. There were fifteen rules that were still not in effect one year after the memo was issued.

The Office of Management and Budget also asked for comments on modifying or rescinding seventy-one rules; it plans to continue to ask the public for suggestions on more rules that it wants to subject to the same treatment. This particular approach is somewhat novel, but it is not unusual for a new administration to take an active role in implementing regulatory policy; each hopes that the changes it makes will be a template for the future management of the regulatory state.

A Go for Snowmobiling

One of the rules that was swept into the Card memo dragnet was a ban imposed by the Clinton administration on snowmobiling in Yellowstone Park, a highly charged issue that had been dividing environmentalists and the snowmobiling industry for years. This rule, like the arsenic decision, will be considered a bellwether for how environmental disputes are settled in the future under Republican administrations.

The snowmobiling rule to ban use of the machines by winter 2003–2004 actually went into effect but was challenged even before it was published. In the settlement of a court case brought by the snowmobiling industry, the Bush administration signaled that it was considering all but reversing a ban on snowmobiling in Yellowstone Park. In the end, it did decide to push aside the ban, proposing that snowmobilers use Yellowstone and Grand Teton National Parks with some restrictions, such as requiring the latest noise- and emissions-reduction technology, imposing daily limits on the numbers of snowmobiles in the parks, and requiring guided travel.

The Bush administration's decision to let snowmobilers continue running in the parks was a victory for those who believe that public lands should be open to the mechanized sleds and to businesses around the park, whereas environmentalists continued to oppose the decision. It also signaled that the administration was likely to make decisions about uses of public lands differently than the preceding administration had, taking into account regional preferences for how much presence the federal government should have in issues like these.

The column that follows examined the strenuous lobbying that was done on the part of green groups to persuade the Clinton administration to ban snowmobiling in the park, an issue that had been studied exhaustively over many years. The Clinton administration concluded that a ban was best to protect the park environment from noise and pollution. With its decision, it hoped to silence the roar of snowmobile engines in the park in perpetuity—a wish that did not come true.

Snowmobiles in National Parks: Can You Bear It?

The Washington Post, January 22, 1999—So much for dashing though the snow on a snowmobile in the national parks.

A group of 60 environmental groups yesterday asked five federal agencies to prohibit or regulate snowmobiling in the nation's parks, alleging that the vehicles pollute, cause health problems and endanger wildlife.

Led by Blue Network, a San Francisco–based environmental group that also opposes the use of water scooters in the parks, snowmobile foes signed a petition asking the Interior Department's National Park Service to ban an estimated 270,000 snowmobiles that enter the national parks annually, calling operation of the high-speed sleds "one of the most environmentally devastating recreational activities permitted by the Park Service."

"Ultimately, the prohibition on recreational snowmobile use in national parks, if accepted and implemented by the Park Service, will result in substantial benefits to park wildlife, ecology, air and water quality, and will restore the sanctity and serenity of the national park experience," the petition said.

Snowmobile advocates regard this attempt at a regulatory blockade as part of an effort to restrict or eliminate any kind of motorized traffic in parks and wilderness areas.

"These are deep-pocketed elitists," said Edward Klim, president of the International Snowmobile Manufacturers Association in Haslett, Mich. "It doesn't surprise me. They want to keep people out of the parks."

The environmental groups also want the Occupational Safety and Health Administration to investigate the health effects of inhaling fumes from snowmobiles. In its petition to that agency, Blue Network claims that park rangers and employees have become dizzy, nauseated and fatigued from inhaling the fumes.

The Environmental Protection Agency is being asked to look at regulating the emissions from snowmobile engines, which cause "noxious blue haze and raw fuel residues," the groups alleged.

The coalition, which includes the Natural Resources Defense Council, the Wilderness Society and Friends of the Earth, wants the Consumer Product Safety Commission and the National Transportation Safety Board to investigate deaths and injuries caused by snowmobiling.

"Anecdotal evidence indicates that snowmobile riders often exhibit the symptoms of carbon monoxide poisoning, reportedly experiencing dizziness, nausea, headaches, fatigue, blurred vision, slowed reaction and impaired judgment," said the petition to the CPSC.

Alan Brown, president of the Montana Snowmobile Association, said reports of sickness from fumes and snowmobiles harming bison in parks such as Yellowstone are exaggerated. Brown said the snowmobile industry is working on more efficient, cleaner engines while it conducts a three-year study on emissions.

The clash between those who seek the solitude of the parks in winter on skis or snowshoes and those who want to ride to sights such as Old Faithful has become more intense as the number of snowmobiles entering parks has grown. In Yellowstone, for example, the number rose from six snowmobiles in 1964 to 60,110 snowmobiles last winter.

Russell Long, executive director of Blue Network, said the Park Service has incorrectly interpreted presidential executive orders that prohibit off-road activities in the parks if they adversely affect natural, aesthetic or scenic values. The Park Service, however, does not consider snowmobiles that are operated on existing roads in parks to be off-road vehicles.

The Interior Department's current policy is to allow individual park superintendents to decide whether snowmobiles are appropriate for their parks. "Superintendents have discretion to allow them on roads or lakes that have cars or boats in the summer," said David Barna, spokesman for the Park Service.

There are 378 parks, monuments and seashores, but the snowmobiling issue is relevant at only a handful of the 28 parks where it is permitted. Denali National Park and Preserve in Alaska is contemplating closing some 2 million acres to snowmobiling to preserve an "intact ecosystem" filled with bears, wolves, lynxes and wolverines, said Steve Martine, Denali superintendent. Skis and dogsleds provide access to that area of the park, he said.

In Yellowstone, where the snowmobile controversy is at fever pitch, the sleds are restricted to the roads used in summer; the Park Service "grooms" them for snowmobile access in winter. Helmets must be worn, the speed limit is 45 mph, and noise levels are checked if they exceed a set minimum.

Yet, with 60,110 snowmobiles in the park last year, "noise and emissions are certainly a problem," said Marsha Karle, spokeswoman for Yellowstone. Fans have been installed in tollbooths to lessen the effect of the exhaust. On top of that, there are 40 to 50 snowmobile accidents each year and, occasionally, a fatality.

The debate at Yellowstone highlights the dual mission—and dilemma—of the Park Service: Provide access to the parks as well as preserve them. As Barna points out, huge recreational vehicles lumber through the park in the summer, as do cars: "It's tough to say flat-out yes or no," to snowmobiles.

Tom Kiernan, president of the National Parks and Conservation Association, supports a temporary ban on the sleds until the Park Service determines what "appropriate use" might be. Some of the possibilities are to issue permits to limit numbers or use outfitters, which are companies that arrange tours.

But Jim Gentz, president of the Motorsports Group for Yamaha Motor Corp., said snowmobiling "is a pretty wonderful way" to see Yellowstone in winter. "The parks are for everybody to enjoy," he said.

And remember: Wildlife has the right of way.

The reversal was a high-profile signal that, on social and environmental issues, the Bush administration was going to consider the views of business and give them considerable weight in regulatory decision making—a stance that is not unusual for a business-oriented, Republican administration.

Another prominent rule, one to increase the efficiency of air condition-ers that was issued in the dusk of the Clinton administration, had a similar fate. Instead of allowing the rule to proceed, the Bush administration decided to substitute another rule, calling for a 20 percent improvement in efficiency, instead of 30 percent, a level that was chosen after deliberation by three pre-vious administrations, a decision challenged in court by environmental groups. As in the case of snowmobiling, industry opposition to the new rule played a decisive role in the future of how the rule would be applied. The fol-lowing column tracks the efforts of most manufacturers to have the rule weakened, even though numerous states supported the tougher standard.

A Matter of Degrees: Air-Conditioning Standards Chilled

The Washington Post, May 8, 2001—Supporters of a Clinton-era regula-tion to increase the efficiency of residential and commercial air condi-tioners want to turn up the heat on a less ambitious proposal favored by the Bush administration and most cooling manufacturers.

As gasoline prices increase and electricity shortages loom, environ-mentalists, conservation advocates and some members of Congress are preparing to battle the Bush administration's effort to roll back the Clinton rule, which was issued three days before Bill Clinton left the White House.

On April 13, the Department of Energy announced it wanted manu-facturers of air-conditioning units to increase their efficiency by 20 per-cent—instead of the 30 percent the Clinton rule ordered. In industry lingo, that meant a seasonal energy efficiency ratio (SEER) of 12, instead of the 13 the Clinton rule mandated.

That announcement sent groups wanting more efficient air condi-tioners scurrying to find reasons the Bush action shouldn't stand.

"Our preliminary analysis is DOE doesn't have the authority to roll back the rule, and we are looking at options that include a lawsuit if the research supports it," said David B. Goldstein, energy program director for the Natural Resources Defense Council. "This is a stupid action that compro-mises the nation's energy needs and increases the likelihood of blackouts."

Though most of the industry lobbied for the Bush stance, a couple of manufacturers take the energy conservationists' side, agreeing that they can meet the Clinton standard. No matter who wins, industry won't have to meet the new efficiency standards until 2006.

Goldstein said he questions whether a final rule can be rolled back—a legal issue that has been raised in other cases where the Bush administration has withdrawn "midnight regulations" issued in the last days of the Clinton era.

He cites a provision in the National Appliance Energy Conservation Act that stressed that DOE "may not prescribe any amended standard which increases the maximum allowable energy, use, or decreases the minimum required energy efficiency, of a covered product."

Prepared for that argument, DOE said it isn't amending the Clinton rule but is getting rid of it altogether. Since the current standard is 10 SEER, an increase to 12 would not be a diminution in the standard at all, but an increase, officials said.

"We're not amending a previous rule, we are withdrawing it and offering our own separate and different regulation," said DOE spokesman Joe Davis.

The Air-Conditioning and Refrigeration Institute has made the same argument.

In its petition asking DOE to reconsider the Clinton rule, Ed Dooley, spokesman for the Institute, said that "in its haste to achieve high efficiency" Clinton regulators set a standard that made new units too expensive for low-income people and hurt small manufacturers. The group also challenged the Clinton rule in court—an action that is now on hold.

Rep. Edward J. Markey (D-Mass.), a co-sponsor of the 1987 law that set new efficiency standards for 13 major household appliances, chastised the manufacturers for being technologically inept and lazy in opposing the Clinton rule.

Markey said offering an amendment protecting the more stringent standard on the House floor in the middle of July—when gas prices might be $3 a gallon and electricity prices quadrupled—would be an "efficient" way to address the problem. It would also be a major embarrassment for the Bush administration and the industry, he added. Markey expects supporters of the Clinton rule to file a lawsuit first.

For the NRDC, this episode is reminiscent of battles it fought in the late 1980s, when the Reagan administration tried to avoid issuing energy standards. First, officials tried to delay them. Then they claimed that federal rules would not save a significant amount of energy compared with what the market could accomplish.

As a result, it set the standards at zero, an approach that came to be known as the "no-standard standard." NRDC sued and won.

Those who believe they may have a case this time have two air-conditioning manufacturers on their side.

On May 1, Daniel H. Burke of Goettl Air Conditioning Inc., a small manufacturer in Phoenix, wrote to Karl Rove, the president's senior adviser, setting him straight on a point Rove made in the media.

Burke wrote, "Your main concern in supporting the lower standard was that going to 13 SEER would cause 'an anticompetitive meltdown' for companies, especially small manufacturers. As a small manufacturer in this industry, I do not believe a higher energy efficiency standard . . . would drive small manufacturers out of business. In fact, given on-going energy concerns nationwide, Goettl . . . supports implementing a 13 SEER standard."

Burke added that his company has been making the higher-efficiency units for four years.

Goodman Manufacturing Co. in Houston, the second-largest manufacturer of residential cooling units in the country and owner of the Amana brand, said that the industry has the technology now to produce units at 13 SEER and that costs to consumers will not be prohibitively high.

Goodman executives wrote a letter to Energy Secretary Spencer Abraham in April, encouraging him to go with the tougher rule.

In an interview, John B. Goodman, chairman and chief executive of Goodman Holding Co., which owns Goodman Manufacturing, was optimistic the Bush administration would cool down and change its mind.

"It's just the right thing, and it's something our industry can do to help," he said.

Looking to the Future

The Bush administration took several opportunities to pursue deregulation and set aside for high-priority review some significant Clinton-era rules. These decisions not only have an immediate impact on current regulatory policy but, if they result in final rules, will determine the future of some significant initiatives. In little more than a year, the Bush administration proposed to change rules guarding the confidentiality of medical records, allow industry to pay user fees to the Food and Drug Administration to review applications and inspect plants that make medical devices, weaken pollution standards for electric utilities, open public lands to mining and timbering, and reverse some restrictions on how wetlands can be developed.

The ergonomics standard, discussed earlier, was invalidated by the Bush administration, and in spring 2002 the Labor Department announced that it would develop voluntary guidelines for companies to follow, beginning with the nursing home industry. At independent agencies such as the Federal Communications Commission, votes to further deregulate the telecommunications industry continued apace. The commission decided that telephone companies did not have to open their Internet networks to competing providers and that cable companies could offer high-speed access to the Internet, cutting out access of competing providers to their networks. The Federal Trade Commission decided not to pursue legislative initiatives that may have resulted in privacy protections for Internet users; instead, the agency said it would concentrate on the enforcement of existing laws. The administration issued safety warnings in lieu of new rulemakings, such as warning about the safety hazards of tipping over in fifteen-passenger vans. It handed out grants to faith-based organizations to do job training and worker relocation, rather than instituting new regulatory programs. In some cases, it encouraged voluntary compliance by industry, rather than rule-based enforcement programs.

The course the administration set for the future, however, was not one that it viewed as purely deregulatory. John Graham, administrator of the Office of Information and Regulatory Affairs at the Office of Management and Budget, stressed in numerous speeches that the Bush White House would take a reasoned, not rash, approach to regulating and deregulating. "A high-quality regulatory process is not uniformly pro-regulation or anti-regulation. Instead, a smart process adopts new rules when market and local choices fail, modifies existing rules to make them more effective or less costly, and rescinds outmoded rules whose benefits no longer justify their costs," Graham said in a speech.[2]

But in the budget that it prepared for the 2003 fiscal year, there were other indications of what the future would hold. The Bush administration took steps to curb what it considered wasteful spending by the federal government. As is mentioned earlier, cutting the funds to programs and to agencies is one way to curb regulatory activity. It is also a way to direct funds to other activities that conservative administrations, in particular, support, such as defense spending and, more recently, homeland security.

The Bush administration budget is a blueprint for understanding how the White House planned to manage regulatory activity at some of the most activist agencies within the federal government. For example, for the Occupational Safety and Health Administration—the agency responsible for workplace safety and the author of the ergonomics rule—the administration requested a $9 million decrease. The National Institute for Occupational Safety and Health also would take a budget cut. The Consumer Product Safety Commission would get a smaller increase in its budget than it requested. The agency said that it would have to cut staff positions as a result.[3] Budget requests are just that, and Congress often decides to restore or increase funding to programs. But the numbers chosen by any administration are an indicator of what policy makers would like to happen at a particular agency or department. And once funds and programs are cut by Congress, it often takes years to restore an agency's capabilities. In the case of the National Highway Traffic Safety Administration, cuts made during the Reagan administration and a subsequent lack of adequate funding increases were widely viewed as one of the reasons why the agency was slow to react to the crisis that developed when Bridgestone/Firestone tires started separating and causing fatal accidents. "If you don't have the budget to cast a big net, you can't catch these defects," said Clarence Ditlow, executive director of the Center for Auto Safety, a safety group in Washington, D.C., that pushed for a wider recall of Firestone tires.[4]

Unexpected Events

This pattern of tightening the regulatory spigot may have continued unabated if the uncontrollable events of September 11 and the collapse of the Enron Corp. had not happened. Those two occurrences were defining moments for the future of regulation, and they changed the direction of a conservative Republican administration that hoped to curb the growth and influence of the regulatory bureaucracy. In fact, the immediate answer to both problems—one of them a security issue and one a financial issue—was to turn to regulatory mechanisms to come up with answers. This approach was taken partly to assuage the fears of Americans shaken by both events, but it also was the most expeditious way for the government to step in and exert its authority. The federal government found that the only way to answer citizens' fears about life in America after the collapse of the New York World Trade Center and other terrorist threats was to increase regulatory safeguards.

Instead of a contraction in the number of rules and cuts in agency appropriations for rulemaking, the federal government grew by leaps and bounds in rules and expenditures related to September 11. In a matter of months, the regulatory bureaucracy was tapped—and expanded—as never before to staff new agencies, take on new duties, promulgate new rules, and plan for new initiatives to safeguard the country. Between September 11, 2001, and March 2002, the government issued forty-one new regulations dealing with national security and relief for individuals affected in some way by the attacks. "After the shocking terrorist attacks of September 11, 2001, the American public looked to the federal government to take action not only to prevent future security threats but also to provide relief for individuals affected by the tragedies," the Bush administration stated in a report prepared by the Office of Management and Budget.[5]

In that extraordinarily short period of time, the Office of Homeland Security was proposed, the biggest expansion of the bureaucracy in fifty years. The Department of Transportation took airport security functions under its wing, one of a dozen new DOT rules related to the events of September 11. The federal government now would be responsible for screening passengers and bags at airports, a function that traditionally was handled by the airlines. A new agency was created: the Transportation Security Administration. Banking rules were tightened, including a raft of new rules to spot money laundering and tax evasion that also applied to mutual funds, credit card companies, jewelers, and others. The Labor Department had to rethink its unemployment regulations to help thousands of people thrown out of jobs as a result of the attacks. The Justice Department had to formulate rules for the administration of the September 11th Victim Compensation Fund of 2001, which Congress created to compensate individuals harmed or killed by the terrorist-related airplane crashes. The Immigration and Naturalization Service was under pressure from Congress and the White House to alter the immigration landscape. New rules to change student visa approvals and limit the stay of foreign tourists in the United States were in place seven months after the tragedies happened. Many more regulatory initiatives were expected to reform the INS after Congress and the Bush administration were left aghast at mistakes the agency made in issuing visas both before and after September 11. And a continuing stream of new rules would trickle out of various agencies well into the future, shaping how privacy, financial, and immigration issues would be regulated.

The Enron Scandal

Barely had government planners executed new rules on security and other safeguards when the country was rocked by a major financial crisis of a proportion not seen since the crash on Wall Street in 1929. Suddenly, many of the regulatory safety nets that had been put in place fifty years ago were tearing. Rules governing pensions, executive compensation, stock and commodity trading practices, accounting standards and disclosures, and financial conflicts of interest came under scrutiny in Congress and at the agencies. The reforms that Arthur Levitt had called for unsuccessfully as chairman of the Securities and Exchange Commission in the Clinton administration suddenly seemed reasonable to many. Harvey Pitt, chairman of the agency in the Bush administration, who started his tenure as a "reluctant regulator," was under great pressure to become a reformer of the accounting industry that he had represented as an attorney in private practice. In the wake of the Enron scandal and the ensuing investigation of it, Pitt proposed a tightening of disclosure standards for companies, more scrutiny of how stock options are doled out to executives, and changes in accounting rules—though some of these changes would be overseen by private sector entities. His proposals were judged as lacking by his critics, and he was watched closely for conflicts of interest because of his prior professional relationship with the accounting industry and investment banks. There were repeated calls for his resignation, which finally came in November 2002.

The Securities and Exchange Commission became a focal point for reform. The agency, perennially understaffed and underfunded, was being prodded by congressional overseers and consumer groups to discipline and regulate wrongdoers. In the aftermath of the Enron collapse and the problems that surfaced with its accounting firm, Arthur Andersen LLP, there were no fewer than a dozen congressional committees and subcommittees examining the scandal and clamoring for regulation to fix the problem. The subsequent bankruptcy of Worldcom Inc. added to the list of problems that needed to be addressed, as Americans watched the value of their stock holdings and pension nest eggs dwindle.

This seemingly uncontrolled burst of regulation concerned reform-minded conservatives who hoped that the future held less, not more, regulation. Thomas D. Hopkins, dean of the College of Business at the Rochester Institute of Technology, a proponent of regulatory restraint, said,

In the wake of September 11, and the more recent Enron debacle, the entire world is looking to Washington in a way never experienced before. New demands are being placed upon our government, new safeguards for our citizens. Inevitably, and indeed immediately, the tactics include tighter regulation across many facets of life. Given the imperative of adding to our nation's regulatory burdens in ways that protect us from terrorism, and that ensure transparency in corporate accounting, it is crucial to get our nation's priorities straight. Cutting back on needlessly costly existing regulations, and revamping regulations that unjustifiably hit some harder than others, will allow "breathing room," if you will, so that newer regulatory initiatives will not overwhelm businesses that already are struggling through economic turbulence.[6]

Paperwork Burden

By at least one measure, the administration was having a tough time following its own advice to cut back on regulation. Besides tallying *Federal Register* pages and adding up expenditures on regulatory compliance, the Office of Management and Budget examines annually the paperwork burden that business carries as a result of regulation. Despite its desire to ease regulatory burdens for business and its scolding of agencies that violate paperwork rules, the Bush administration found itself reporting that, after one year of its tenure, the time Americans spent filling out forms had risen to 7.65 billion hours in fiscal year 2001, an increase of 290 million hours from the previous years—the largest annual increase since 1995, with most of it attributable to the Internal Revenue Service. The time spent filling out forms is called "burden hours," but even critics of paperwork admit that much of it is necessary for the federal government to carry out projects such as the U.S. Census and social welfare programs. The goal, however, is to minimize it, and attempts to meet annual reduction goals set by the Paperwork Reduction Act since 1980 have not been met (save for a downward blip in 1993). For critics of regulation, this result is dismaying because 95 percent of the 7.65 billion hours has to do with regulatory compliance and two-thirds of the "burden" fell on business. Table 6.1, for example, illustrates the amount of time it takes businesses and individuals to fill out forms for various federal agencies.

TABLE 6.1. **Non–Internal Revenue Service Paperwork Over 10 Million Hours**

Department/Agency	Regulatory Paperwork	Paperwork Burden in Millions of Hours
Department of Labor	Occupational Safety and Health Administration's Process Safety Management of Highly Hazardous Chemicals	79
Securities and Exchange Commission	Confirmation of Securities Transactions	56
Department of Transportation	Hours of Service of Drivers Regulations	42
Department of Transportation	Inspection, Repair, and Maintenance	35
Securities and Exchange Commission	Record Keeping by Registered Investment Companies	21
Federal Trade Commission	Truth-in-Lending Regulation	20
Department of Health and Human Services	Food and Drug Administration's Investigational New Drug Regulations	17
Environmental Protection Agency	Standards for the Use or Disposal of Sewage Sludge	13
Department of Labor	Occupational Safety and Health Administration's Bloodborne Pathogens Standard	13
Federal Trade Commission	Fair Packaging and Labeling Act Regulation	12
Department of Treasury	Record Keeping and Reporting of Currency and Foreign Financial Accounts	12
Department of Labor	Office of Federal Contract Compliance Programs Record Keeping and Reporting Requirements	11

TABLE 6.1. **(cont.)**

Department/Agency	Regulatory Paperwork	Paperwork Burden in Millions of Hours
Department of Health and Human Services	Medicare and Medicaid for Home Health Agencies	10
Department of Health and Human Services	Food and Drug Administration's Clinical Laboratory Improvement Amendments	10
Department of Education	Federal Family Education Loan Program	10

Source: Office of Management and Budget, 2001.

Rules of the Future

Besides addressing the fallout from financial scandals, there are new fronts of regulation on the horizon growing out of new technologies, security concerns that took hold of the country after September 11, and advances in health care. Staring regulators in the face are issues such as Internet online privacy. What role should the federal government play in protecting individuals from online snooping and personal intrusions from Internet companies that collect information about them and use it for marketing purposes? Should the government promote and mandate online electronic surveillance—so-called cybersurveillance—to head off would-be terrorists? The nation's panoply of immigration rules, which were found to offer inadequate protection after September 11, will be the source of ongoing future revisions. The food industry will find itself subject to many more safeguards, some that it already has opposed as too far-reaching and expensive. Financial institutions will face increasing regulatory scrutiny as the federal government tries to combat the financial underpinnings of terrorism. What should the rule book say for the emerging biotechnology industry?

Yet to be settled is the question of taxing Internet sales—a key issue of the new Internet economy. And the deregulation of the electrical industry, which was well under way until the bankruptcy of Enron and the disastrous results in the state of California, is an ongoing regulatory challenge. States have stepped in to regulate cellular telephone use, but there are other electronic devices now used in cars that might one day warrant standards. Even in seemingly old-line industries such as tobacco there are new products that might warrant future rulemaking—like tobacco lozenges. It is likely that the federal government will have to lay down rules for how to conduct stem cell research or uphold a ban on it. The regulation of irradiated foods, a growing part of the food supply, is being debated.

The future of regulatory policy in the United States will be determined by many of the issues discussed at the start of this book: the continuing growth of federal regulation and attempts by various administrations, Congress, and special interests to influence and control it. The minutia of everyday life, including breath mints, Swiss cheese, and toilet flushing, will continue to be regulated by a huge federal establishment of highly specialized bureaucrats. And after several decades of efforts to deregulate and reduce the role of the federal government, the pendulum has swung back toward more government intervention and regulation in key areas such as corporate governance, accounting, and homeland security, though de-emphasizing health and environmental regulation continued apace. In short, in the space of one year there was an unprecedented expansion in the regulatory state.

What also will become apparent in the future is how well the new bureaucracy that was created by the Bush administration and Congress will fare. Will a new Department of Homeland Security—the combination of twenty-two federal agencies with separate missions and histories—be an effective regulator or an inefficient, bloated reshuffling of the regulatory deck? The prospect of executing the most significant reorganization of the federal government in a half century is one that will either reform a system of intelligence and safeguards that is now broken or will simply repeat the mistakes of the past. Those with good memories recall that the Defense Department, the Transportation Department, and the Energy Department—each roiled by power struggles and classic bureaucratic inefficiencies—took years to begin functioning as coherent, capable regulators. Ironically, the Republican ideal of a lean federal regulatory machine has been overtaken by the idea that a new Department of Homeland Security, with at least 169,000 federal employees and a complicated organization chart, will result in less duplication and sharper regulatory focus—even as a dozen congressional committees fought to approve, shape, and fund the new department.

The International Front

Finally, there is a whole new frontier of regulation that is even less well understood and more obscure than domestic rulemaking, especially because much of the negotiating is done behind closed doors in foreign countries.

Some of these issues, which involve environmental protection, food safety, and worker protections, are being discussed in the context of the provisions of the North American Free Trade Agreement and other trade pacts negotiated by the United States and other countries. These international trade agreements often strive to "harmonize" the regulations that the United States operates under with those of other countries. Currently, there are efforts to harmonize standards for pharmaceuticals, meat and poultry inspection, automobile safety, and medical devices—to name a few. Business is involved in setting many of these standards and often supports them as a way to increase international trade and reduce regulation. Certain terms of NAFTA also provide legal avenues for corporations to challenge the regulatory policies of a country if the rule or regulatory decision infringes on the rights of foreign investors provided for in the agreement.

Consumer and environmental groups have expressed opposition to many of the terms of these agreements if they believe that they will result in less stringent standards than those that already exist in the United States. "These are not public health agreements. These are legal agreements," said Bruce Silverglade, director of legal affairs for the Center for Science in the Public Interest, referring to the negotiations that have taken place over food safety standards. He argues that the establishment of the World Trade Organization and agreements pertaining to food regulation such as the WTO's Agreement on Sanitary and Phytosanitary Measures have had a significant impact on the Food and Drug Administration and the Department of Agriculture and their policies when domestic regulations that are more stringent than those found in other countries are considered trade barriers. Developing countries that do not have a comparable level of health and safety standards exert pressure for "downward harmonization" of rules, Silverglade has maintained in speeches and articles.

Other international regulatory quandaries are decided by agreeing to disagree over whose rule is best. The United States preferred that the terms of one agreement require the pasteurization of cheese, as the FDA now requires of most cheese sold in this country. The standard that was agreed on calls for control measures that might include, but would not require, pasteurization. In other cases, subjective determinations are made that regulatory systems among various countries are equivalent, allowing goods to move freely into those countries.

Trade agreements also serve as ways to export various regulatory regimes. For example, under the WTO, the United States wanted other nations to accept the regulatory policy postulated by the Federal Communications Commission,

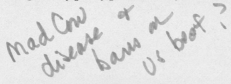

a position that would have significant impact on a country such as Japan, which has its own set of highly developed telecommunications standards. What standards should apply to the flow of data across borders also has developed into a trade-related regulatory tussle, as Europe and the United States struggle over the standards that companies doing business in those countries will have to comply with. Those who support free trade maintain that less regulation of information, rather than more, as imposed by European countries, would benefit businesses and consumers. Europeans want their concerns for privacy respected.

These divisions have created special interests of their own: antiglobalists who oppose the reach of various trade agreements and free traders who are trying to "fast-track" trade negotiating authority directly to the president and limit the role of Congress in the creation of the agreement. In each of these agreements are questions that loom large about the future of the many rules and standards that now govern health and safety in the United States and how they will be applied—if at all—around the world.

Mexican Trucks

A recent example of how a trade agreement—in this case, NAFTA—can create a heated regulatory debate involved whether to allow Mexican commercial trucks full access to the United States. At issue was whether Mexican trucks were as safe as U.S. rigs and whether Mexico's safety standards were equivalent to those imposed on truckers here—classic safety questions that will determine, in part, truck safety in the United States in the future. A battle was set off among the trucking industry, organized labor, members of Congress, highway safety groups, the Mexican government, and the Clinton and Bush administrations. Much of the controversy was settled when Congress stipulated in the agency's 2002 funding how the rules should be written to toughen safety requirements for the trucks and to guide audits and inspections of them. But before that happened, the following column was written to look at the controversy that erupted when the Department of Transportation—under pressure from the terms of the NAFTA treaty and the Mexican government to move forward—issued a proposal in summer 2001 for what kind of rules would apply to Mexican carriers.

The Trucking Tiff with Mexico:
Lift Safety Standards at the Border?

The Washington Post, July 17, 2001—The Mexican trucks that the Bush administration wants to see rolling over the border starting next year would be subject to looser rules than their American counterparts under an administration proposal. That prospect is what's behind the current fracas over the safety of Mexican trucks.

Mexican President Vicente Fox met in Detroit yesterday with union leaders who oppose giving the foreign trucks full freedom to carry goods across American highways. (They are now limited to operating in a 20-mile zone near the border.) And President Bush has threatened to veto recent congressional attempts to block the controversial rule.

The proposal the Department of Transportation issued in May would let thousands of Mexican trucking companies certify, without verification, that they have systems in place to comply with U.S. trucking rules on the qualifications of drivers, how many hours they can be on the road, the upkeep of vehicles, and drug and alcohol testing. A similar system of safety requirements does not currently exist in Mexico.

If approved, the Mexican carriers then would receive conditional operating authority and be subject to a "safety review" within 18 months, or perhaps longer. Under U.S. rules, government inspectors examine the books, and vehicles, of American truckers to ensure compliance. But under the proposed regulation, the review of the Mexican companies wouldn't necessarily be at their headquarters across the border. Instead it could be a paperwork review at a border location in the United States.

The prospect of the rule being finalized and the border opening in January has galvanized safety groups and members of Congress to scrutinize its fine print.

For instance, currently there is no systematic tracking of the 11,787 Mexican carriers that have limited operating authority in the United States. "We do not currently have this type of information on Mexican carriers," the proposed regulation said.

"We do not have abundant information on their safety record, out-of-service rates, or other overall safety." It also noted that Mexico doesn't have a safety inspection program comparable to the one U.S. regulators use on American truckers.

Concerned about the certification proposal, the House voted on June 26 to ban Mexican trucks from traveling into the United States. The Senate is expected to vote soon on a package that toughens the DOT proposal, including requiring a full safety audit before operating authority is granted.

Hearings are scheduled tomorrow in the House and Senate over the safety implications of allowing Mexican trucks into the United States.

The trucking issue has been simmering since the 1990s, when the Clinton administration, under pressure from the International Brotherhood of Teamsters, decided not to allow trucks from Mexico to roll into the United States.

The union is now asking that Mexican drivers be given proficiency exams and their companies undergo a safety review before they are given operating authority. The Mexican government has accused the Teamsters of trying to block the rule because the union fears the loss of jobs to lower-paid, nonunionized Mexican drivers.

Several reports by the General Accounting Office and the DOT inspector general documented the high number of Mexican trucks that had to be taken off the road for safety violations and the weak system of inspection that exists at the border.

But the Bush administration put the issue on fast-forward after a tribunal that decides grievances under the North American Free Trade Agreement agreed with Mexico that keeping its trucks out of widespread commerce violated the terms of the treaty.

That led to the DOT proposal in May and the congressional efforts since to block it.

The administration thinks it can meet "reasonable safety concerns" without throwing out the whole rule. "We think we can work within the rulemaking process," said Chet Lunner, a spokesman for the Department of Transportation.

Some safety and insurance groups have joined organized labor in calling for more stringent standards for the Mexican trucks.

Advocates for Highway and Auto Safety said in comments that the DOT agency in charge of the program, the Federal Motor Carrier Safety Administration, "intends to openly experiment with the health and safety of the American people by permitting operation of Mexican-domiciled motor carriers to begin on the basis of invalidated affidavits."

The American Insurance Association, whose members are faced with writing insurance for the Mexican trucks, said in comments: "The proposed system for Mexican motor carriers relies on check-the-box self-certifications at the front end, to gain operating authority, and little real enforcement after the Mexican motor carriers begin operating."

David Snyder, general counsel of the insurance group, added in an interview: "The rule comes nowhere near assuring the levels of safety and a system to guarantee that safety that the Congress says the public wants."

The American Trucking Associations, which represents domestic trucking companies, has a different take. With an eye on eventually being able to operate more cheaply out of Mexico, it said the Bush administration is making a good-faith effort to implement the provisions of NAFTA.

"It's to the benefit of both countries . . . to allow long-haul carriers to move back and forth across the border," said Martin Rojas, director of cross-border operations for the ATA.

Like many regulatory issues, this one has a postscript that says something about how regulatory issues are likely to unfold on a global stage in the future. The fine print of regulatory policy, once hammered out exclusively in this country, now is also crafted by international tribunals and international committees where the United States has a seat and a major role but is not the only player. The Mexican truck case continued to be so contentious that, just days before the rules allowing the Mexican trucks over the border were to take effect, a lawsuit was filed by environmental and consumer groups contending that the trucks would not be able to meet U.S. emission standards and would pollute. The federal appeals court declined to stop border crossings, but it will let the case go forward as it examines whether the regulators adequately studied the environmental effects of the rule. In late 2002, the Bush administration lifted the moratorium on truck crossings, which led to another legal challenge to keep the border closed. Whatever the court decides, this will be one decision of many that speaks to a regulatory state that is increasingly becoming one without borders.

Summary

This chapter looks ahead to the regulatory issues of the future, many of which will grow out of environmental, security, and business issues in which the

George W. Bush administration has been involved. Setting levels of allowable arsenic in drinking water, deciding whether to allow snowmobiling in Yellowstone, and debating the appropriate level of energy efficiency for air conditioners are discussed to bring to life the debates among special interests, Congress, environmentalists, and various administrations in setting national regulatory policy. The chapter also considers the effects that the terrorist attacks of September 11, 2001, and the collapse of the Enron Corp. had in setting the course for aggressive rulemaking in a Republican era that otherwise may have pursued a course of heavier deregulation. The chapter predicts some of the areas that will be ripe for regulation in the future: health care, genetics, telecommunications, immigration, and homeland security. Finally, it analyzes how the terms of international trade pacts will influence domestic regulatory policy in the future, making questions about regulatory policy global as well as domestic.

To Learn More

The two rules issued by the Department of Transportation governing how Mexican trucks must operate in the United States illustrate the border conflict over regulation. One covers trucks that operate in a commercial zone close to the U.S.–Mexican border, and the other rule is for trucks that want to travel throughout the United States. Go to the electronic version of the *Federal Register* (www.access.gpo.gov/nara) or to the Department of Transportation's "Docket Management System" (dms.dot.gov) to see the full text of the rules. This is an opportunity to read a rule in its entirety; notice the technical language and legalese that permeate rules such as these. If you use the DOT "Docket Management System," you also will be able to trace the history of the rule from its proposal to the final stage, as well as the comments that were filed with DOT about the proposal. For both rules, use docket numbers to find them in DOT's "Docket Management System":

> TITLE: Revision of application form for Mexico-Domiciled Motor carriers to operate in US Municipalities and commercial zones; published: March 19, 2002 (67 FR 12652) 50 pp. Final Rule [Docket No. FMCSA-98-3297] RIN 2126-AA33

> TITLE: Application by certain Mexico-Domiciled Motor carriers to operate beyond US Municipalities and commercial zones published:

March 19, 2002 (67 FR 12701) 55 pp. Interim final rule [Docket No. FMCSA-98-3298]; RIN 2126-AA34

To read more about the challenges awaiting regulators in the future, consult the *Congressional Quarterly* weekly magazine for a special outlook piece called "Can Congress Regulate the New Economy?" published on November 10, 2001. This piece is available in hard copy only through public and academic libraries.

An excellent insight into the cause and effect of regulatory lobbying in the aftermath of September 11, 2001, can be found in a *National Journal* article called "Behind the Bailout," published on September 29, 2001, pages 2996–97. This publication also can be found in libraries and online (www.nationaljournal.com) for a subscription fee. This article follows the intensive lobbying done on Congress and the White House to get a package of emergency financial relief from the federal government to compensate for losses associated with terrorism.

To see how a congressional committee prepares for a regulatory oversight hearing, go to www.house.gov/reform/reg. Go to "Hearings" and click on April 11, 2002, to see all the background documents, testimony, and briefing memos for the hearing held by the Subcommittee on Paperwork Inflation.

Notes

1. Don Van Natta Jr. and Neela Banerjee, "Bush Policies Have Been Good to Energy Industry," *New York Times,* April 21, 2002: A24.

2. John D. Graham, remarks prepared for delivery to the National Economists Club, Library of Congress, Washington, D.C., March 7, 2002.

3. Kathy Chen, Jill Carroll, Greg Ip, and John J. Fialka, "Regulators Face Tight Curbs on Spending; Business Groups Are Likely to Be Pleased," *Wall Street Journal,* February 5, 2002: A8.

4. Cindy Skrzycki, "NHTSA Will Share Hearing Spotlight," *Washington Post,* September 5, 2000: E1.

5. Office of Management and Budget, Office of Information and Regulatory Affairs, "Draft Report to Congress on the Costs and Benefits of Federal Regulations," *Federal Register* 67 (March 28, 2002): 15015.

6. Thomas D. Hopkins, *Regulatory Accounting: Costs and Benefits of Federal Regulations,* prepared for the Subcommittee on Energy Policy, Natural Resources and Regulatory Affairs, House Government Reform Committee (105th Cong., 2d sess., March 12, 2002).

Index

recision

About the Author

Cindy Skrzycki writes "The Regulators" column, which focuses on the nexus among government, business, and federal regulation, for *The Washington Post*. For nearly a quarter century, she has covered some of the most arcane and important regulatory issues in Washington as well as public policy makers involved in those issues. In positions at *The Washington Post, U.S. News and World Report*, and the Washington Bureau of the *Fort Worth Star-Telegram*, she has reported on virtually every federal agency, its relationship with Congress, and the influence of lobbying and special interests on public policy. She has covered stories that range from how the federal government has handled tire safety problems to congressional attempts to revamp the entire regulatory system.

She began her career at the *Buffalo Evening News* where she developed a career-long interest in writing about business issues. A native of Buffalo, N.Y., she holds degrees from Canisius College and an advanced degree from American University. She lives in Washington, D.C., with her husband and two daughters.